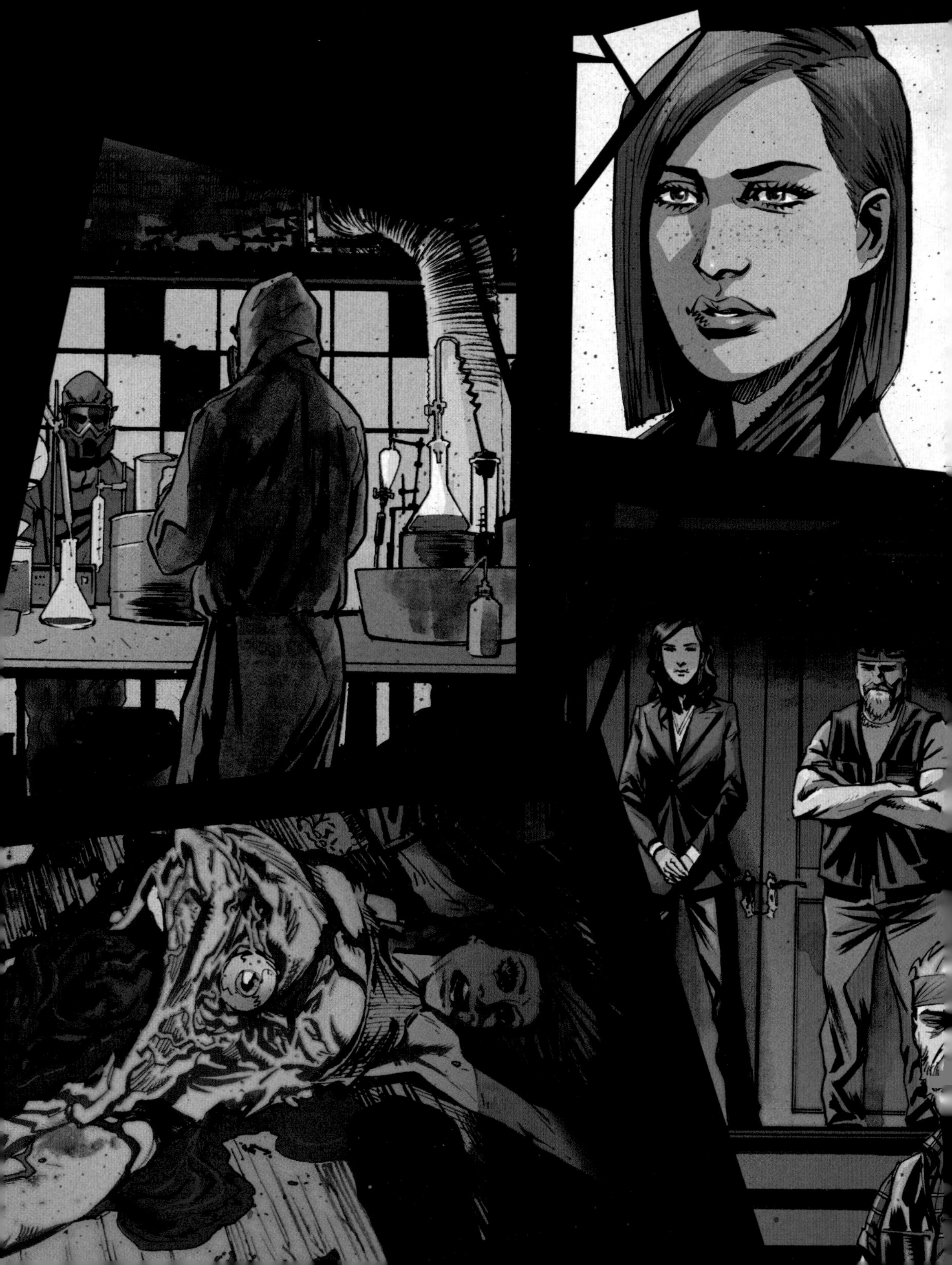

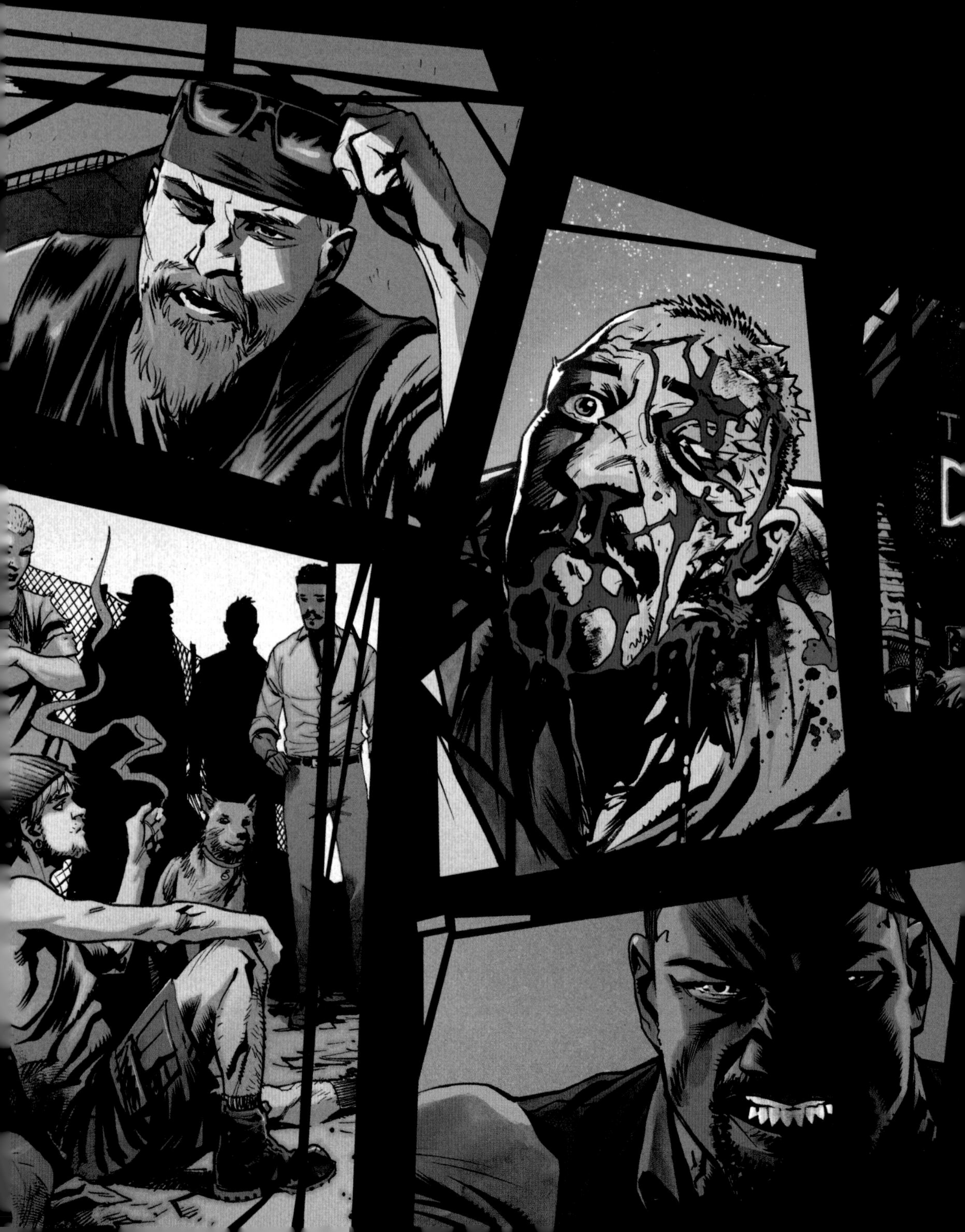

Written by
CULLEN BUNN

Illustrated by
JONAS SCHARF

Colored by
ALEX GUIMARÃES

Lettered by
ED DUKESHIRE

Cover by
LEE GARBETT

Series Designer
MICHELLE ANKLEY

Collection Designer
JILLIAN CRAB

Editor
ERIC HARBURN

BONE PARISH Created by
CULLEN BUNN & JONAS SCHARF

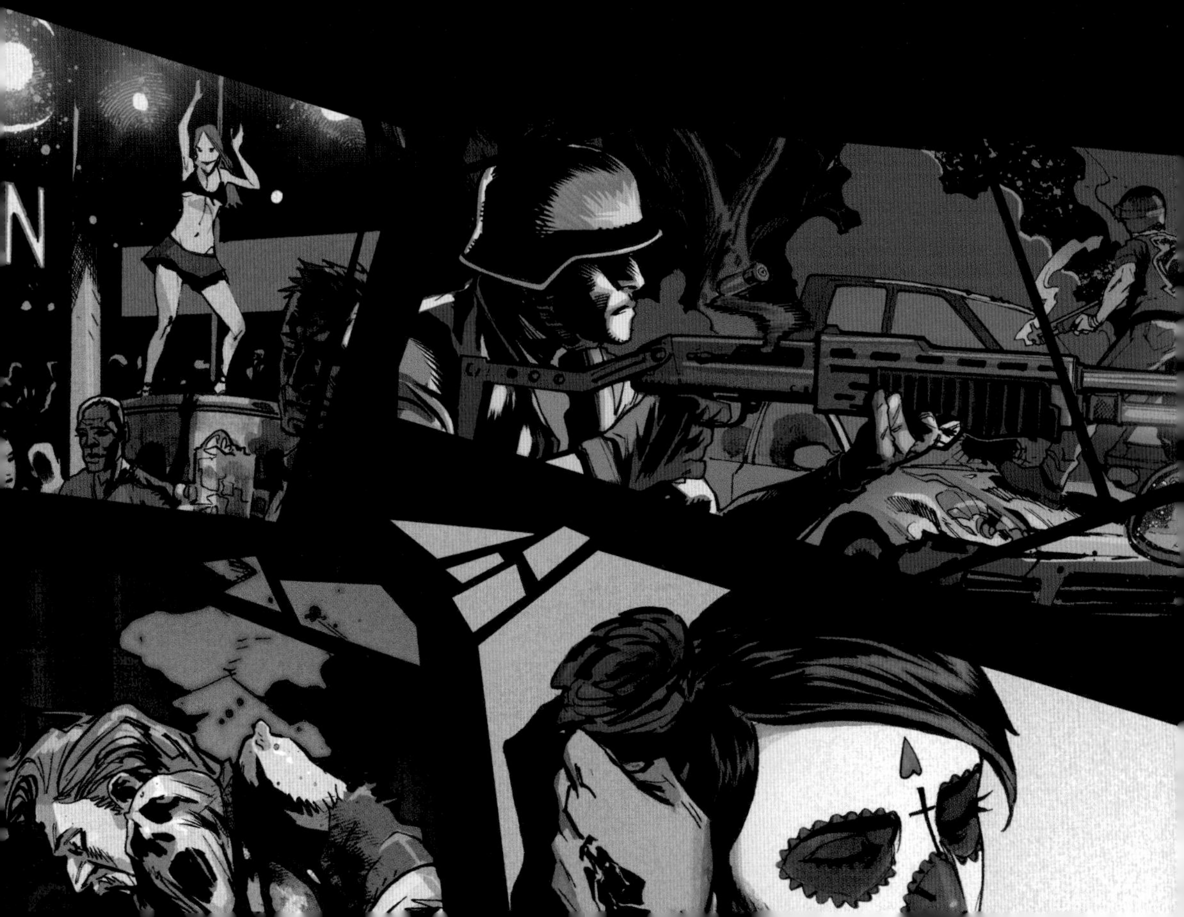

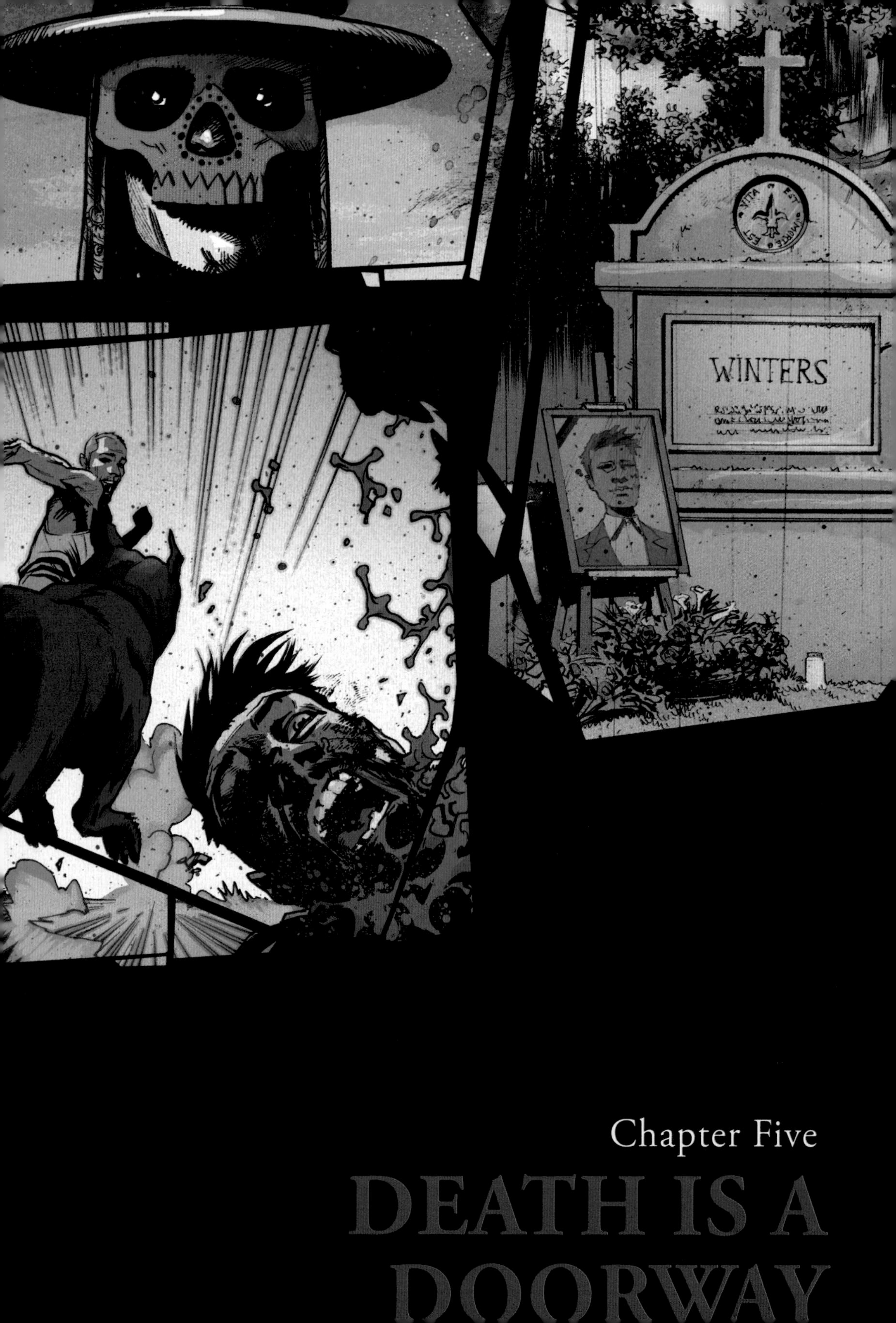
WINTERS

Chapter Five

DEATH IS A DOORWAY

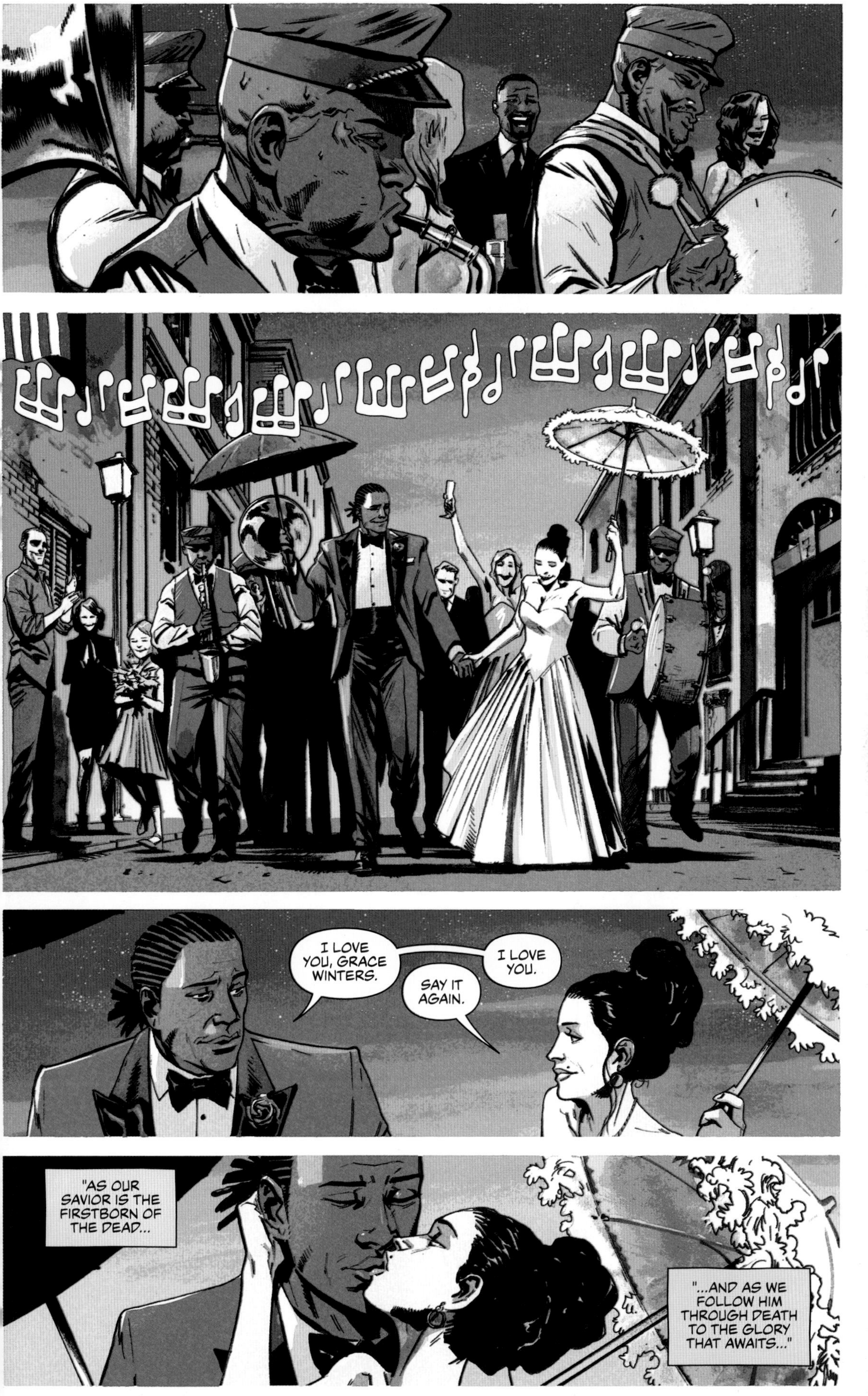
I LOVE YOU, GRACE WINTERS.
I LOVE YOU.
SAY IT AGAIN.
"AS OUR SAVIOR IS THE FIRSTBORN OF THE DEAD...
"...AND AS WE FOLLOW HIM THROUGH DEATH TO THE GLORY THAT AWAITS..."

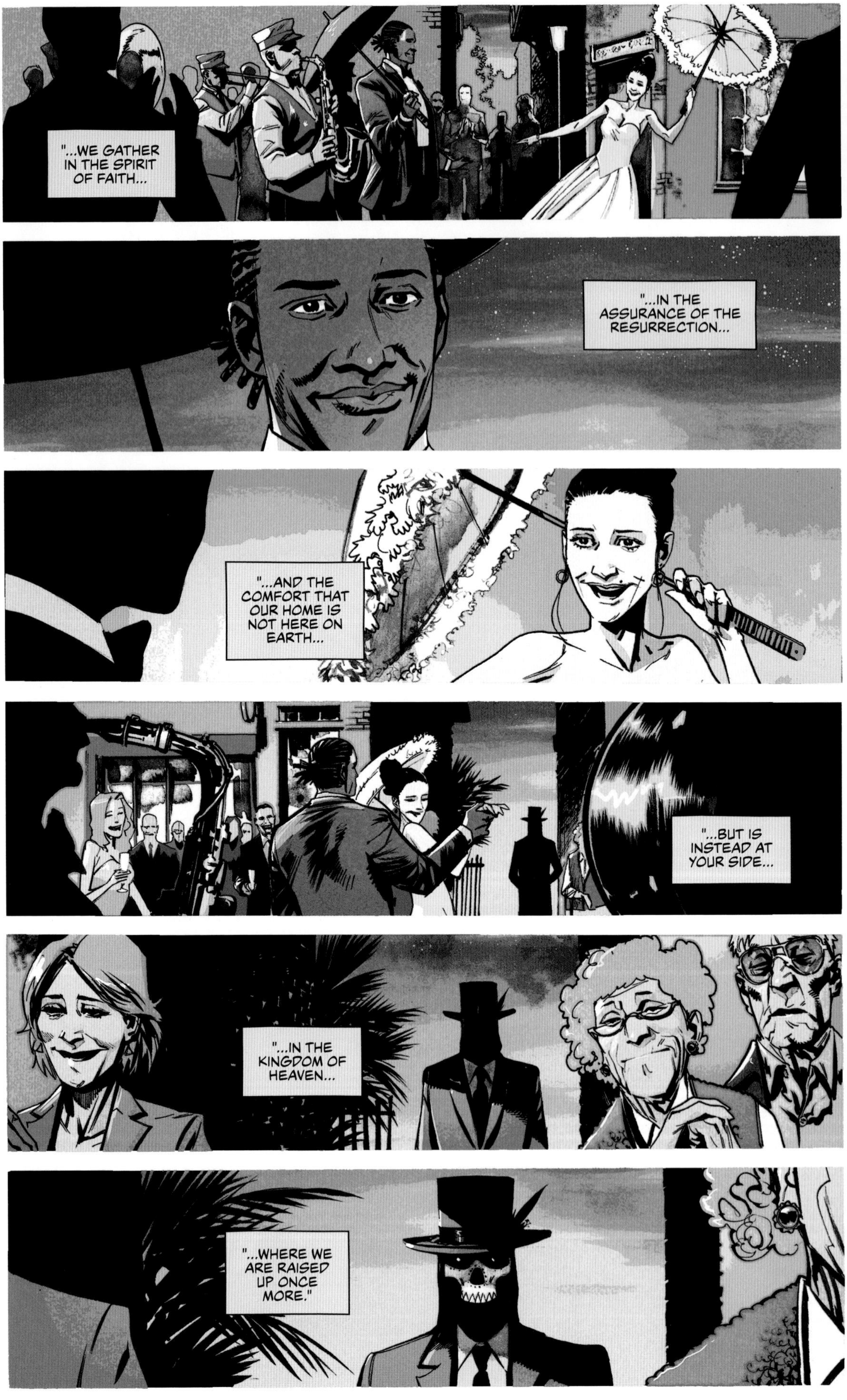
"...WE GATHER IN THE SPIRIT OF FAITH...
"...IN THE ASSURANCE OF THE RESURRECTION...
"...AND THE COMFORT THAT OUR HOME IS NOT HERE ON EARTH...
"...BUT IS INSTEAD AT YOUR SIDE...
"...IN THE KINGDOM OF HEAVEN...
"...WHERE WE ARE RAISED UP ONCE MORE."

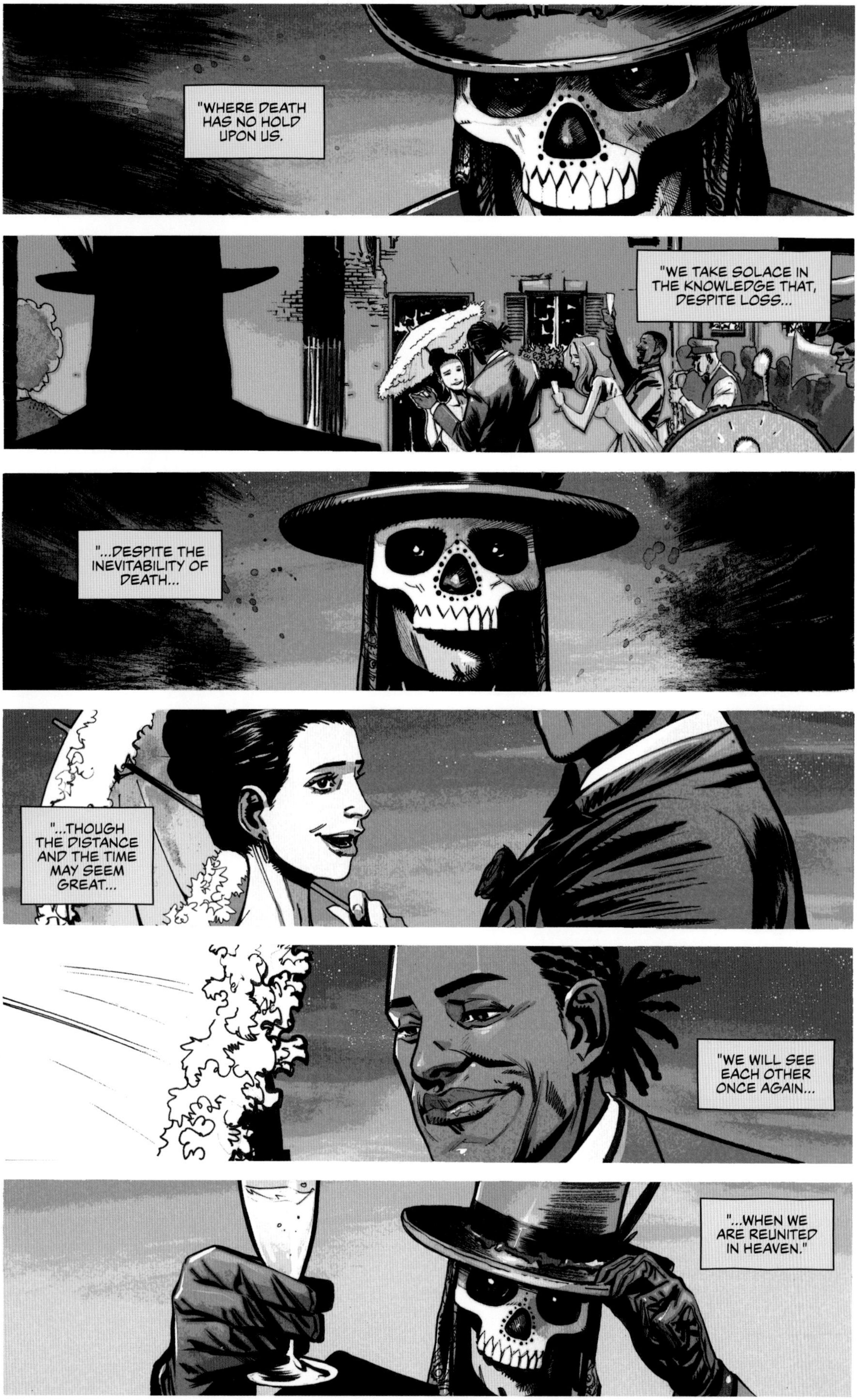
"WHERE DEATH HAS NO HOLD UPON US.
"WE TAKE SOLACE IN THE KNOWLEDGE THAT, DESPITE LOSS...
"...DESPITE THE INEVITABILITY OF DEATH...
"...THOUGH THE DISTANCE AND THE TIME MAY SEEM GREAT...
"WE WILL SEE EACH OTHER ONCE AGAIN...
"...WHEN WE ARE REUNITED IN HEAVEN."

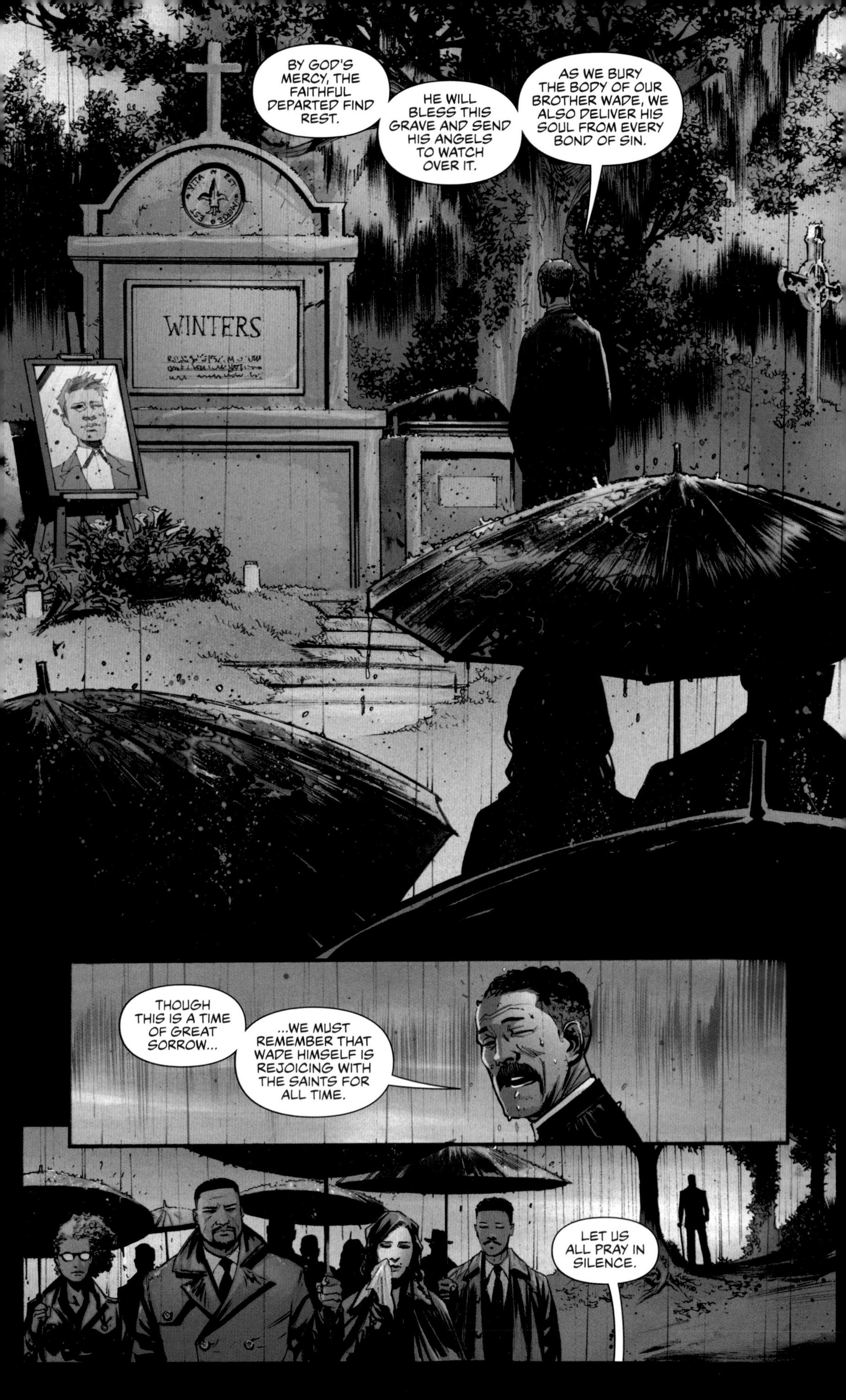
BY GOD'S MERCY, THE FAITHFUL DEPARTED FIND REST.
HE WILL BLESS THIS GRAVE AND SEND HIS ANGELS TO WATCH OVER IT.
AS WE BURY THE BODY OF OUR BROTHER WADE, WE ALSO DELIVER HIS SOUL FROM EVERY BOND OF SIN.
WINTERS
THOUGH THIS IS A TIME OF GREAT SORROW...
...WE MUST REMEMBER THAT WADE HIMSELF IS REJOICING WITH THE SAINTS FOR ALL TIME.
LET US ALL PRAY IN SILENCE.

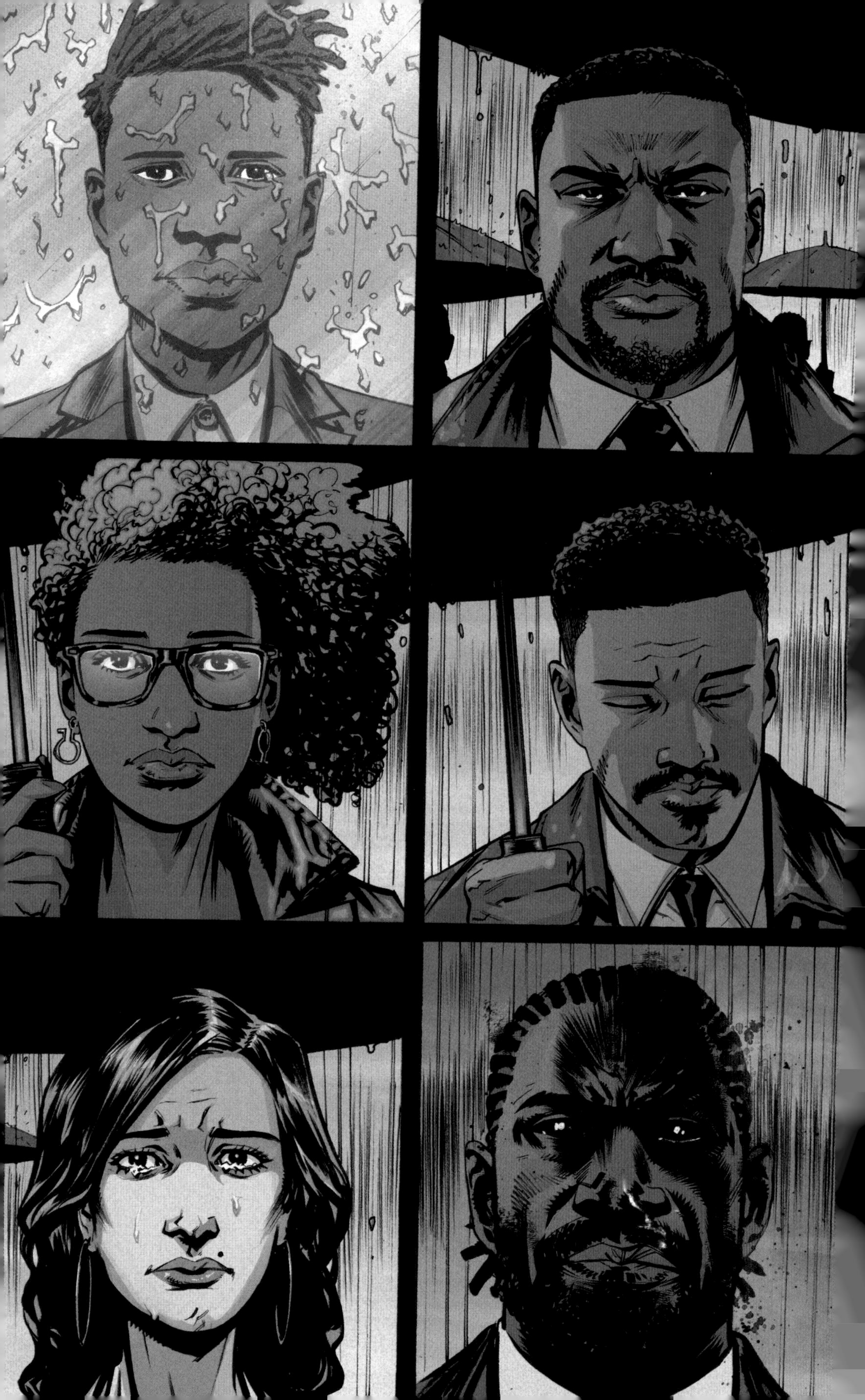

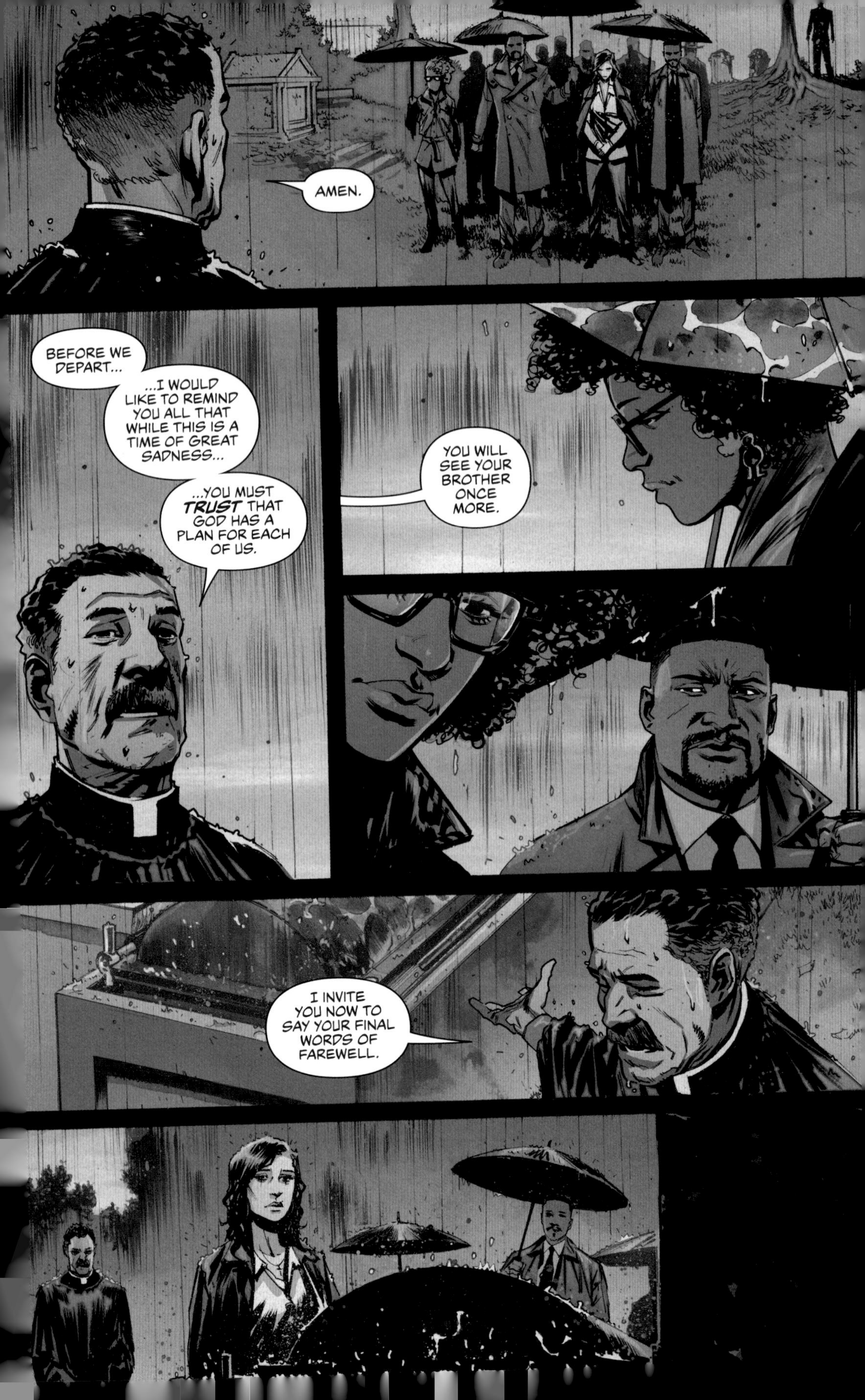
AMEN.
BEFORE WE DEPART...
...I WOULD LIKE TO REMIND YOU ALL THAT WHILE THIS IS A TIME OF GREAT SADNESS...
...YOU MUST TRUST THAT GOD HAS A PLAN FOR EACH OF US.
YOU WILL SEE YOUR BROTHER ONCE MORE.
I INVITE YOU NOW TO SAY YOUR FINAL WORDS OF FAREWELL.

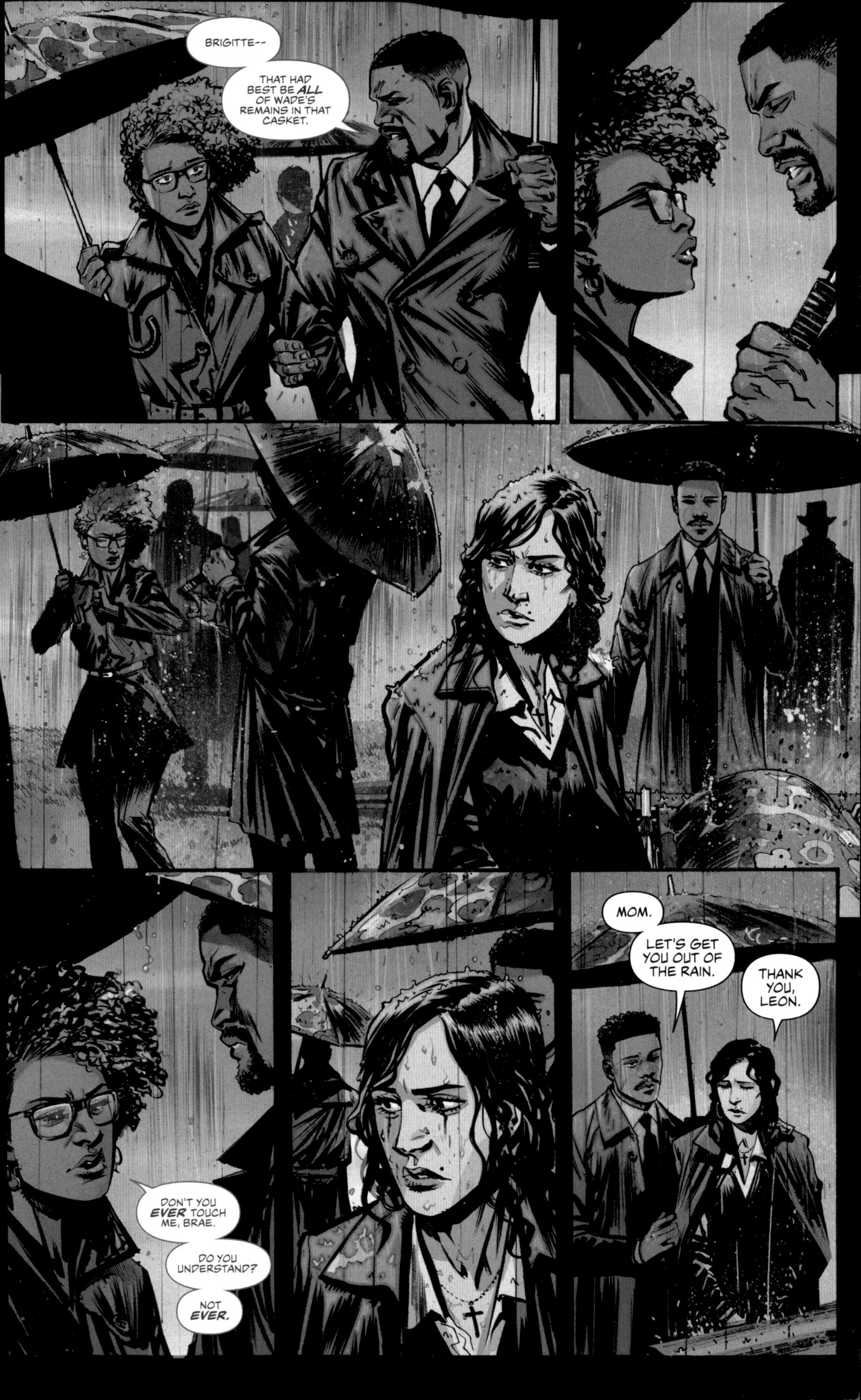

BRIGITTE--
THAT HAD BEST BE ALL OF WADE'S REMAINS IN THAT CASKET.
DON'T YOU EVER TOUCH ME, BRAE.
DO YOU UNDERSTAND?
NOT EVER.
MOM.
LET'S GET YOU OUT OF THE RAIN.
THANK YOU, LEON.

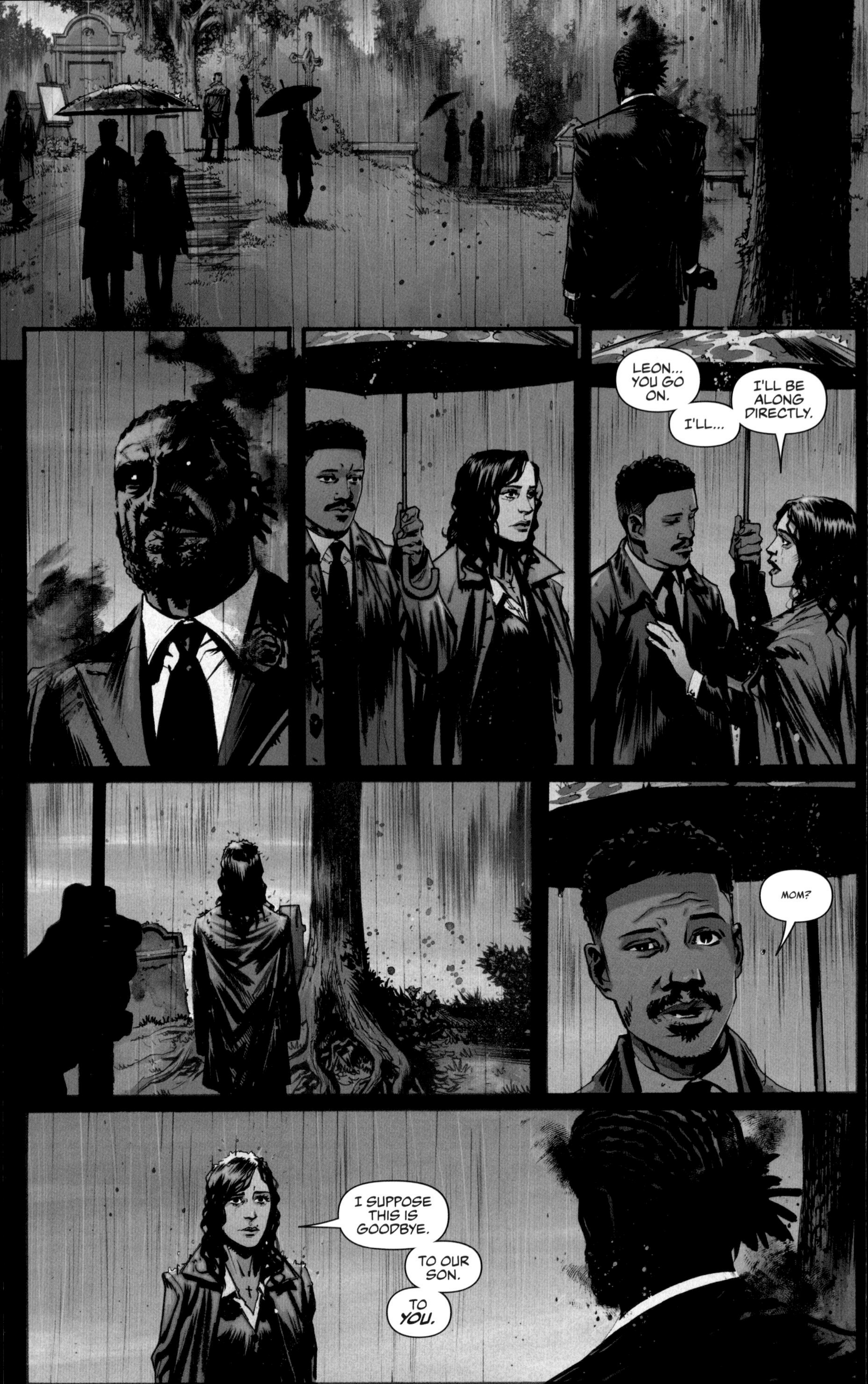
LEON... YOU GO ON.
I'LL...
I'LL BE ALONG DIRECTLY.
MOM?
I SUPPOSE THIS IS GOODBYE.
TO OUR SON.
TO YOU.

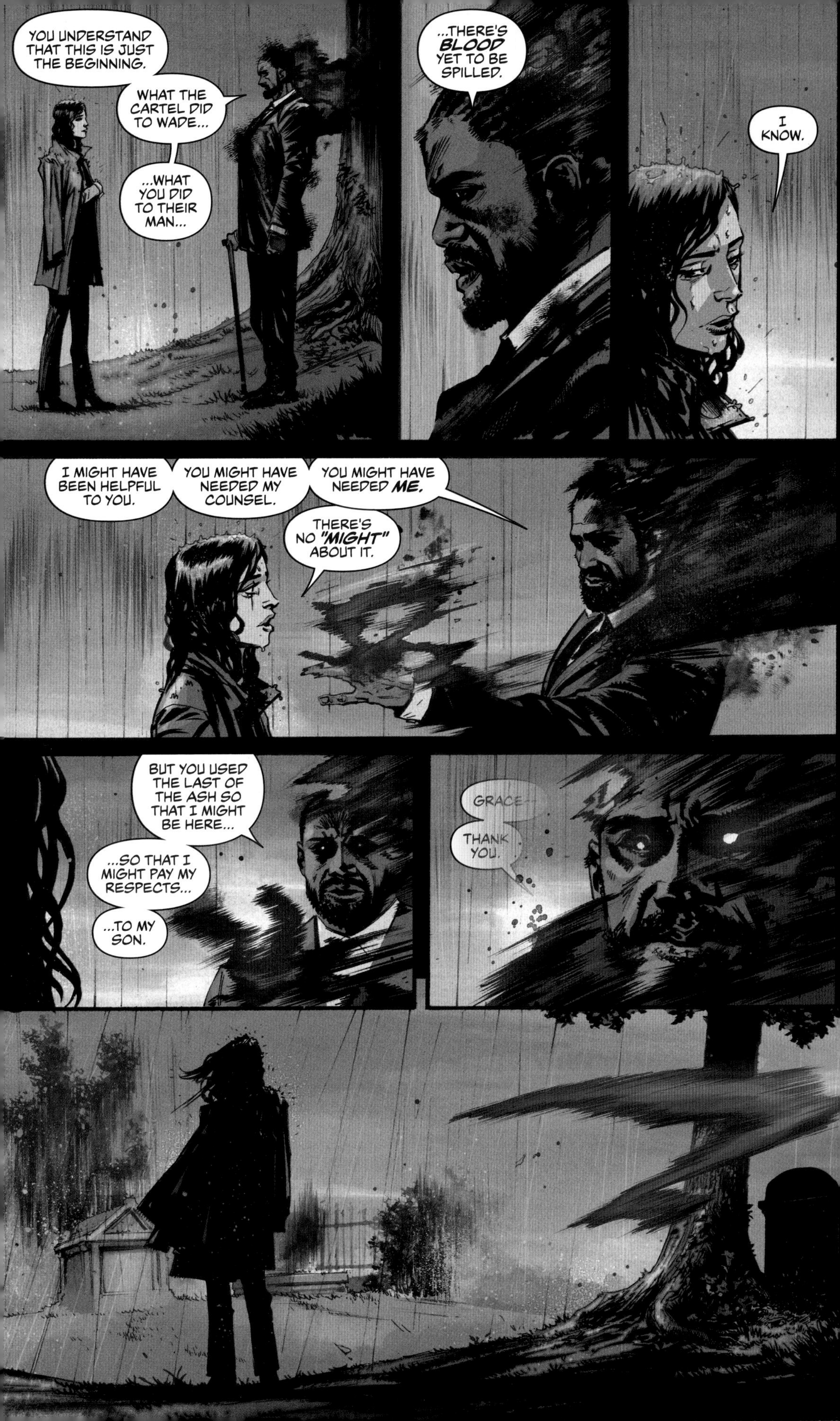
YOU UNDERSTAND THAT THIS IS JUST THE BEGINNING.
WHAT THE CARTEL DID TO WADE...
...WHAT YOU DID TO THEIR MAN...
...THERE'S BLOOD YET TO BE SPILLED.
I KNOW.
I MIGHT HAVE BEEN HELPFUL TO YOU.
YOU MIGHT HAVE NEEDED MY COUNSEL.
YOU MIGHT HAVE NEEDED ME.
THERE'S NO "MIGHT" ABOUT IT.
BUT YOU USED THE LAST OF THE ASH SO THAT I MIGHT BE HERE...
...SO THAT I MIGHT PAY MY RESPECTS...
...TO MY SON.
GRACE--
THANK YOU.

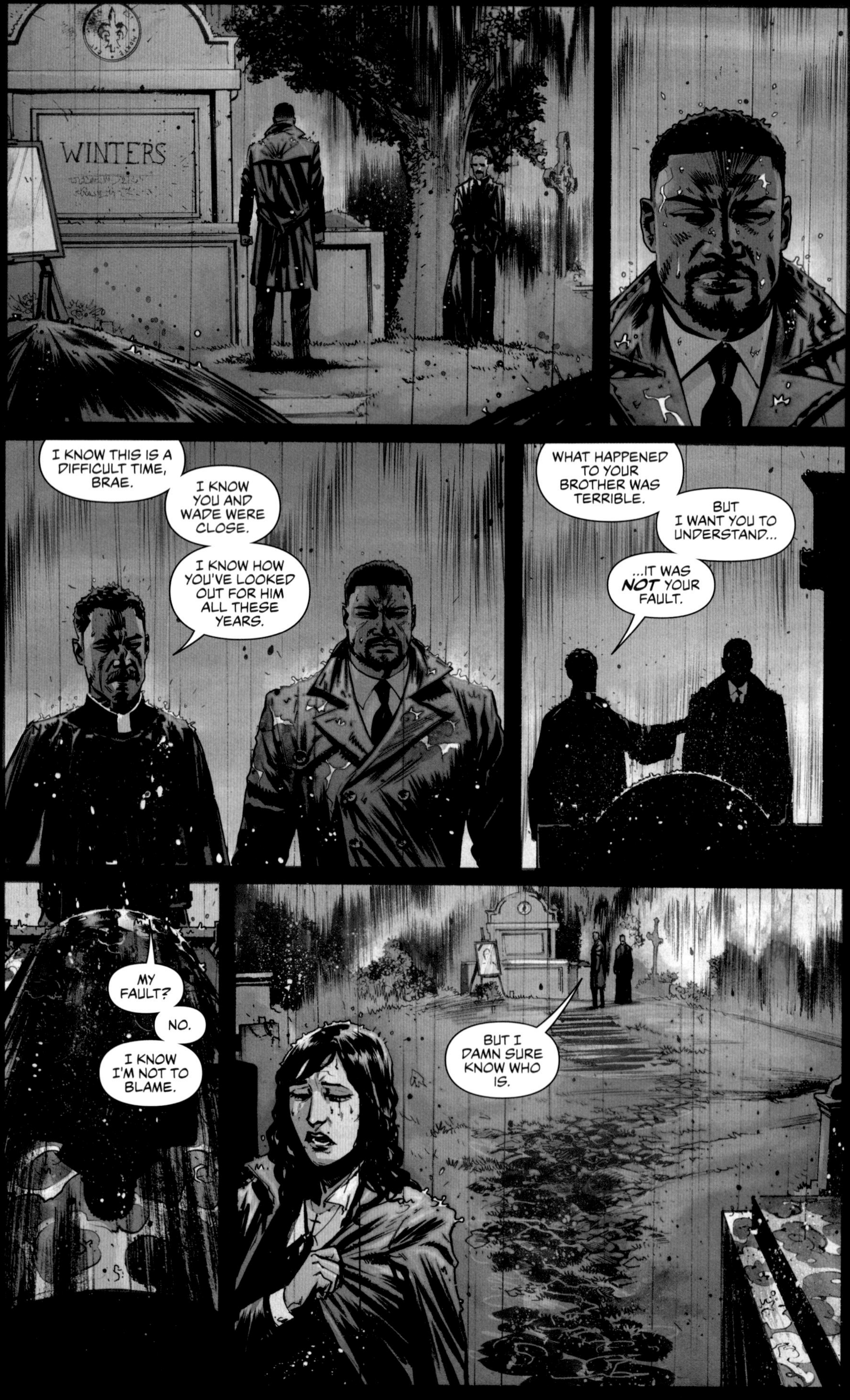
WINTERS
I KNOW THIS IS A DIFFICULT TIME, BRAE.
I KNOW YOU AND WADE WERE CLOSE.
I KNOW HOW YOU'VE LOOKED OUT FOR HIM ALL THESE YEARS.
WHAT HAPPENED TO YOUR BROTHER WAS TERRIBLE.
BUT I WANT YOU TO UNDERSTAND...
...IT WAS NOT YOUR FAULT.
MY FAULT?
NO.
I KNOW I'M NOT TO BLAME.
BUT I DAMN SURE KNOW WHO IS.

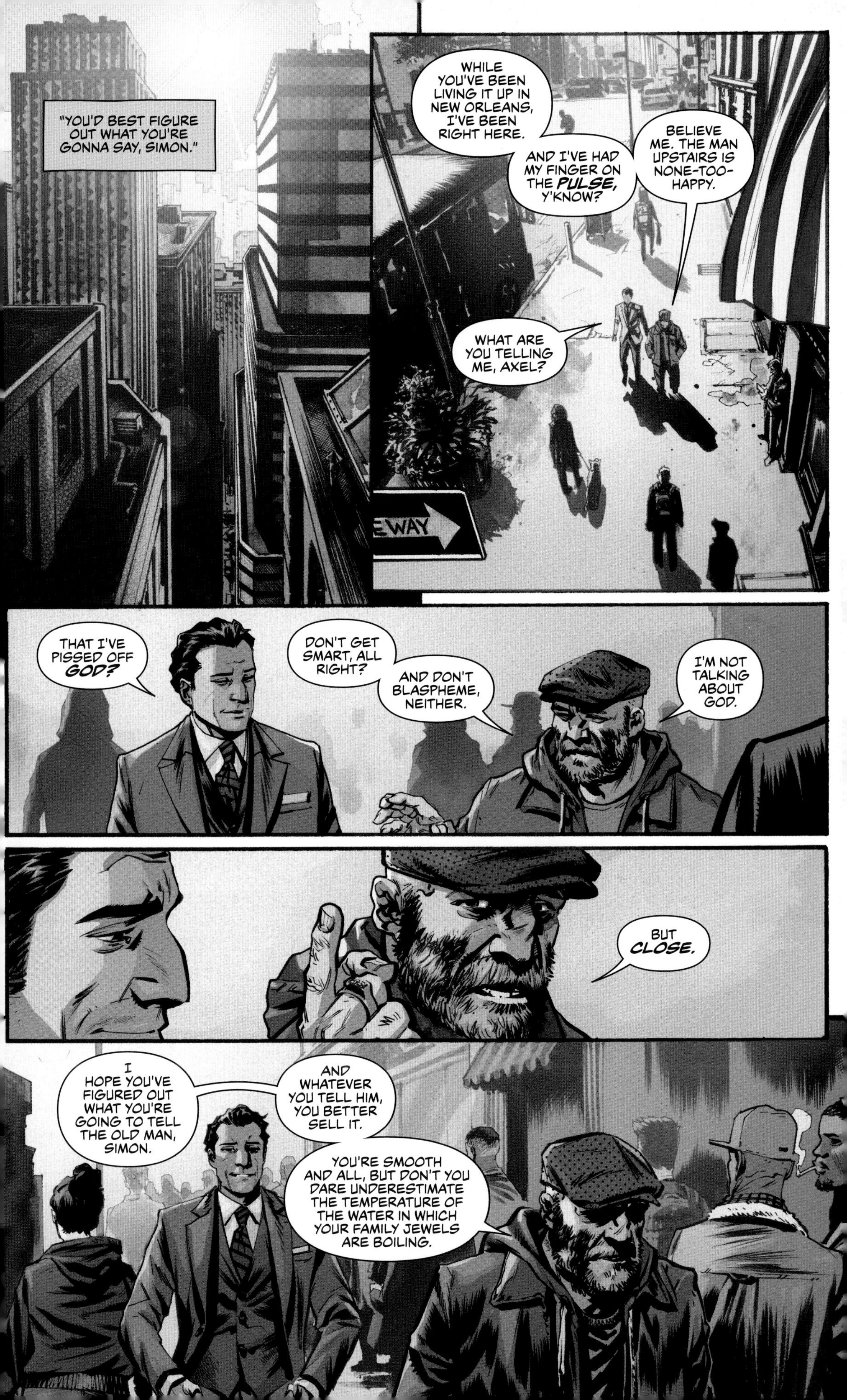
"YOU'D BEST FIGURE OUT WHAT YOU'RE GONNA SAY, SIMON."
WHILE YOU'VE BEEN LIVING IT UP IN NEW ORLEANS, I'VE BEEN RIGHT HERE.
AND I'VE HAD MY FINGER ON THE PULSE, Y'KNOW?
BELIEVE ME. THE MAN UPSTAIRS IS NONE-TOO-HAPPY.
WHAT ARE YOU TELLING ME, AXEL?
THAT I'VE PISSED OFF GOD?
DON'T GET SMART, ALL RIGHT?
AND DON'T BLASPHEME, NEITHER.
I'M NOT TALKING ABOUT GOD.
BUT CLOSE.
I HOPE YOU'VE FIGURED OUT WHAT YOU'RE GOING TO TELL THE OLD MAN, SIMON.
AND WHATEVER YOU TELL HIM, YOU BETTER SELL IT.
YOU'RE SMOOTH AND ALL, BUT DON'T YOU DARE UNDERESTIMATE THE TEMPERATURE OF THE WATER IN WHICH YOUR FAMILY JEWELS ARE BOILING.

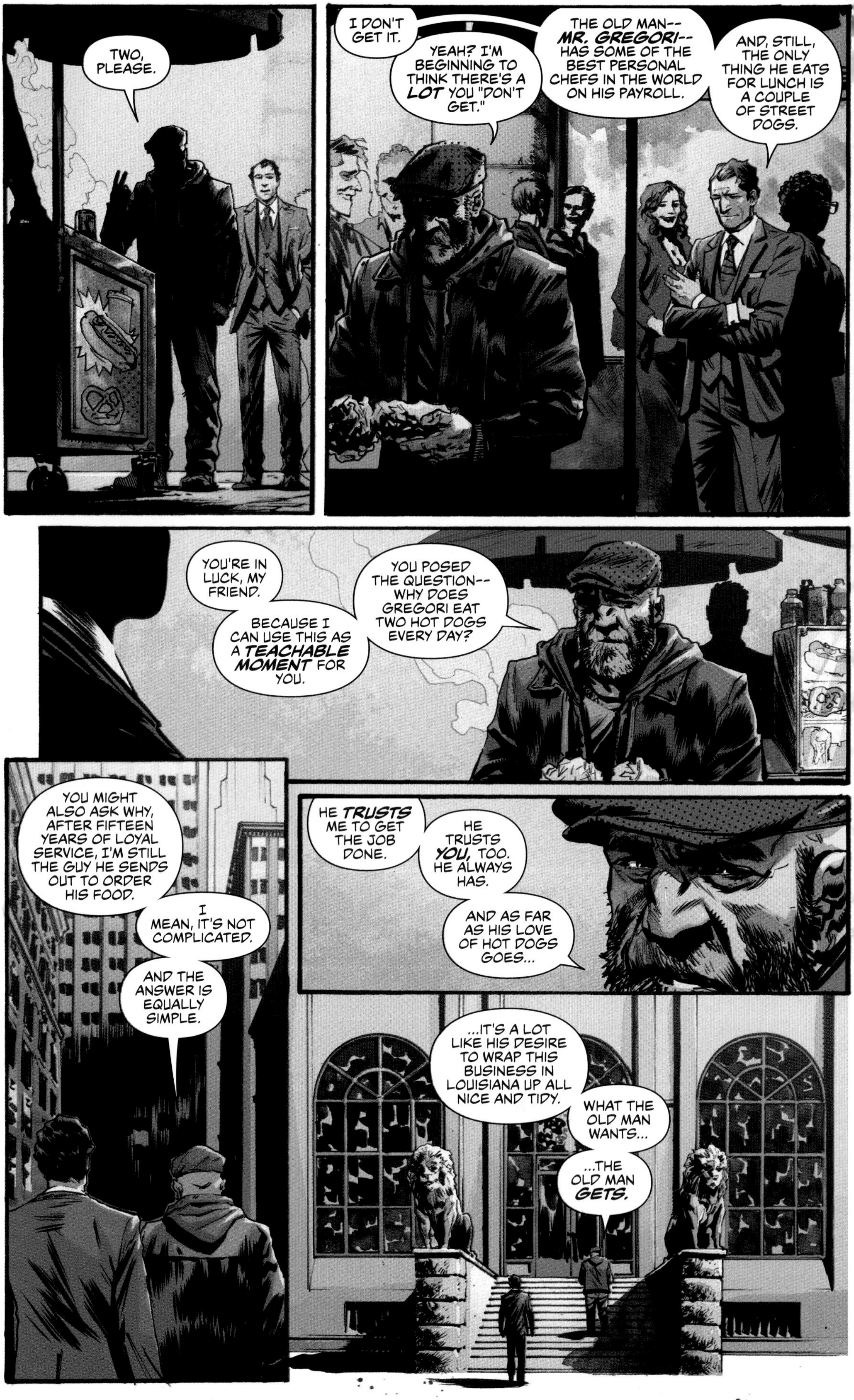

TWO, PLEASE.
I DON'T GET IT.
YEAH? I'M BEGINNING TO THINK THERE'S A **LOT** YOU "DON'T GET."
THE OLD MAN-- **MR. GREGORI--** HAS SOME OF THE BEST PERSONAL CHEFS IN THE WORLD ON HIS PAYROLL.
AND, STILL, THE ONLY THING HE EATS FOR LUNCH IS A COUPLE OF STREET DOGS.
YOU'RE IN LUCK, MY FRIEND.
BECAUSE I CAN USE THIS AS A **TEACHABLE MOMENT** FOR YOU.
YOU POSED THE QUESTION-- WHY DOES GREGORI EAT TWO HOT DOGS EVERY DAY?
YOU MIGHT ALSO ASK WHY, AFTER FIFTEEN YEARS OF LOYAL SERVICE, I'M STILL THE GUY HE SENDS OUT TO ORDER HIS FOOD.
I MEAN, IT'S NOT COMPLICATED.
AND THE ANSWER IS EQUALLY SIMPLE.
HE **TRUSTS** ME TO GET THE JOB DONE.
HE TRUSTS **YOU,** TOO. HE ALWAYS HAS.
AND AS FAR AS HIS LOVE OF HOT DOGS GOES...
...IT'S A LOT LIKE HIS DESIRE TO WRAP THIS BUSINESS IN LOUISIANA UP ALL NICE AND TIDY.
WHAT THE OLD MAN WANTS...
...THE OLD MAN **GETS.**

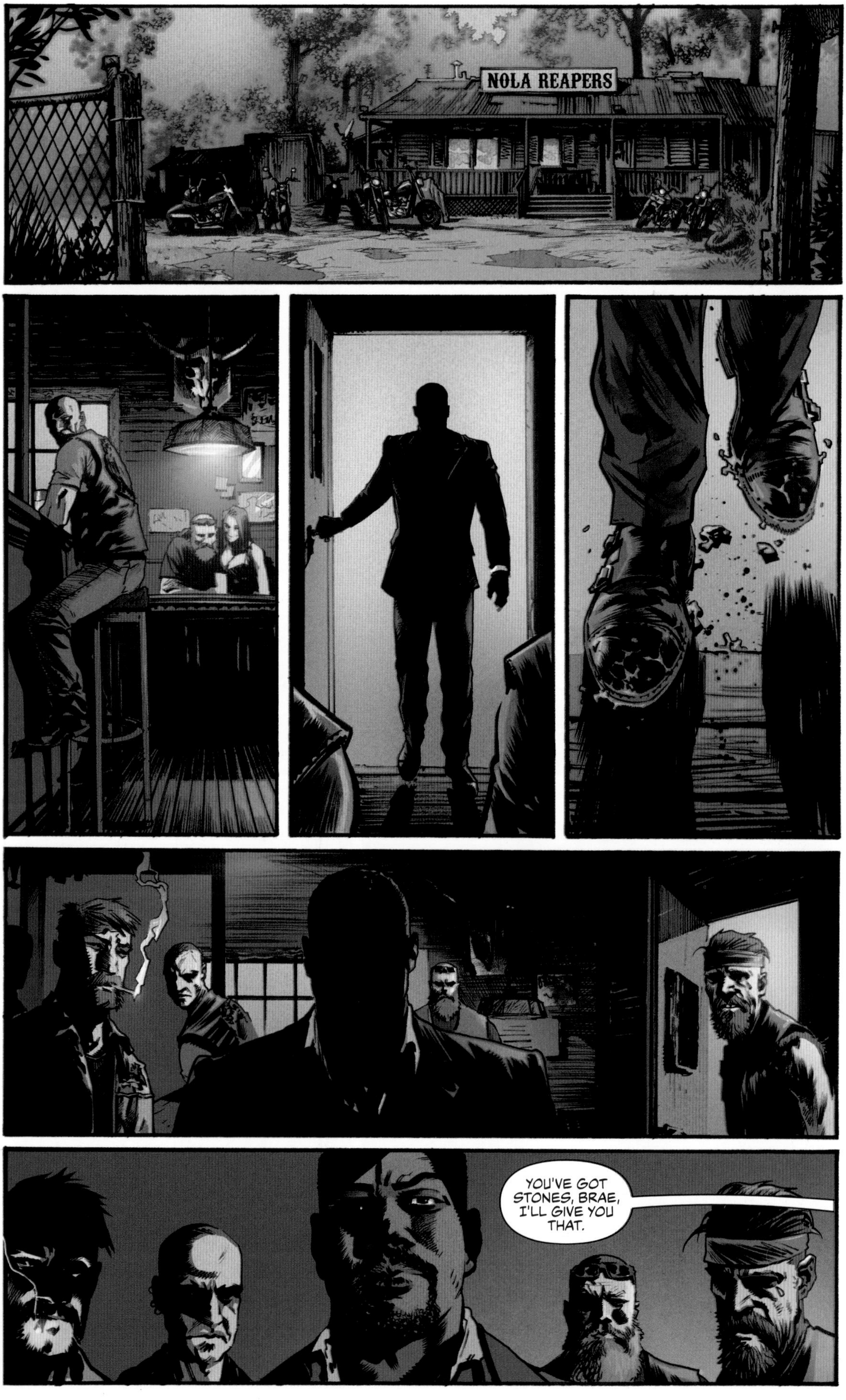
NOLA REAPERS
YOU'VE GOT STONES, BRAE, I'LL GIVE YOU THAT.

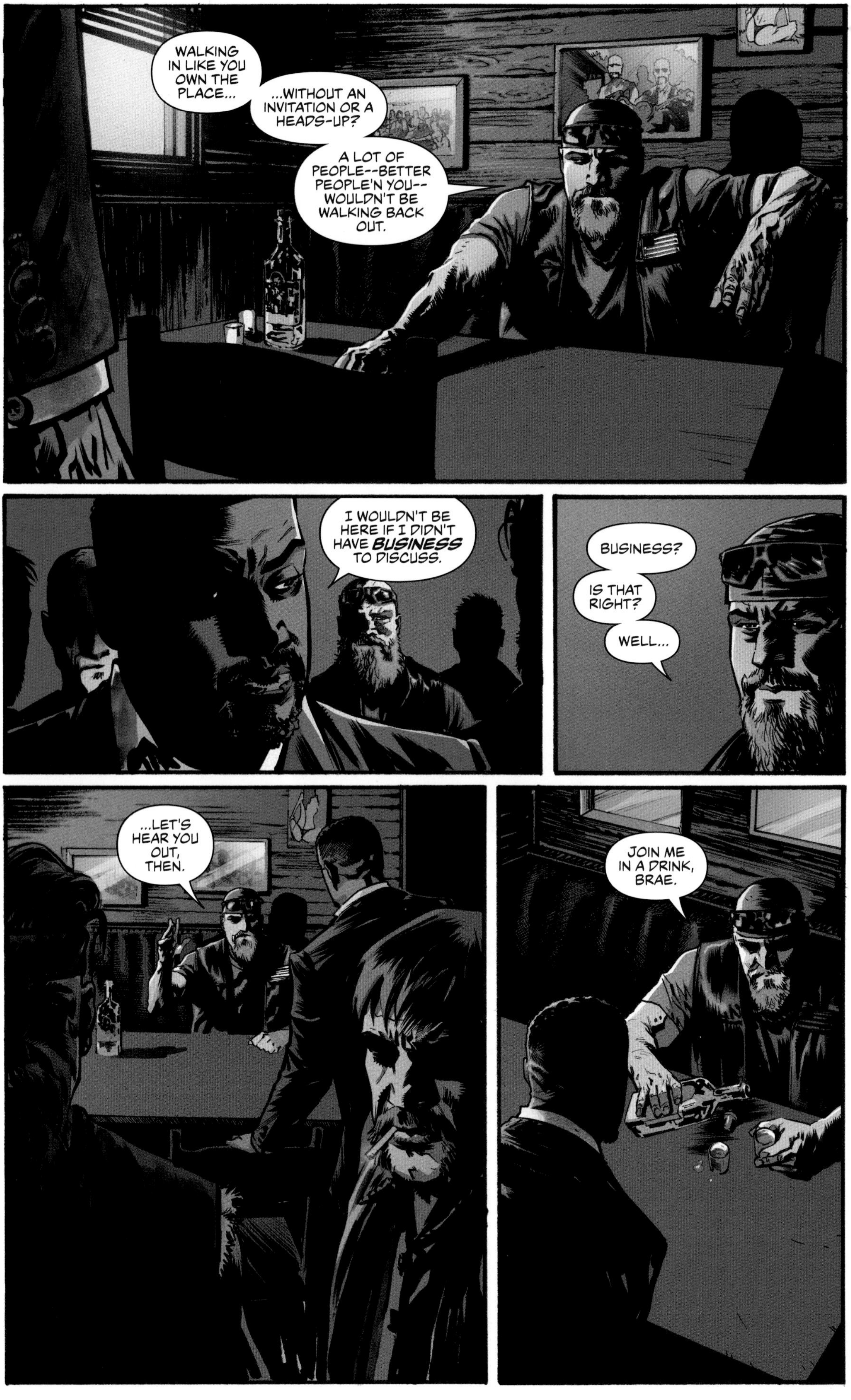
WALKING IN LIKE YOU OWN THE PLACE...
...WITHOUT AN INVITATION OR A HEADS-UP?
A LOT OF PEOPLE--BETTER PEOPLE'N YOU--WOULDN'T BE WALKING BACK OUT.
I WOULDN'T BE HERE IF I DIDN'T HAVE BUSINESS TO DISCUSS.
BUSINESS?
IS THAT RIGHT?
WELL...
...LET'S HEAR YOU OUT, THEN.
JOIN ME IN A DRINK, BRAE.

I HEARD WHAT HAPPENED TO YOUR BROTHER.

THAT WAS A SHAME.

I'VE HAD MY DIFFERENCES WITH YOUR FAMILY, BUT WHAT HAPPENED TO YOUR BROTHER...

...THAT WASN'T RIGHT.

I HEARD WHAT HAPPENED TO THE CARTEL LAPDOG THAT KILLED HIM, TOO.

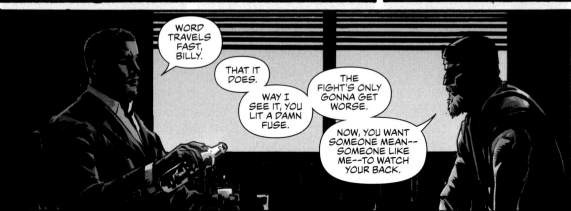

WORD TRAVELS FAST, BILLY.

THAT IT DOES.

WAY I SEE IT, YOU LIT A DAMN FUSE.

THE FIGHT'S ONLY GONNA GET WORSE.

NOW, YOU WANT SOMEONE MEAN-- SOMEONE LIKE ME--TO WATCH YOUR BACK.

MY FATHER AND YOUR FATHER ONCE HAD SIMILAR ARRANGEMENTS.

BUT I THINK THE DETAILS OF THOSE ARRANGEMENTS-- THE FINER POINTS-- CAN BE IMPROVED UPON.

THERE'S ALWAYS ROOM FOR IMPROVEMENT.

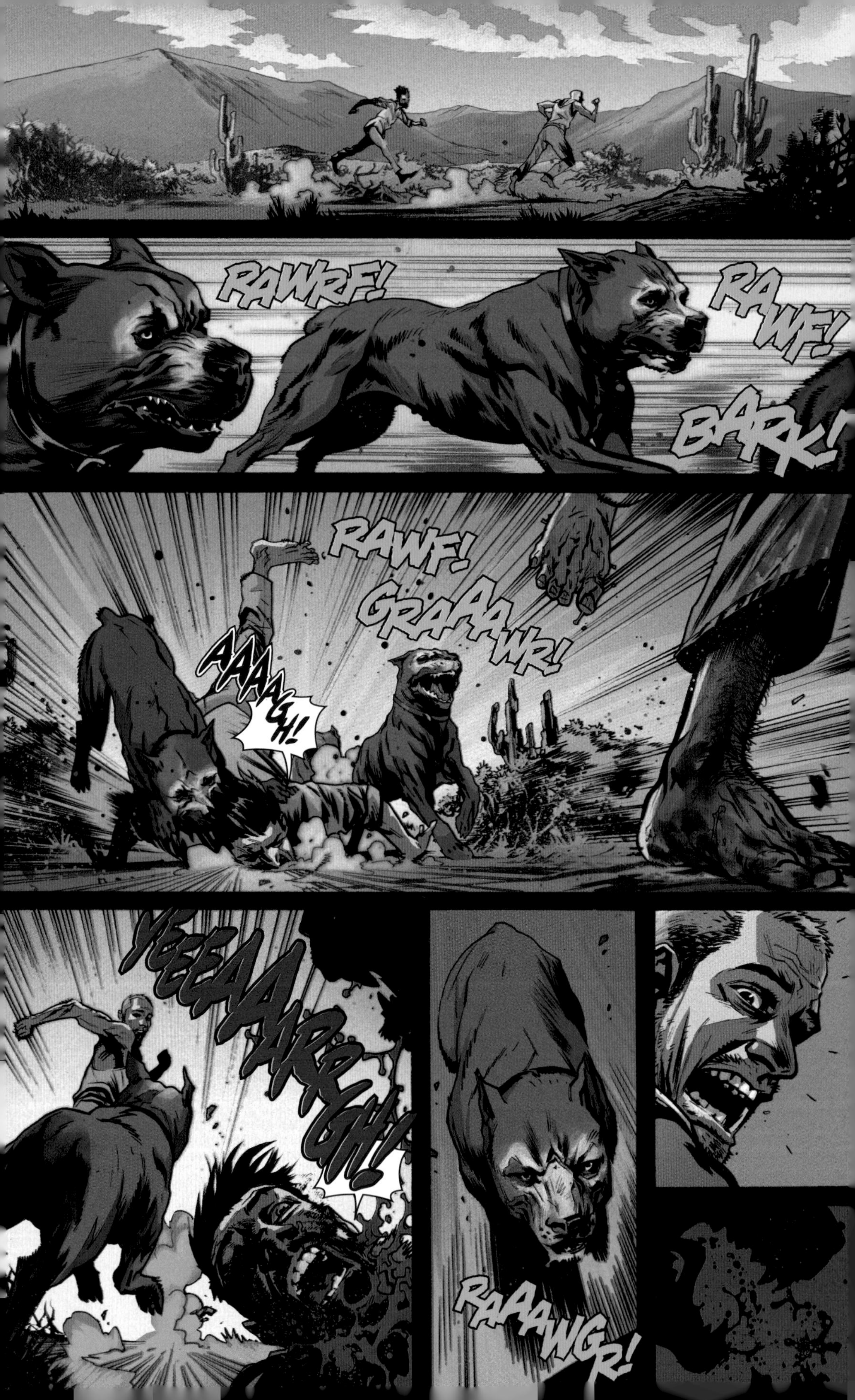
RAWRF!
RAWF!
BARK!
RAWF!
GRAAAAWR!
AAAAGH!
YEEEAAARRGH!
RAAAWGR!

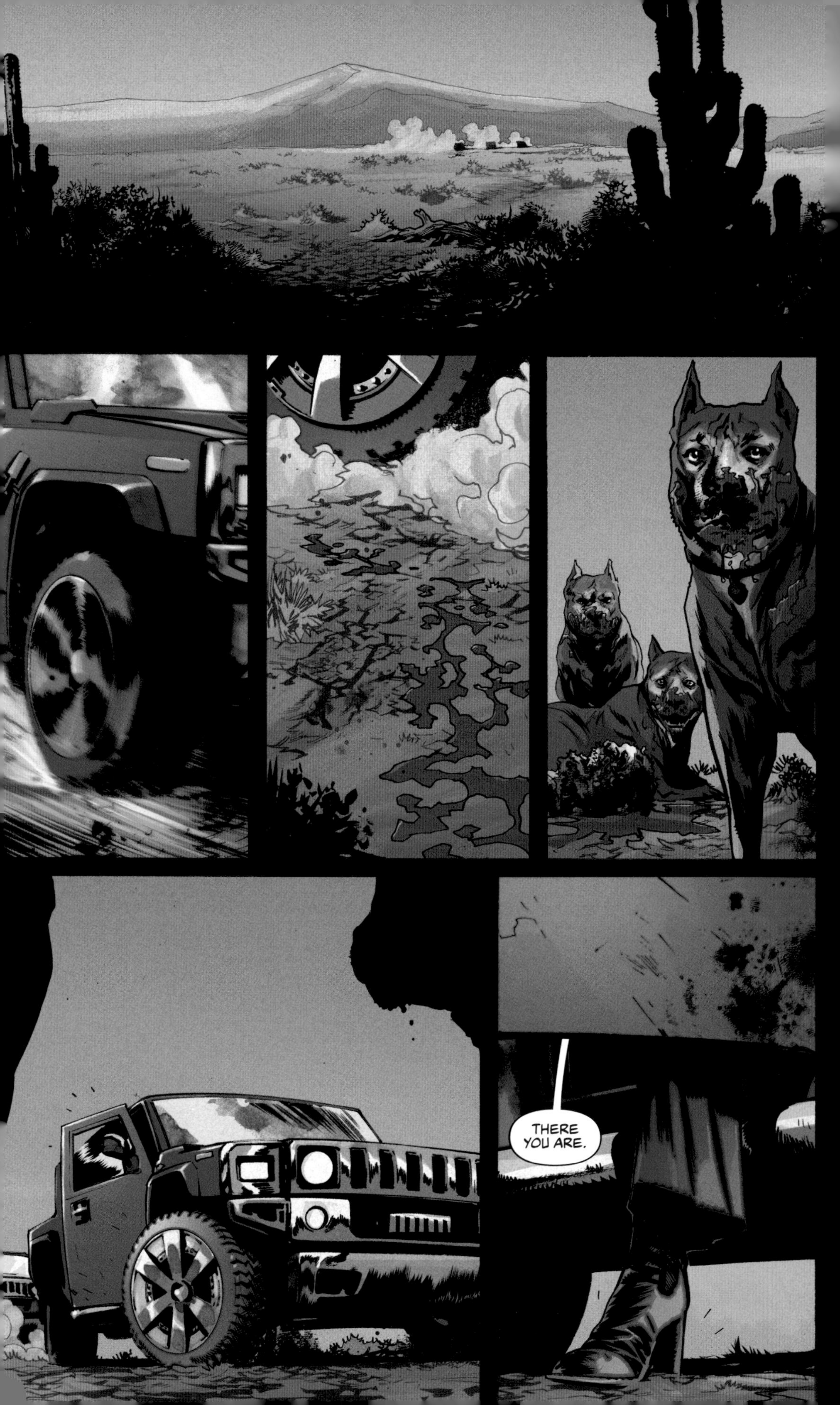
THERE YOU ARE.

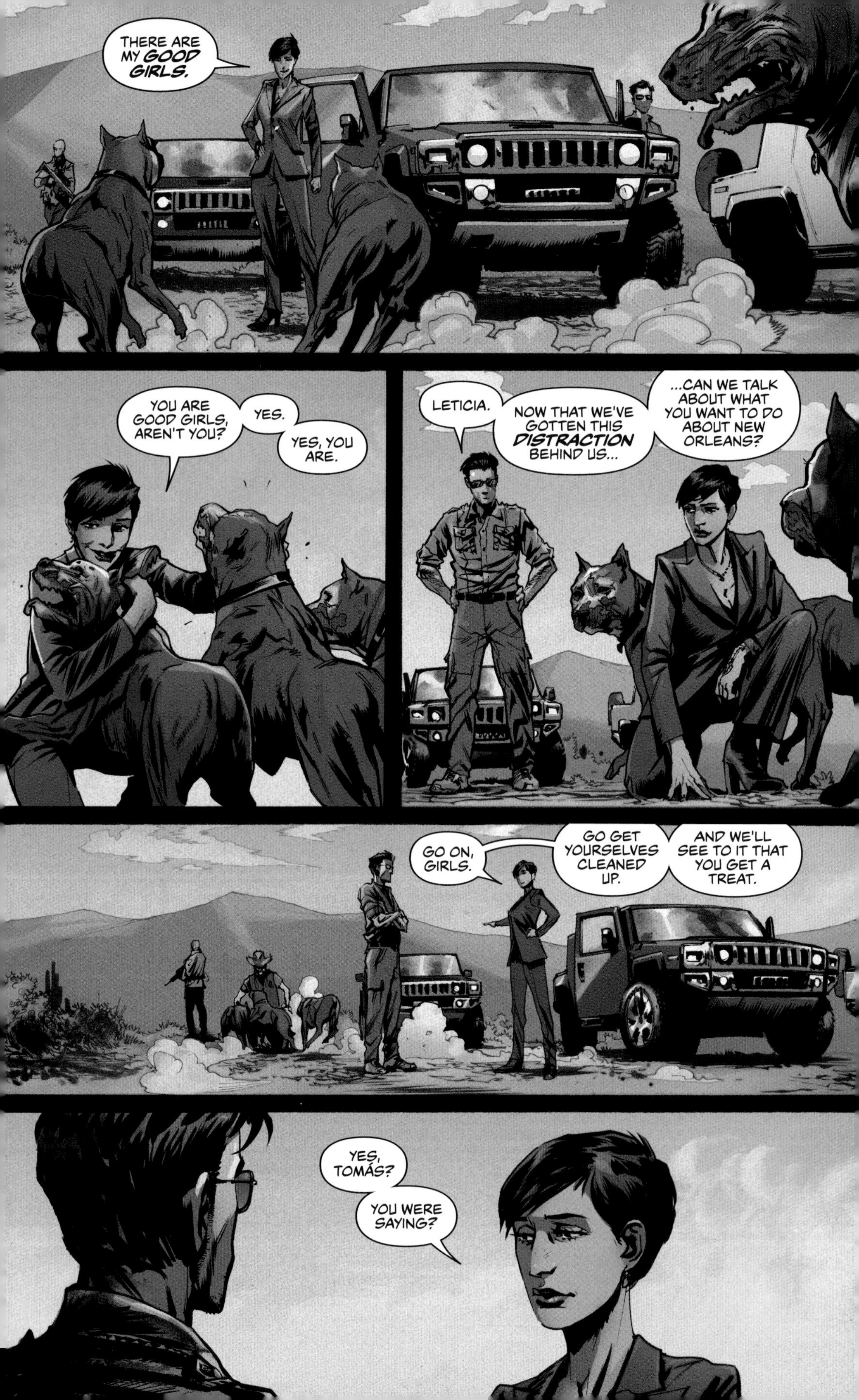
THERE ARE MY GOOD GIRLS.
YOU ARE GOOD GIRLS, AREN'T YOU?
YES.
YES, YOU ARE.
LETICIA.
NOW THAT WE'VE GOTTEN THIS DISTRACTION BEHIND US...
...CAN WE TALK ABOUT WHAT YOU WANT TO DO ABOUT NEW ORLEANS?
GO ON, GIRLS.
GO GET YOURSELVES CLEANED UP.
AND WE'LL SEE TO IT THAT YOU GET A TREAT.
YES, TOMÁS?
YOU WERE SAYING?

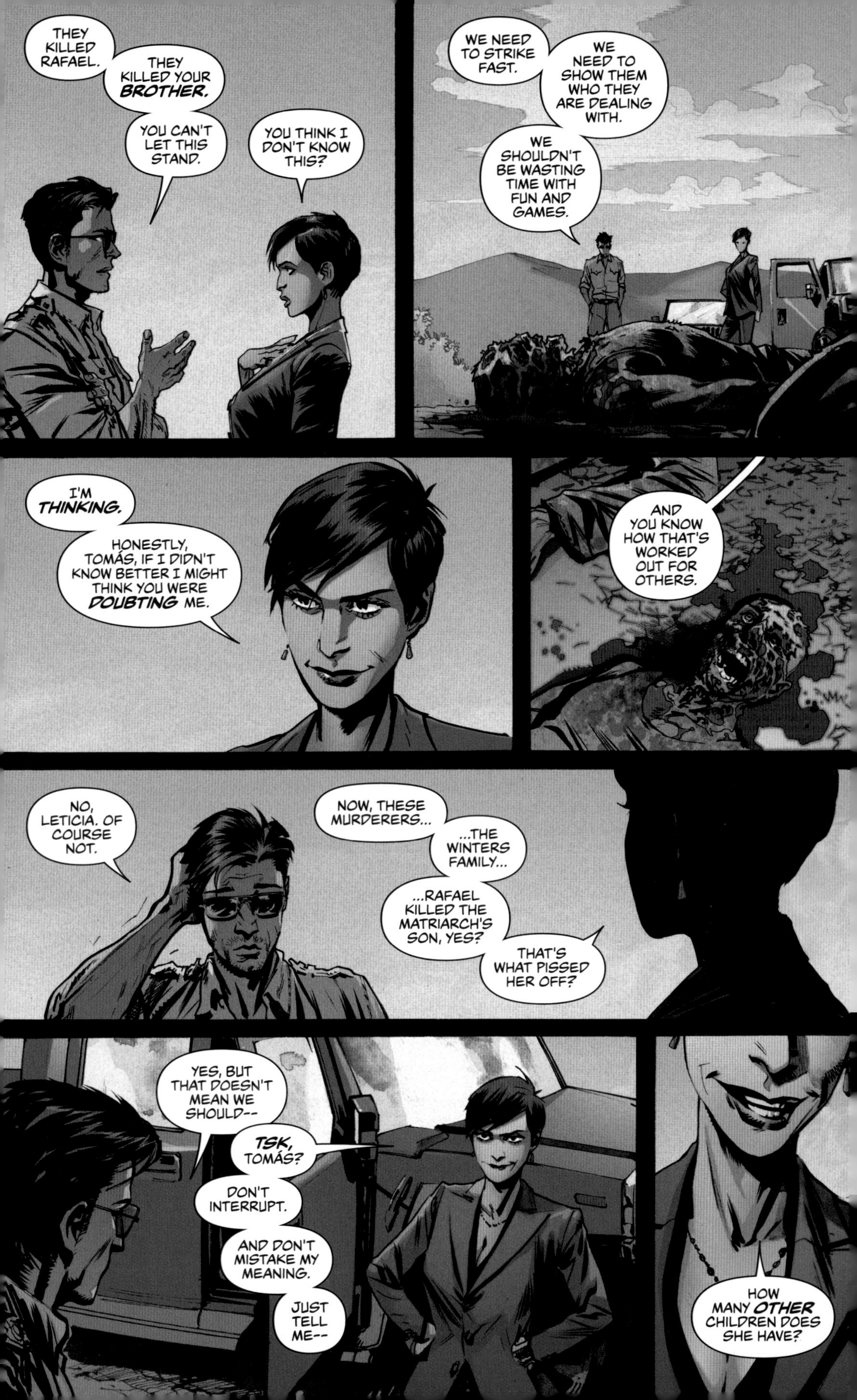

THEY KILLED RAFAEL.
THEY KILLED YOUR BROTHER.
YOU CAN'T LET THIS STAND.
YOU THINK I DON'T KNOW THIS?
WE NEED TO STRIKE FAST.
WE NEED TO SHOW THEM WHO THEY ARE DEALING WITH.
WE SHOULDN'T BE WASTING TIME WITH FUN AND GAMES.
I'M THINKING.
HONESTLY, TOMÁS, IF I DIDN'T KNOW BETTER I MIGHT THINK YOU WERE DOUBTING ME.
AND YOU KNOW HOW THAT'S WORKED OUT FOR OTHERS.
NO, LETICIA. OF COURSE NOT.
NOW, THESE MURDERERS...
...THE WINTERS FAMILY...
...RAFAEL KILLED THE MATRIARCH'S SON, YES?
THAT'S WHAT PISSED HER OFF?
YES, BUT THAT DOESN'T MEAN WE SHOULD--
TSK, TOMÁS?
DON'T INTERRUPT.
AND DON'T MISTAKE MY MEANING.
JUST TELL ME--
HOW MANY OTHER CHILDREN DOES SHE HAVE?

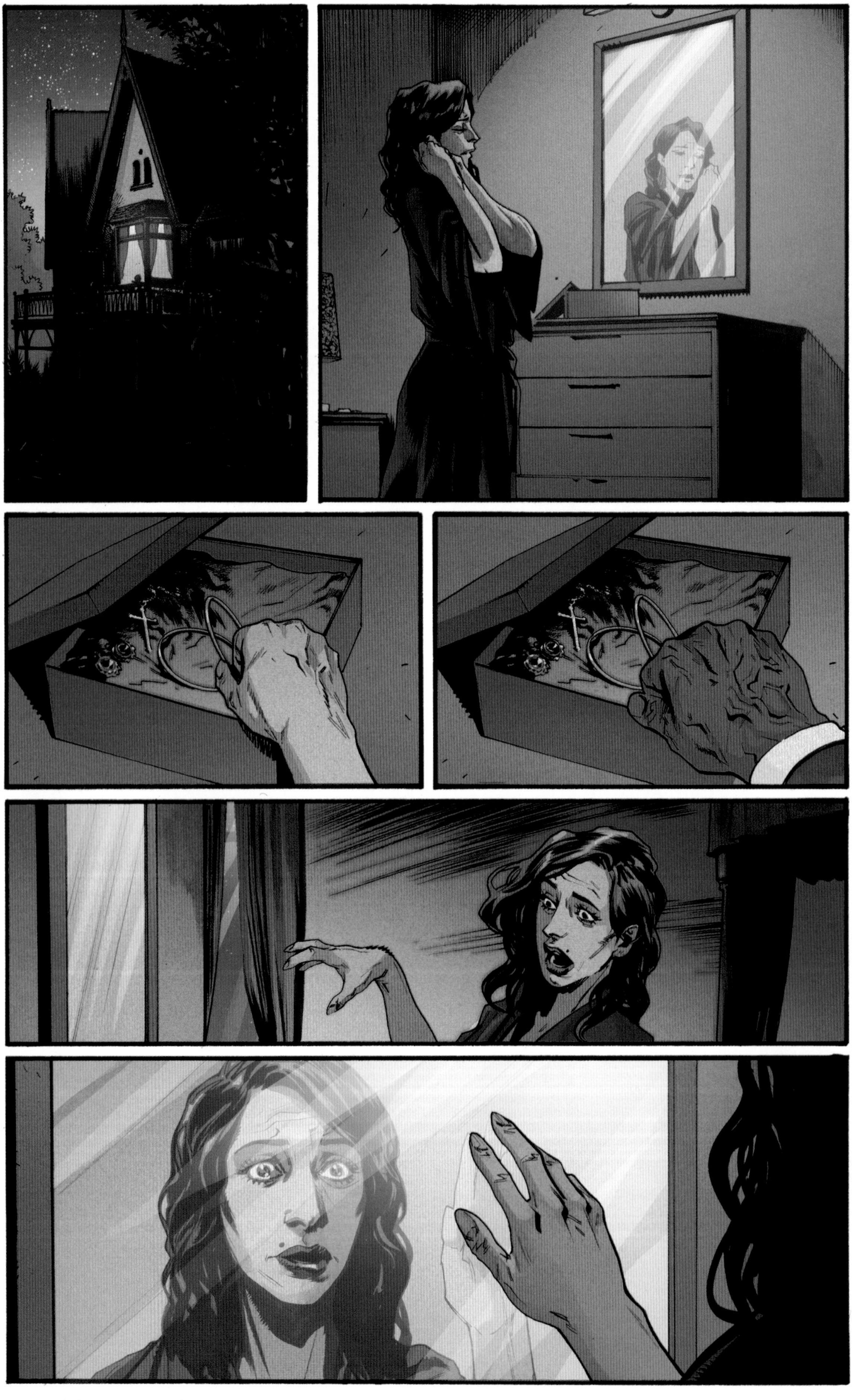

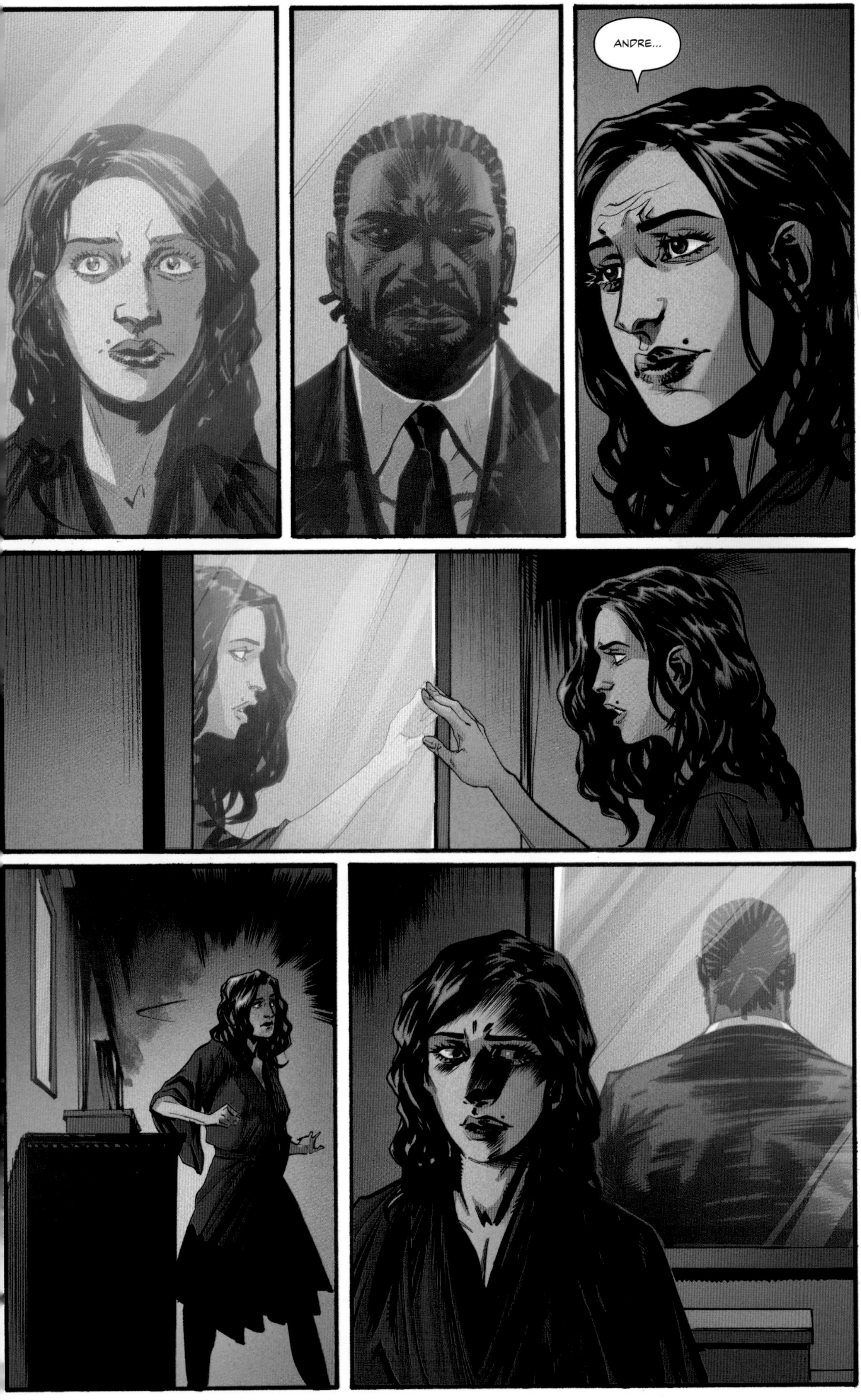
ANDRE...

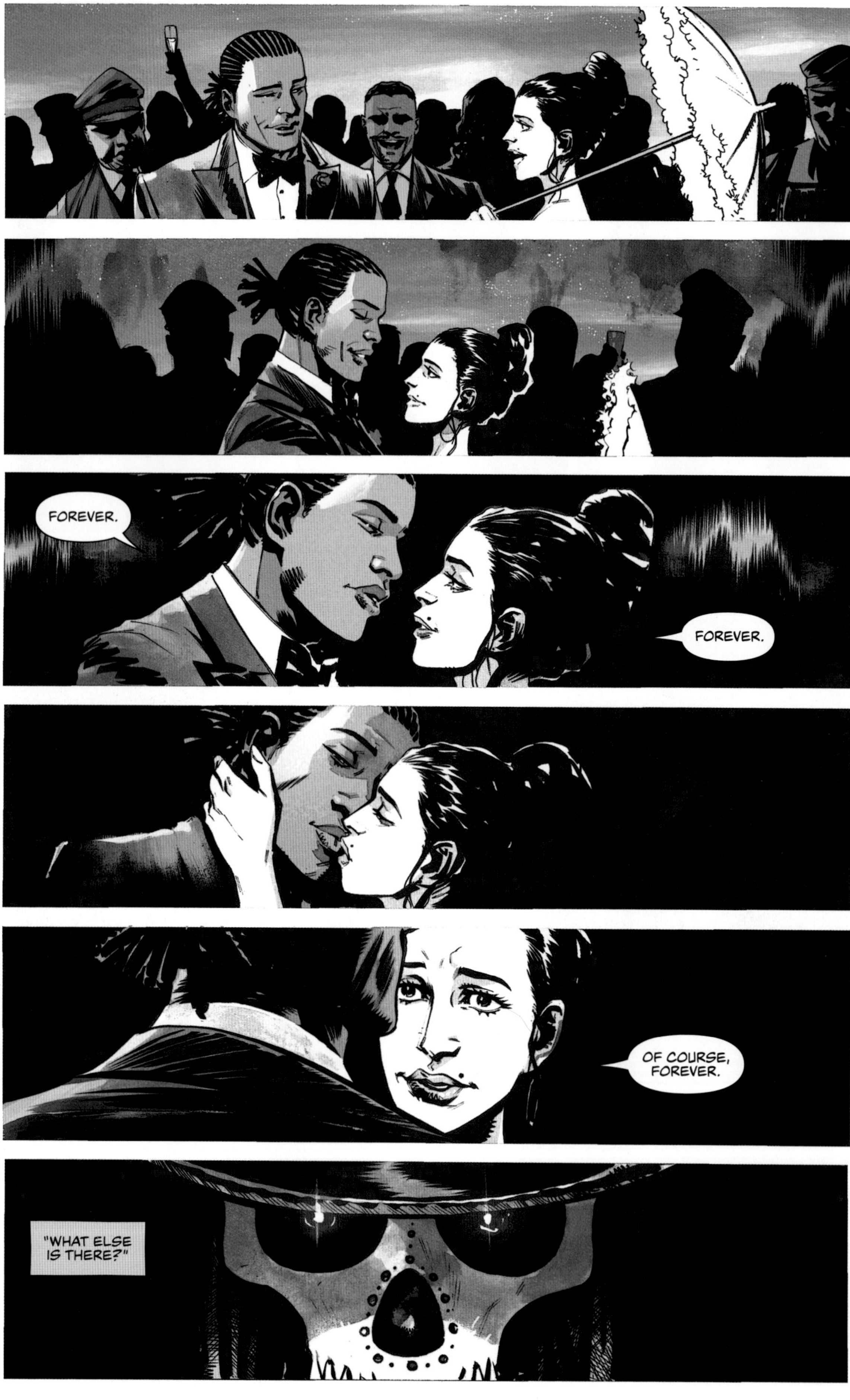
FOREVER.
FOREVER.
OF COURSE, FOREVER.
"WHAT ELSE IS THERE?"

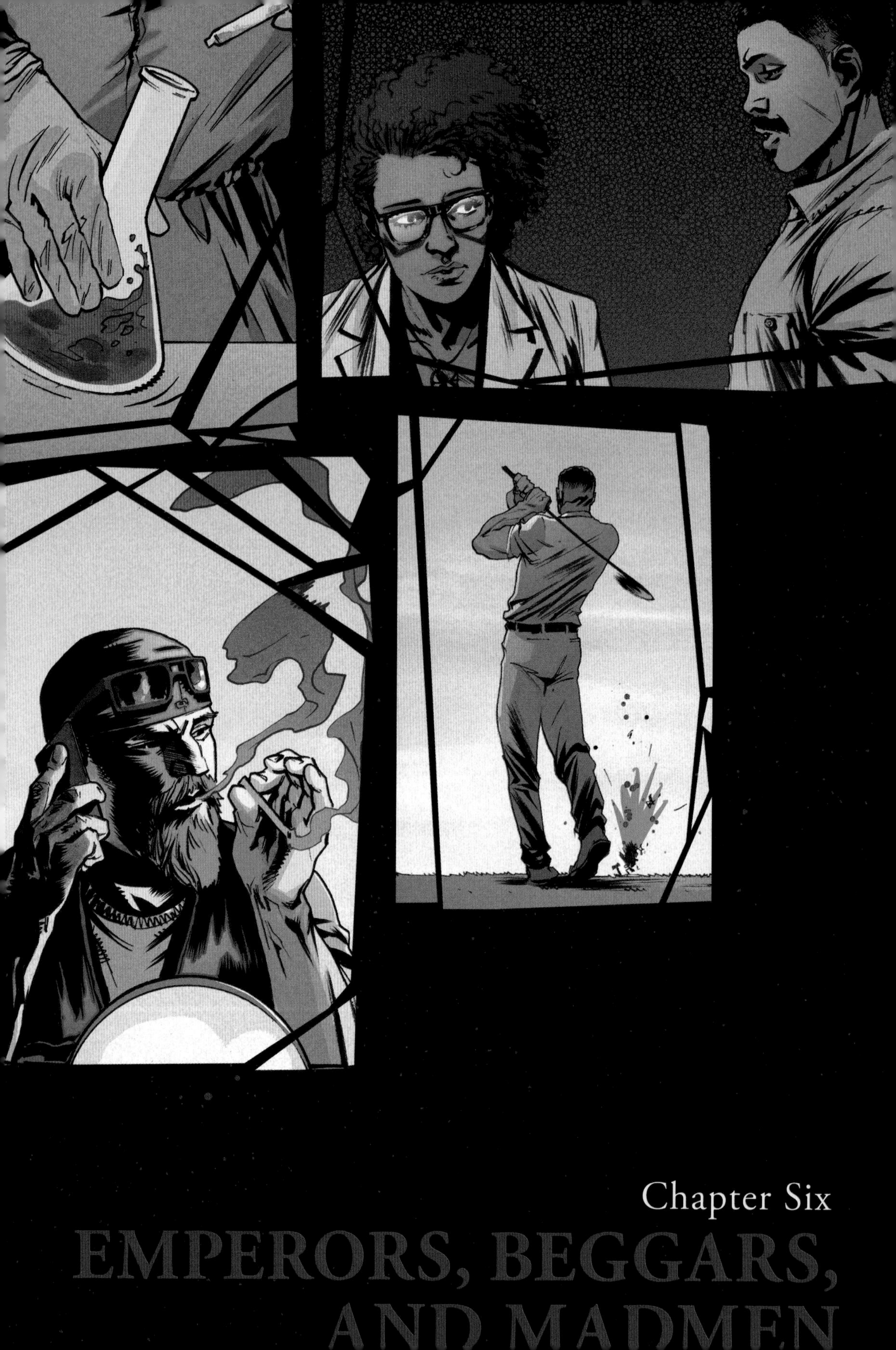

Chapter Six

EMPERORS, BEGGARS, AND MADMEN

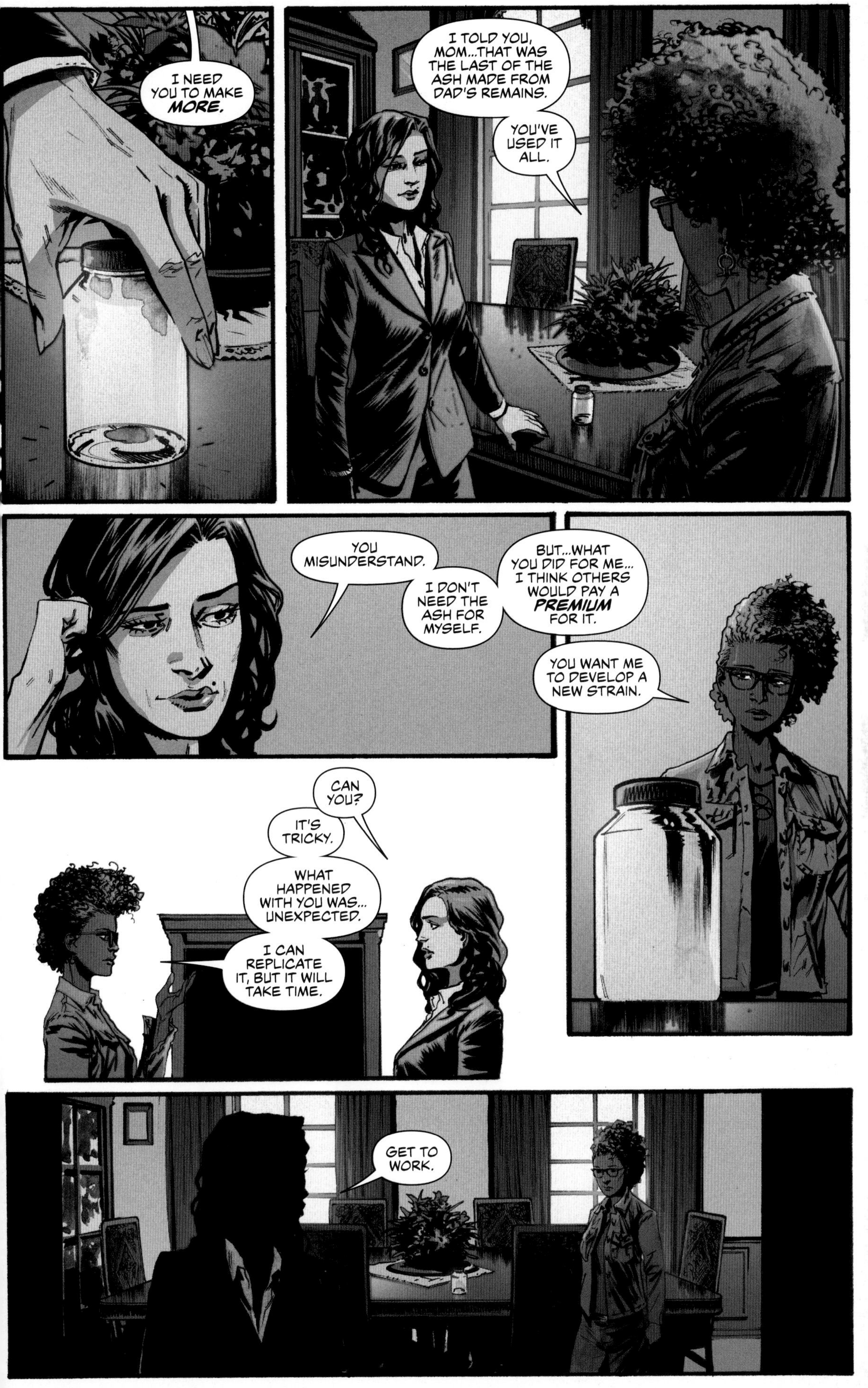
I NEED YOU TO MAKE MORE.
I TOLD YOU, MOM...THAT WAS THE LAST OF THE ASH MADE FROM DAD'S REMAINS.
YOU'VE USED IT ALL.
YOU MISUNDERSTAND.
I DON'T NEED THE ASH FOR MYSELF.
BUT...WHAT YOU DID FOR ME... I THINK OTHERS WOULD PAY A PREMIUM FOR IT.
YOU WANT ME TO DEVELOP A NEW STRAIN.
CAN YOU?
IT'S TRICKY.
WHAT HAPPENED WITH YOU WAS... UNEXPECTED.
I CAN REPLICATE IT, BUT IT WILL TAKE TIME.
GET TO WORK.

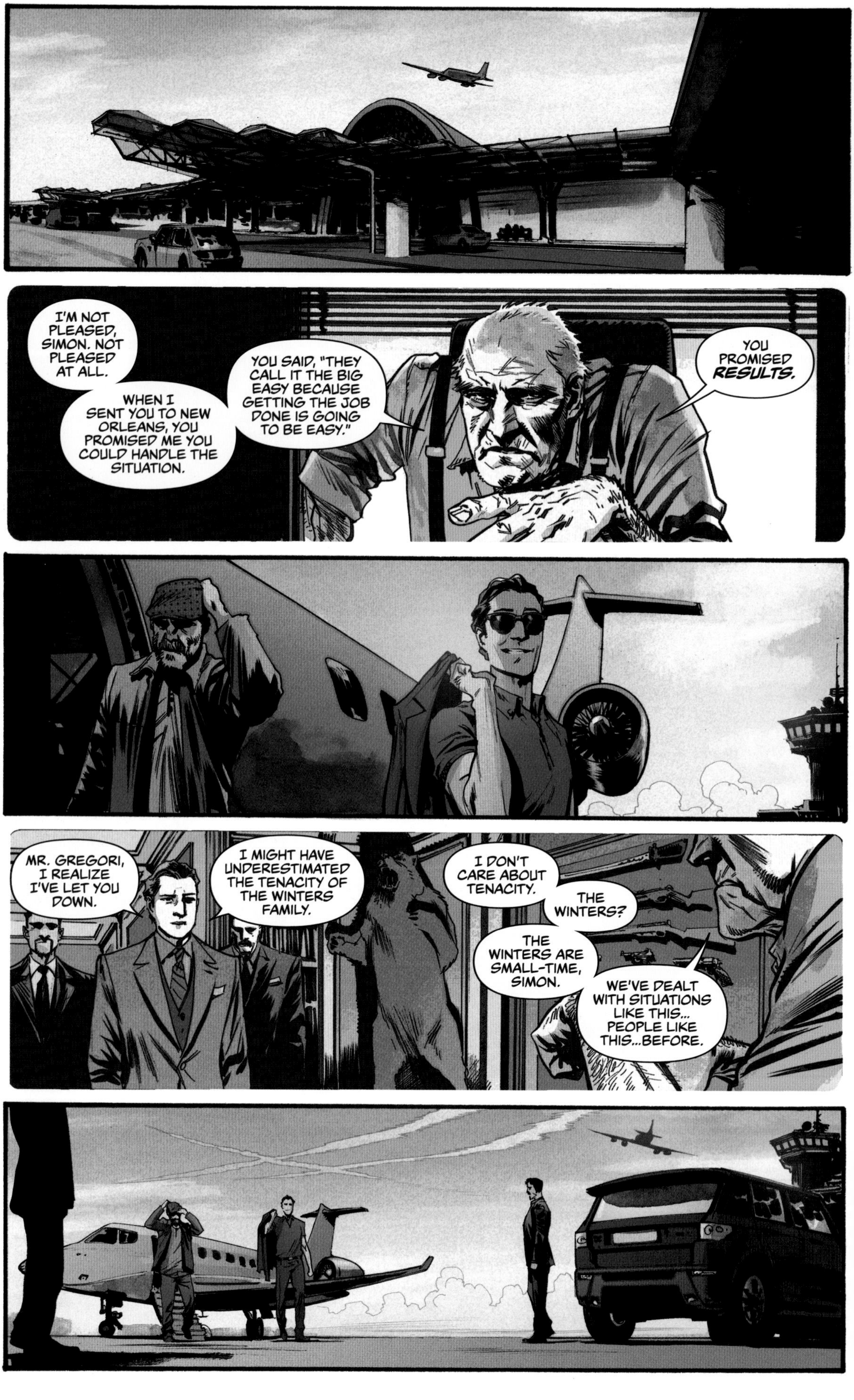
I'M NOT PLEASED, SIMON. NOT PLEASED AT ALL.
WHEN I SENT YOU TO NEW ORLEANS, YOU PROMISED ME YOU COULD HANDLE THE SITUATION.
YOU SAID, "THEY CALL IT THE BIG EASY BECAUSE GETTING THE JOB DONE IS GOING TO BE EASY."
YOU PROMISED RESULTS.
MR. GREGORI, I REALIZE I'VE LET YOU DOWN.
I MIGHT HAVE UNDERESTIMATED THE TENACITY OF THE WINTERS FAMILY.
I DON'T CARE ABOUT TENACITY.
THE WINTERS?
THE WINTERS ARE SMALL-TIME, SIMON.
WE'VE DEALT WITH SITUATIONS LIKE THIS... PEOPLE LIKE THIS...BEFORE.

WELCOME BACK TO NEW ORLEANS, MR. LAMONT.

WE HAVE EVERYTHING READY FOR YOU, SIR.

YEAH?

YOU GOT A/C IN THAT SUV?

BECAUSE IT'S HOT AS A STRIPPER'S UNDERARM OUT HERE.

I WARNED YOU NOT TO WEAR THE LEATHER JACKET, AXEL.

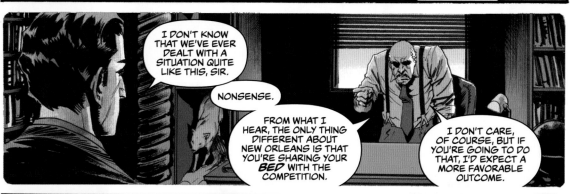

I DON'T KNOW THAT WE'VE EVER DEALT WITH A SITUATION QUITE LIKE THIS, SIR.

NONSENSE.

FROM WHAT I HEAR, THE ONLY THING DIFFERENT ABOUT NEW ORLEANS IS THAT YOU'RE SHARING YOUR **BED** WITH THE COMPETITION.

I DON'T CARE, OF COURSE, BUT IF YOU'RE GOING TO DO THAT, I'D EXPECT A MORE FAVORABLE OUTCOME.

WE'LL START PUTTING THE OPERATION TOGETHER IMMEDIATELY.

I'M GOING TO WANT TO INTERVIEW A FEW POTENTIAL CHEMISTS.

I'LL TAKE ONE MORE RUN AT THE WINTERS WITH A BUY-OUT OFFER, BUT IF THEY DON'T ACCEPT--

SIR?

THE OPERATION IS ALREADY IN FULL SWING.

THE DRUG...THIS ASH...IS ALREADY ON THE STREET, YES? IT'S READILY AVAILABLE?

OUR NEXT STEP IS SIMPLE, SIMON.

WE REVERSE-ENGINEER THE PRODUCT.

ONCE THEY'RE NO LONGER THE ONLY GAME IN TOWN, THEY'LL SELL.

AND CHEAP.

WHAT DO YOU MEAN?

WE RECEIVED WORD FROM MR. GREGORI HIMSELF.

HE SAID YOU DIDN'T WANT TO WAIT FOR FURTHER NEGOTIATIONS, THAT YOU WANTED TO MOVE AHEAD WITH THE NEXT STEPS.

WE'VE ALREADY GOT A COUPLE OF CHEMISTS WORKING ON MAKING SOME ASH OF OUR OWN.

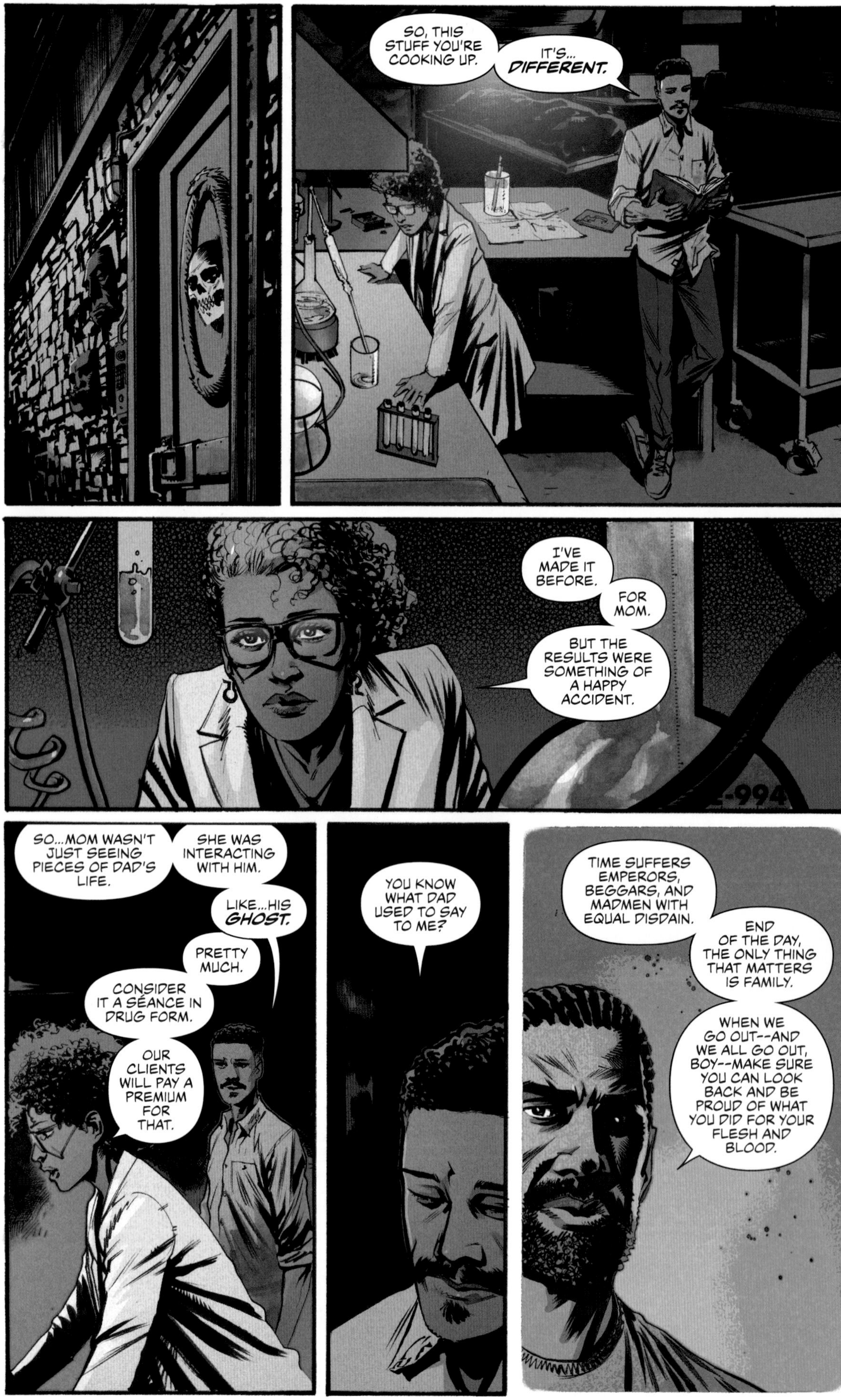
SO, THIS STUFF YOU'RE COOKING UP.
IT'S... DIFFERENT.
I'VE MADE IT BEFORE.
FOR MOM.
BUT THE RESULTS WERE SOMETHING OF A HAPPY ACCIDENT.
-994
SO...MOM WASN'T JUST SEEING PIECES OF DAD'S LIFE.
SHE WAS INTERACTING WITH HIM.
LIKE...HIS GHOST.
PRETTY MUCH.
CONSIDER IT A SÉANCE IN DRUG FORM.
OUR CLIENTS WILL PAY A PREMIUM FOR THAT.
YOU KNOW WHAT DAD USED TO SAY TO ME?
TIME SUFFERS EMPERORS, BEGGARS, AND MADMEN WITH EQUAL DISDAIN.
END OF THE DAY, THE ONLY THING THAT MATTERS IS FAMILY.
WHEN WE GO OUT--AND WE ALL GO OUT, BOY--MAKE SURE YOU CAN LOOK BACK AND BE PROUD OF WHAT YOU DID FOR YOUR FLESH AND BLOOD.

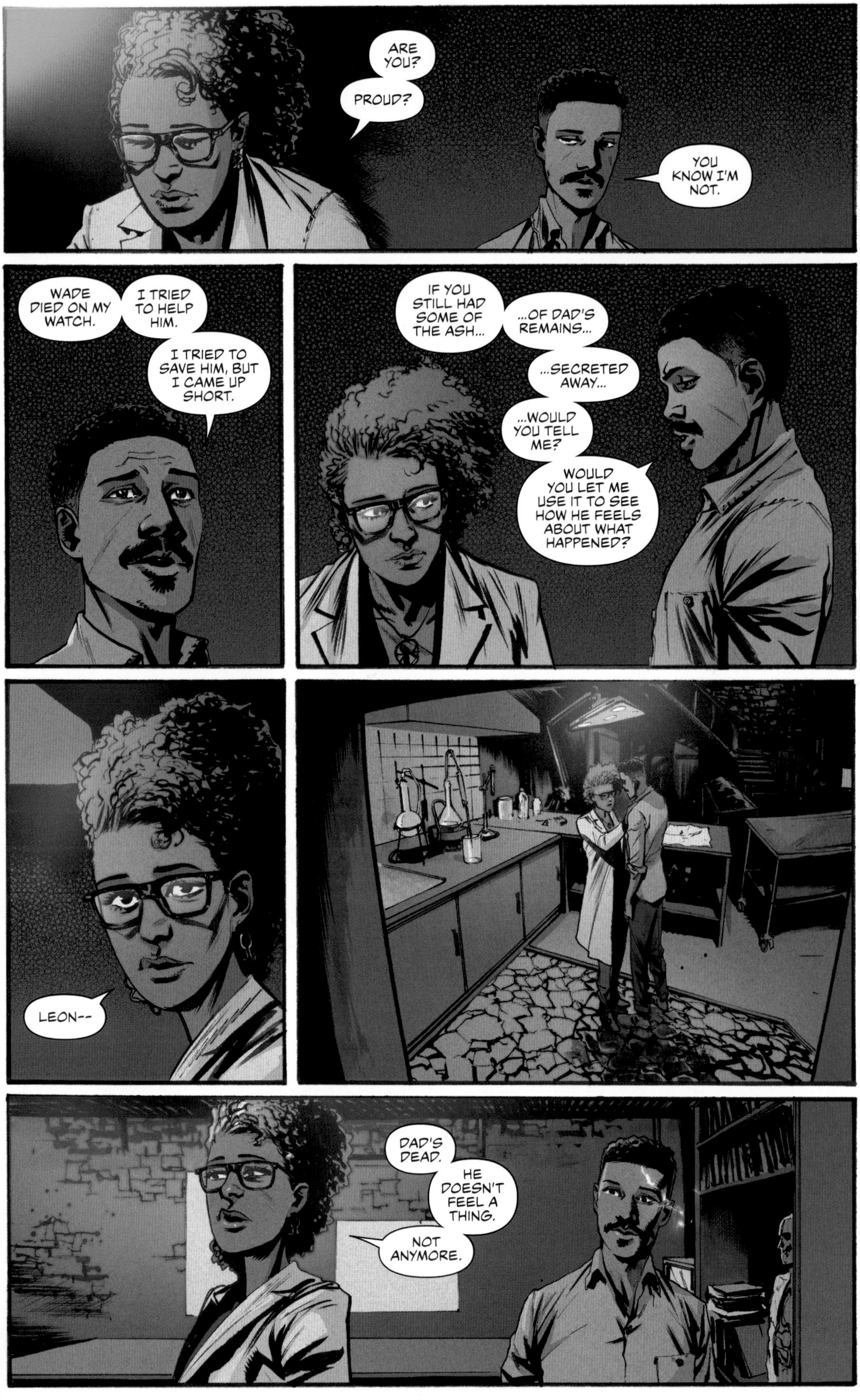

ARE YOU?
PROUD?
YOU KNOW I'M NOT.
WADE DIED ON MY WATCH.
I TRIED TO HELP HIM.
I TRIED TO SAVE HIM, BUT I CAME UP SHORT.
IF YOU STILL HAD SOME OF THE ASH...
...OF DAD'S REMAINS...
...SECRETED AWAY...
...WOULD YOU TELL ME?
WOULD YOU LET ME USE IT TO SEE HOW HE FEELS ABOUT WHAT HAPPENED?
LEON--
DAD'S DEAD.
HE DOESN'T FEEL A THING.
NOT ANYMORE.

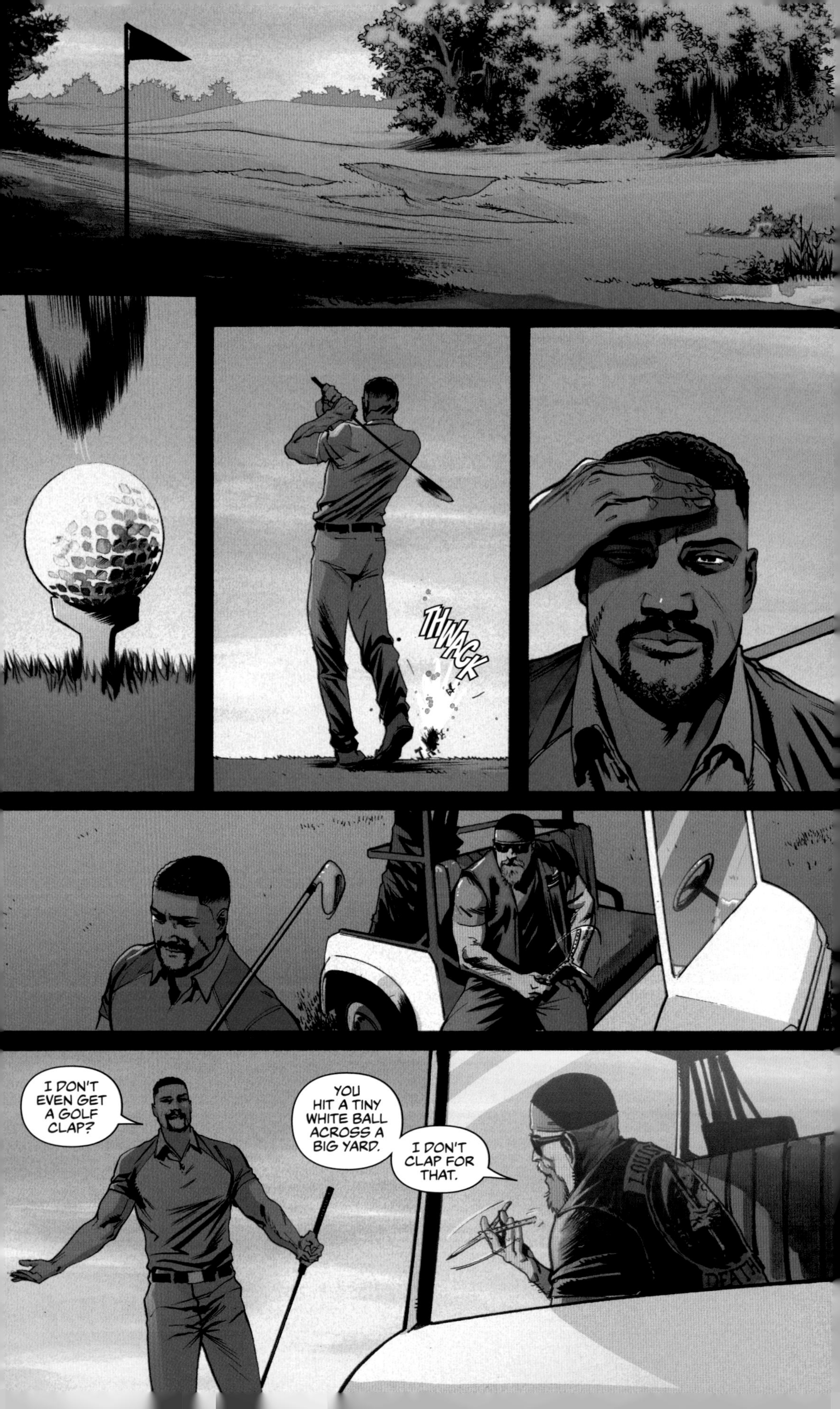
THWACK
I DON'T EVEN GET A GOLF CLAP?
YOU HIT A TINY WHITE BALL ACROSS A BIG YARD.
I DON'T CLAP FOR THAT.
DEATH

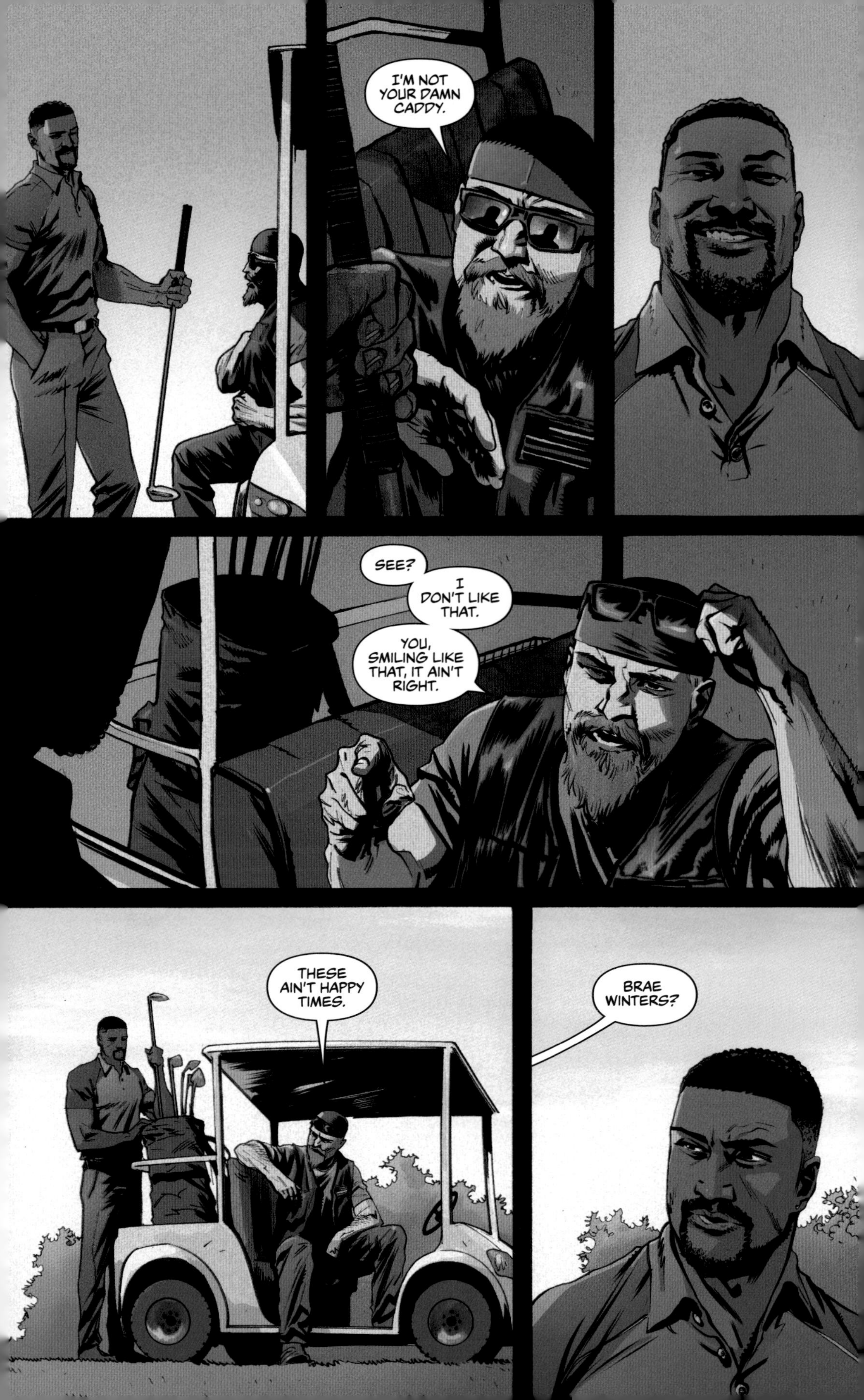
I'M NOT YOUR DAMN CADDY.
SEE?
I DON'T LIKE THAT.
YOU, SMILING LIKE THAT, IT AIN'T RIGHT.
THESE AIN'T HAPPY TIMES.
BRAE WINTERS?

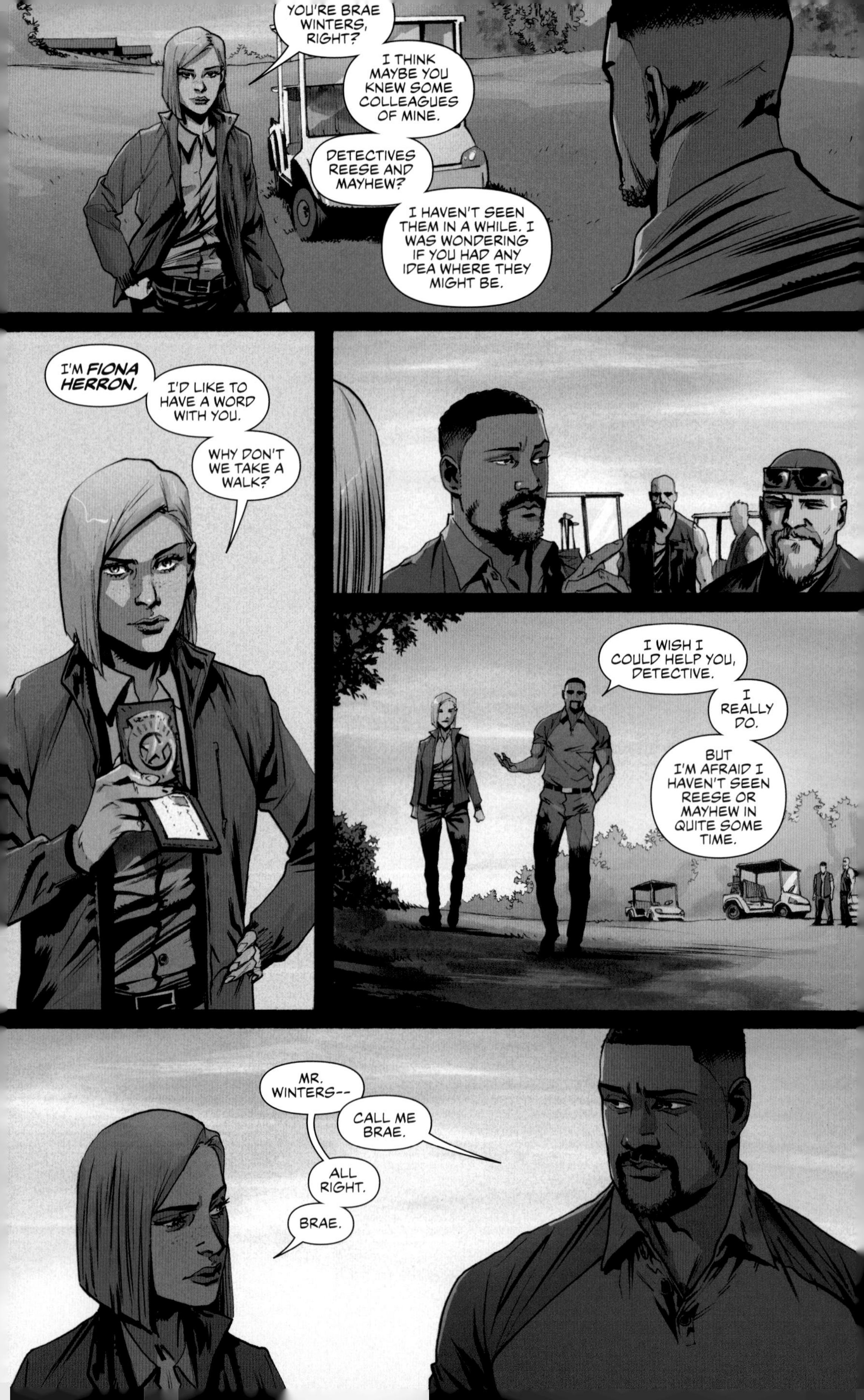
YOU'RE BRAE WINTERS, RIGHT?
I THINK MAYBE YOU KNEW SOME COLLEAGUES OF MINE.
DETECTIVES REESE AND MAYHEW?
I HAVEN'T SEEN THEM IN A WHILE. I WAS WONDERING IF YOU HAD ANY IDEA WHERE THEY MIGHT BE.
I'M FIONA HERRON.
I'D LIKE TO HAVE A WORD WITH YOU.
WHY DON'T WE TAKE A WALK?
I WISH I COULD HELP YOU, DETECTIVE.
I REALLY DO.
BUT I'M AFRAID I HAVEN'T SEEN REESE OR MAYHEW IN QUITE SOME TIME.
MR. WINTERS--
CALL ME BRAE.
ALL RIGHT.
BRAE.

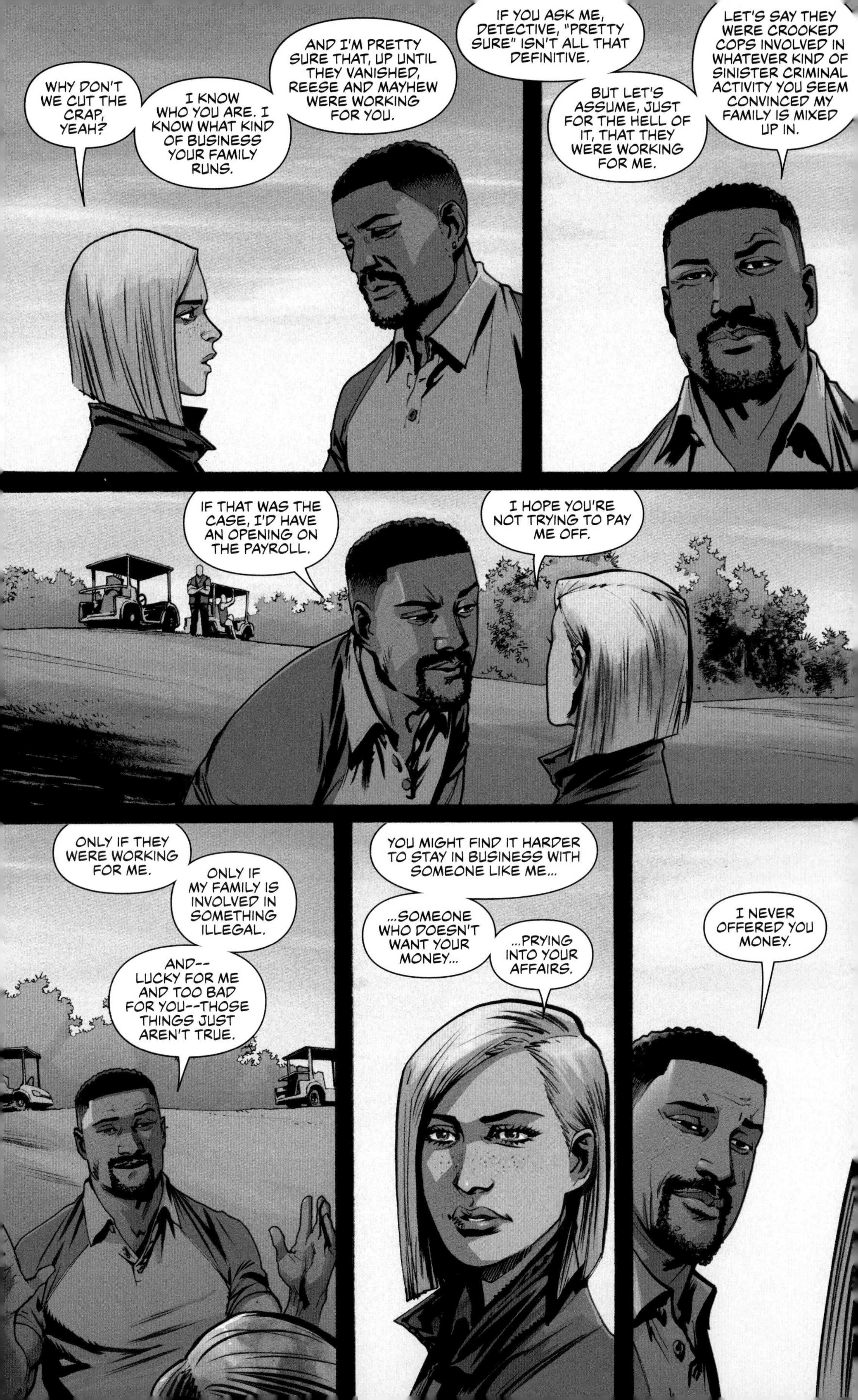
WHY DON'T WE CUT THE CRAP, YEAH?
I KNOW WHO YOU ARE. I KNOW WHAT KIND OF BUSINESS YOUR FAMILY RUNS.
AND I'M PRETTY SURE THAT, UP UNTIL THEY VANISHED, REESE AND MAYHEW WERE WORKING FOR YOU.
IF YOU ASK ME, DETECTIVE, "PRETTY SURE" ISN'T ALL THAT DEFINITIVE.
BUT LET'S ASSUME, JUST FOR THE HELL OF IT, THAT THEY WERE WORKING FOR ME.
LET'S SAY THEY WERE CROOKED COPS INVOLVED IN WHATEVER KIND OF SINISTER CRIMINAL ACTIVITY YOU SEEM CONVINCED MY FAMILY IS MIXED UP IN.
IF THAT WAS THE CASE, I'D HAVE AN OPENING ON THE PAYROLL.
I HOPE YOU'RE NOT TRYING TO PAY ME OFF.
ONLY IF THEY WERE WORKING FOR ME.
ONLY IF MY FAMILY IS INVOLVED IN SOMETHING ILLEGAL.
AND-- LUCKY FOR ME AND TOO BAD FOR YOU--THOSE THINGS JUST AREN'T TRUE.
YOU MIGHT FIND IT HARDER TO STAY IN BUSINESS WITH SOMEONE LIKE ME...
...SOMEONE WHO DOESN'T WANT YOUR MONEY...
...PRYING INTO YOUR AFFAIRS.
I NEVER OFFERED YOU MONEY.

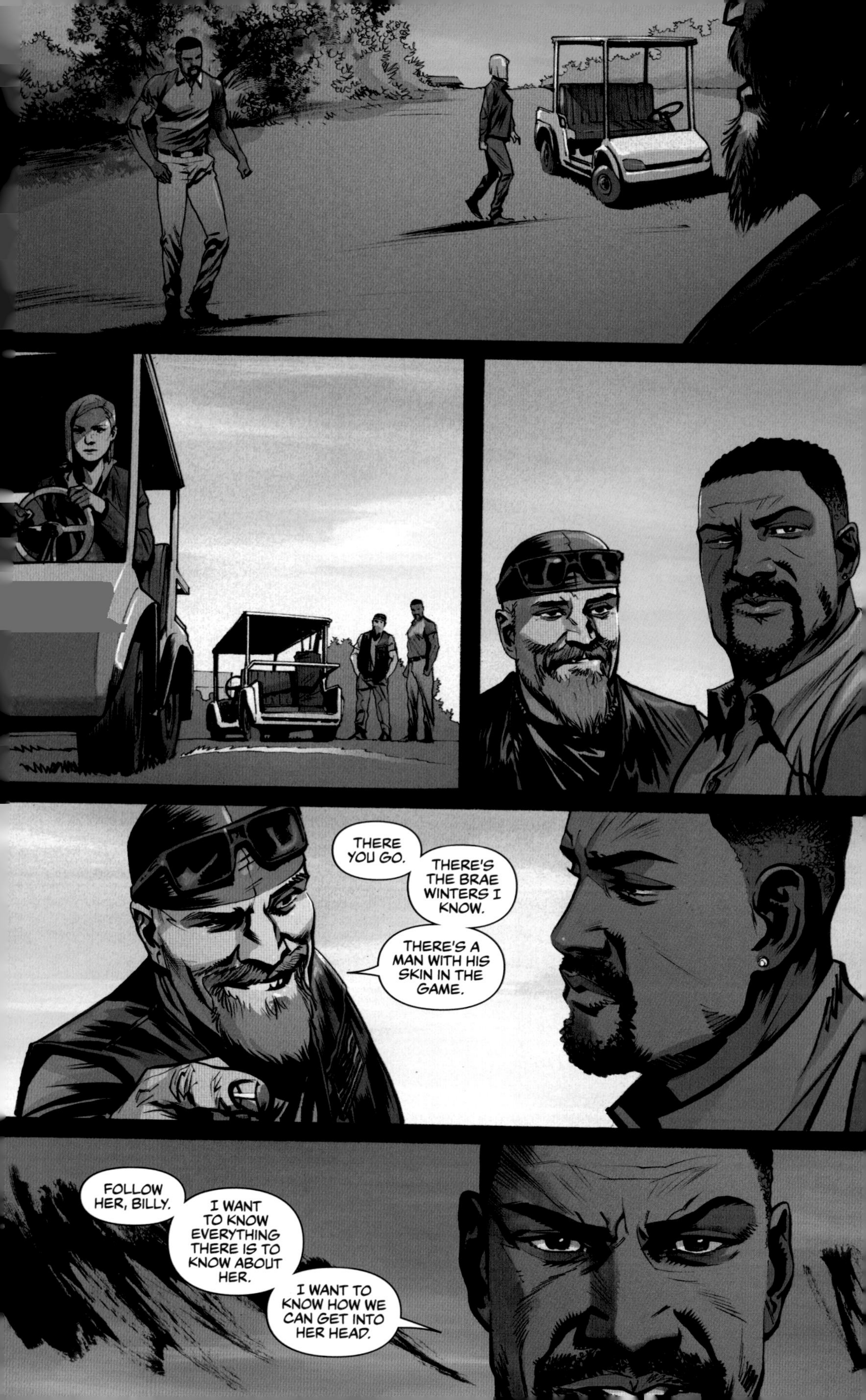
THERE YOU GO.
THERE'S THE BRAE WINTERS I KNOW.
THERE'S A MAN WITH HIS SKIN IN THE GAME.
FOLLOW HER, BILLY.
I WANT TO KNOW EVERYTHING THERE IS TO KNOW ABOUT HER.
I WANT TO KNOW HOW WE CAN GET INTO HER HEAD.

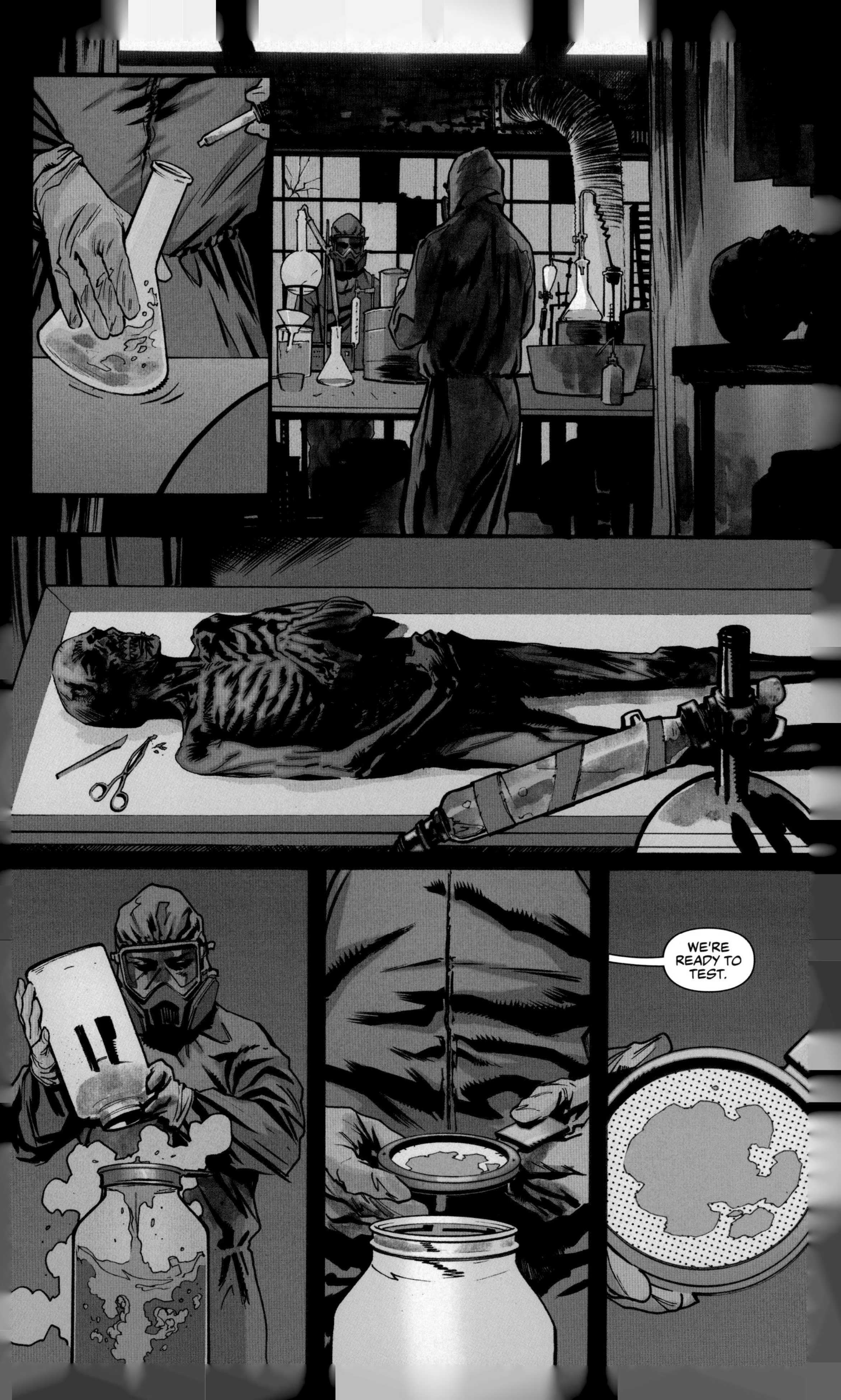
WE'RE READY TO TEST.

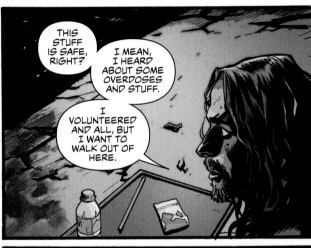

THIS STUFF IS SAFE, RIGHT? I MEAN, I HEARD ABOUT SOME OVERDOSES AND STUFF.

I VOLUNTEERED AND ALL, BUT I WANT TO WALK OUT OF HERE.

WE'RE GOOD AT OUR JOBS.

WHATEVER YOU SAY. I TRIED THIS STUFF A FEW TIMES, YOU KNOW.

ONCE, I WAS, LIKE, FLYING AN F-15 OR SOMETHING.

IT WAS RAD.

UH--

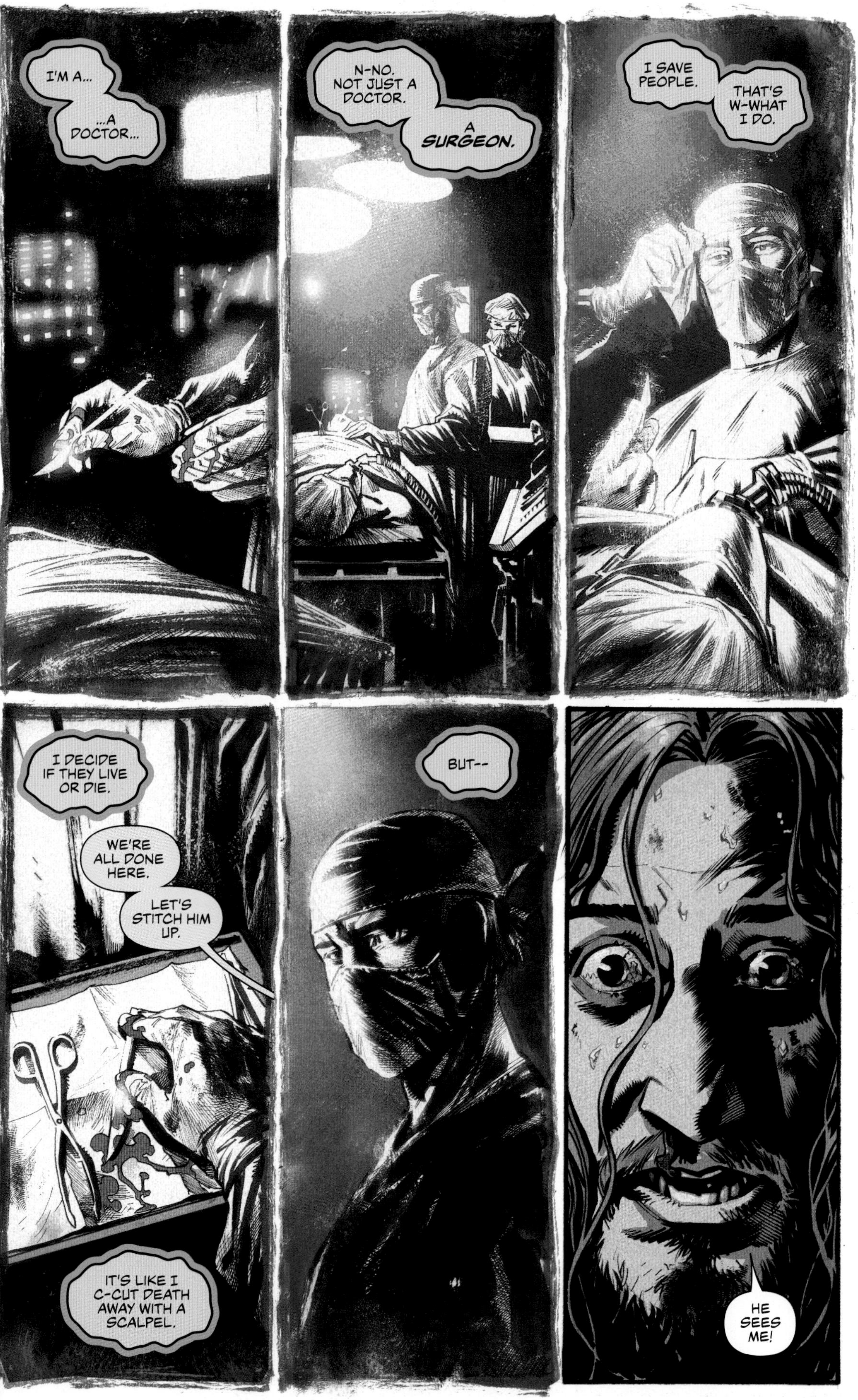
I'M A...
...A DOCTOR...
N-NO. NOT JUST A DOCTOR.
A SURGEON.
I SAVE PEOPLE.
THAT'S W-WHAT I DO.
I DECIDE IF THEY LIVE OR DIE.
WE'RE ALL DONE HERE.
LET'S STITCH HIM UP.
IT'S LIKE I C-CUT DEATH AWAY WITH A SCALPEL.
BUT--
HE SEES ME!

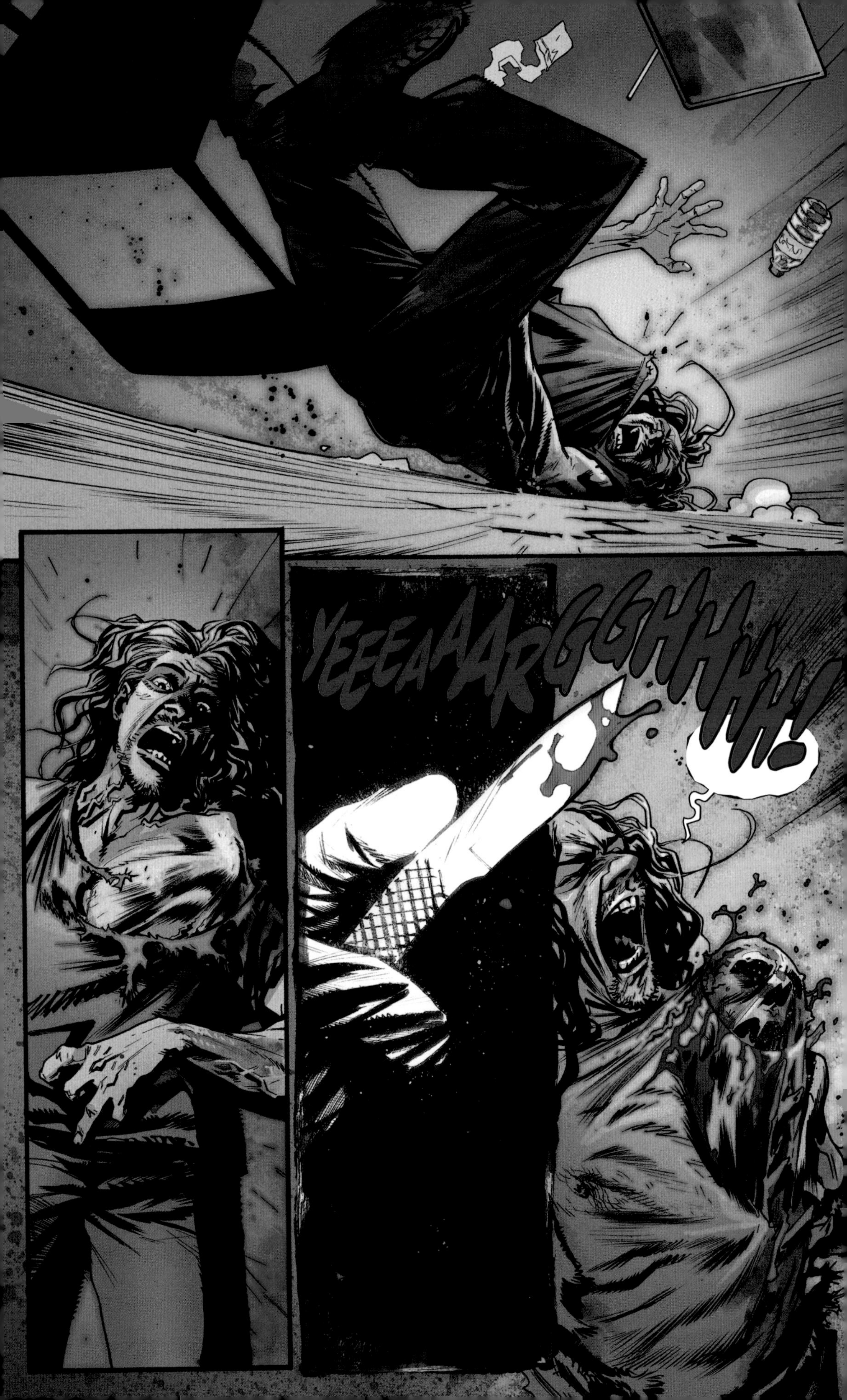
YEEEAAARGGHHHH!

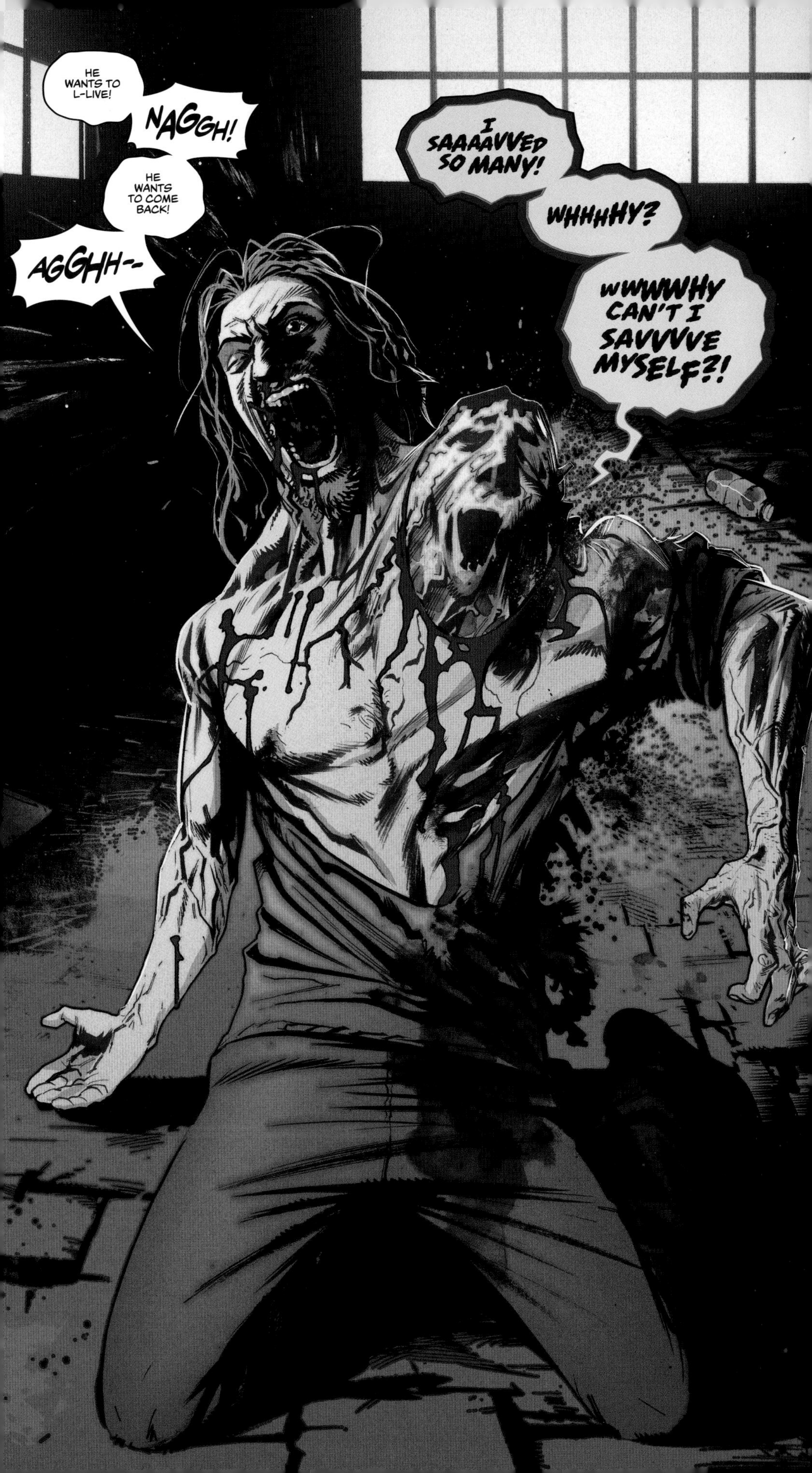
HE WANTS TO L-LIVE!
NAGGH!
HE WANTS TO COME BACK!
AGGHH-
I SAAAAVVED SO MANY!
WHHHHY?
WWWWHY CAN'T I SAVVVVE MYSELF?!

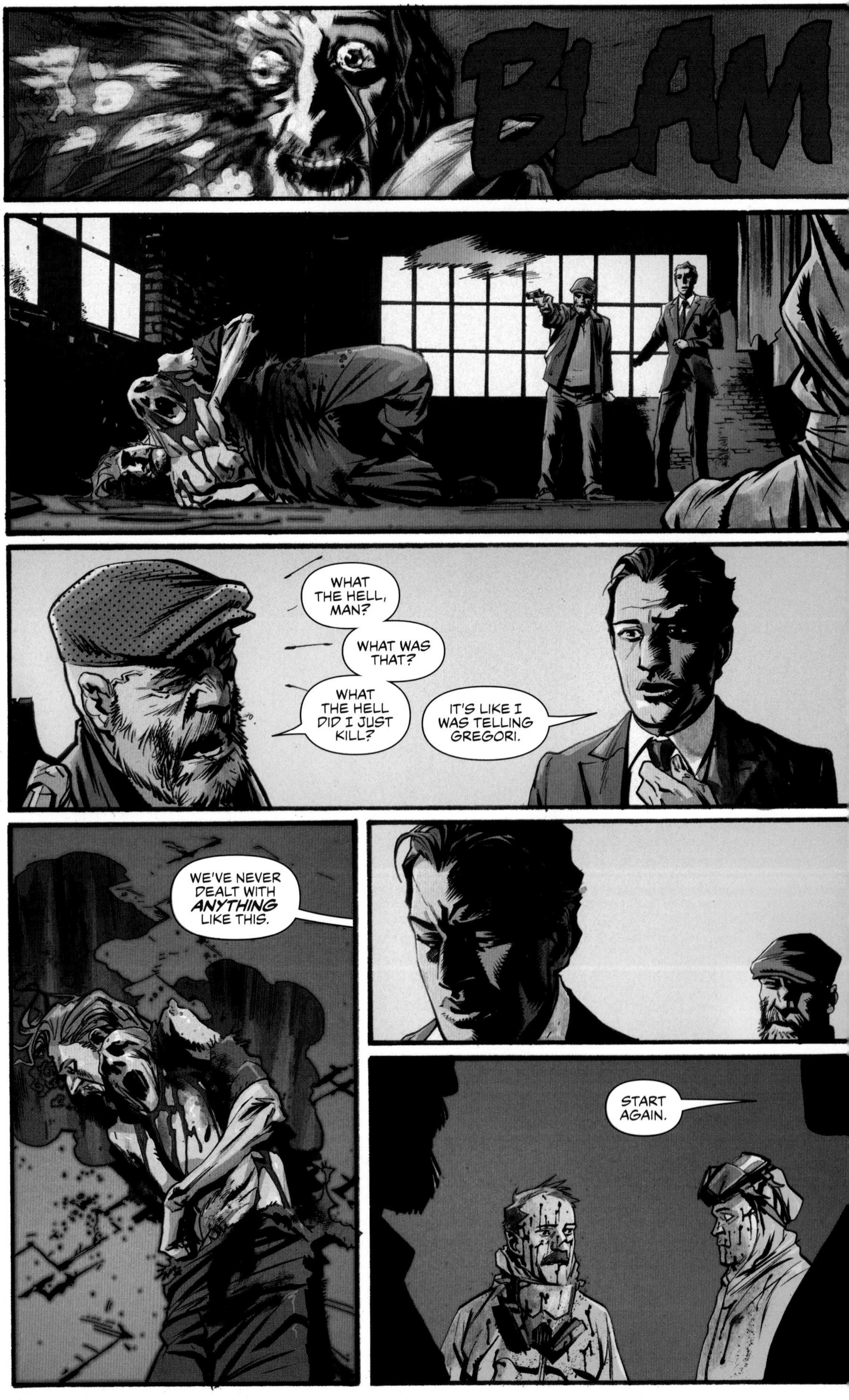
BLAM
WHAT THE HELL, MAN?
WHAT WAS THAT?
WHAT THE HELL DID I JUST KILL?
IT'S LIKE I WAS TELLING GREGORI.
WE'VE NEVER DEALT WITH ANYTHING LIKE THIS.
START AGAIN.

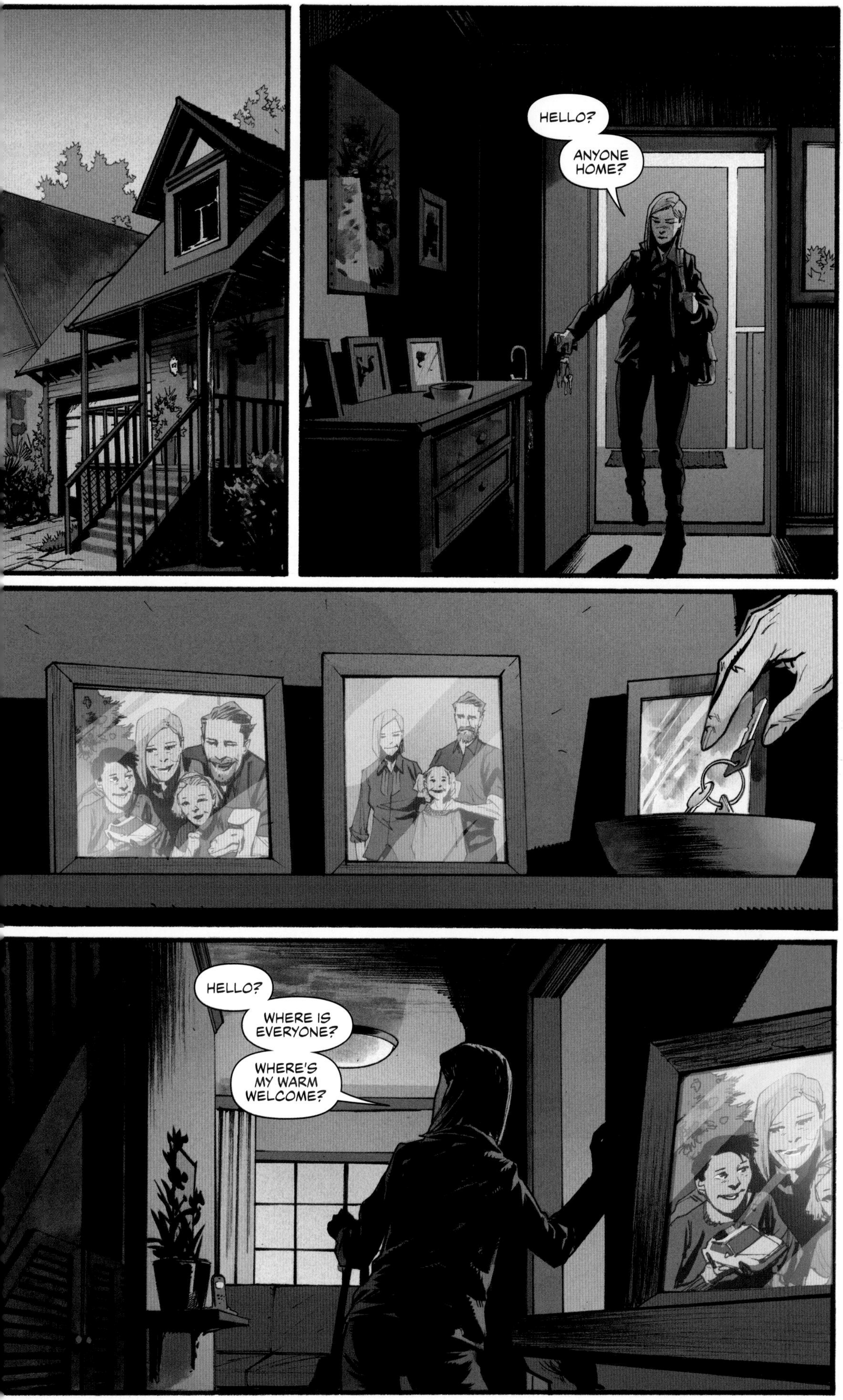
HELLO?
ANYONE HOME?
HELLO?
WHERE IS EVERYONE?
WHERE'S MY WARM WELCOME?

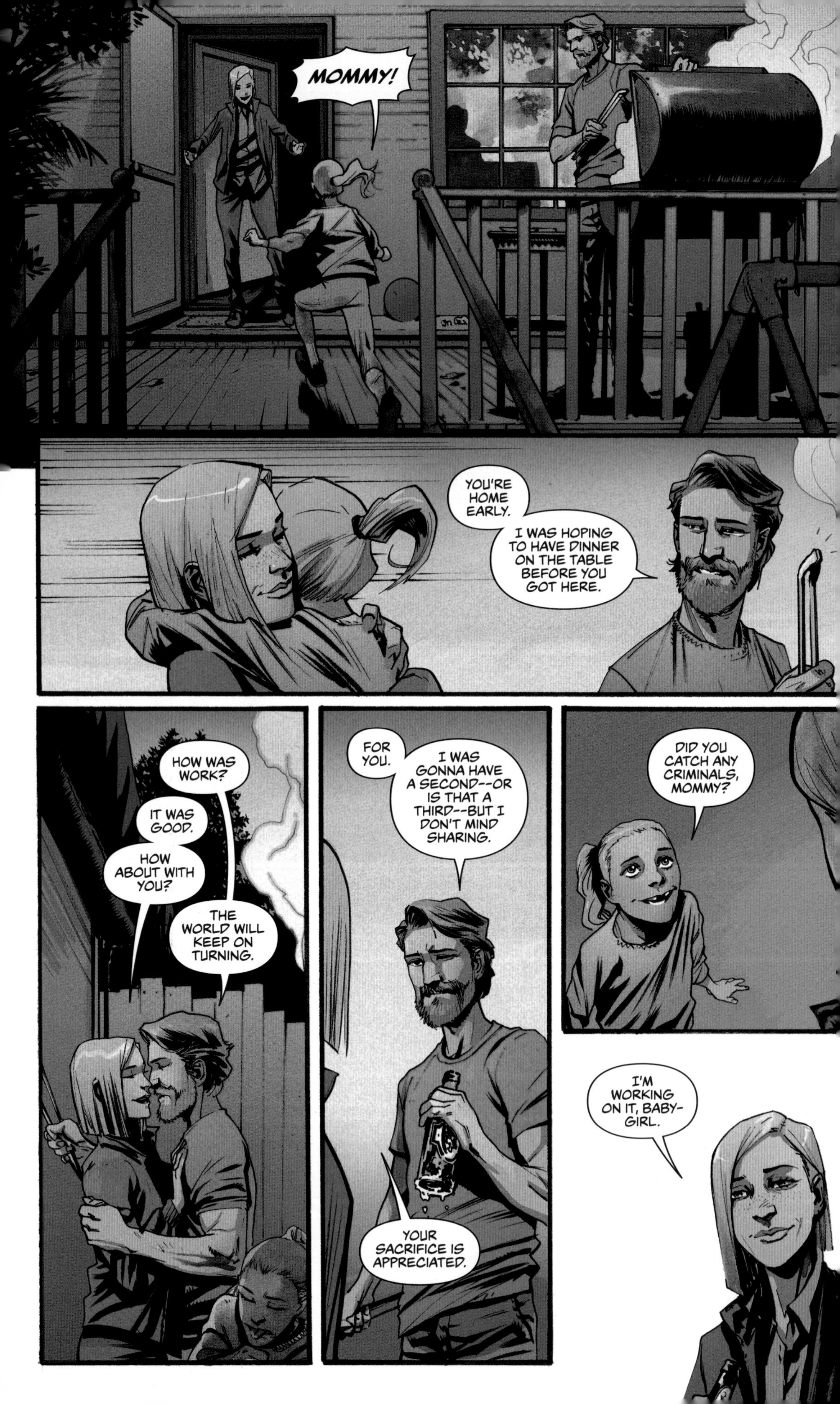
MOMMY!
YOU'RE HOME EARLY.
I WAS HOPING TO HAVE DINNER ON THE TABLE BEFORE YOU GOT HERE.
HOW WAS WORK?
IT WAS GOOD.
HOW ABOUT WITH YOU?
THE WORLD WILL KEEP ON TURNING.
FOR YOU.
I WAS GONNA HAVE A SECOND--OR IS THAT A THIRD--BUT I DON'T MIND SHARING.
YOUR SACRIFICE IS APPRECIATED.
DID YOU CATCH ANY CRIMINALS, MOMMY?
I'M WORKING ON IT, BABY-GIRL.

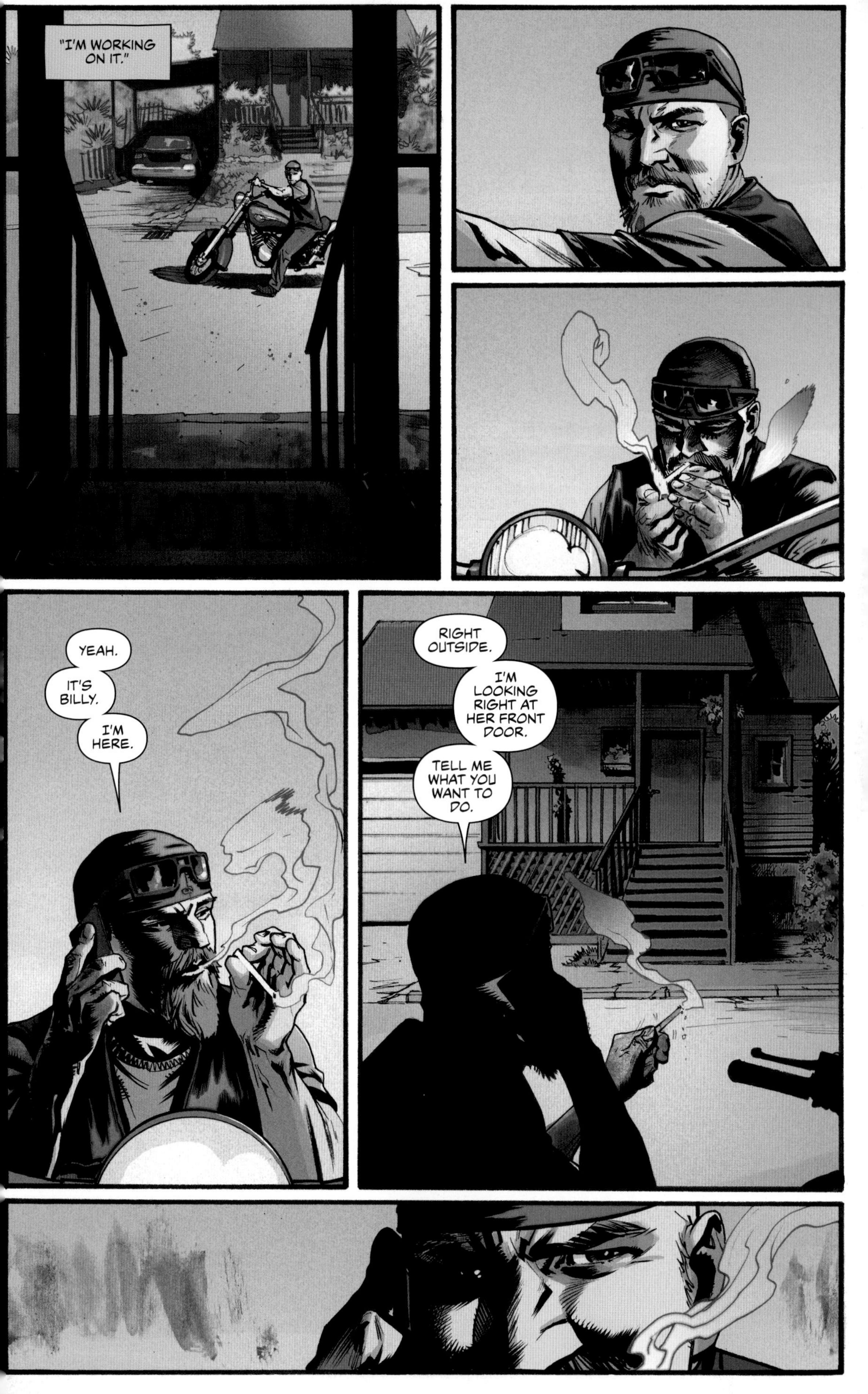
"I'M WORKING ON IT."
YEAH.
IT'S BILLY.
I'M HERE.
RIGHT OUTSIDE.
I'M LOOKING RIGHT AT HER FRONT DOOR.
TELL ME WHAT YOU WANT TO DO.

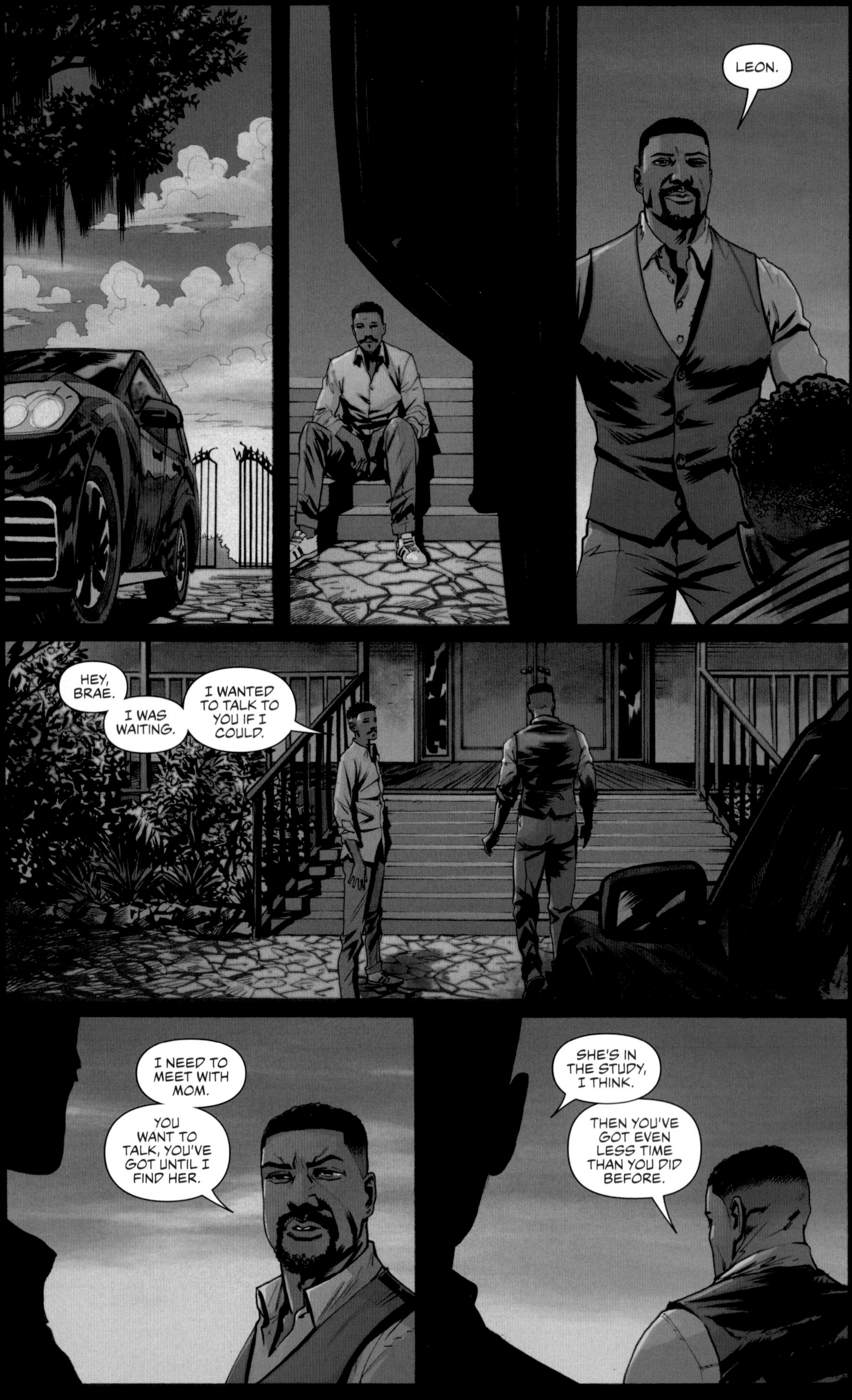
LEON.
HEY, BRAE.
I WAS WAITING.
I WANTED TO TALK TO YOU IF I COULD.
I NEED TO MEET WITH MOM.
YOU WANT TO TALK, YOU'VE GOT UNTIL I FIND HER.
SHE'S IN THE STUDY, I THINK.
THEN YOU'VE GOT EVEN LESS TIME THAN YOU DID BEFORE.

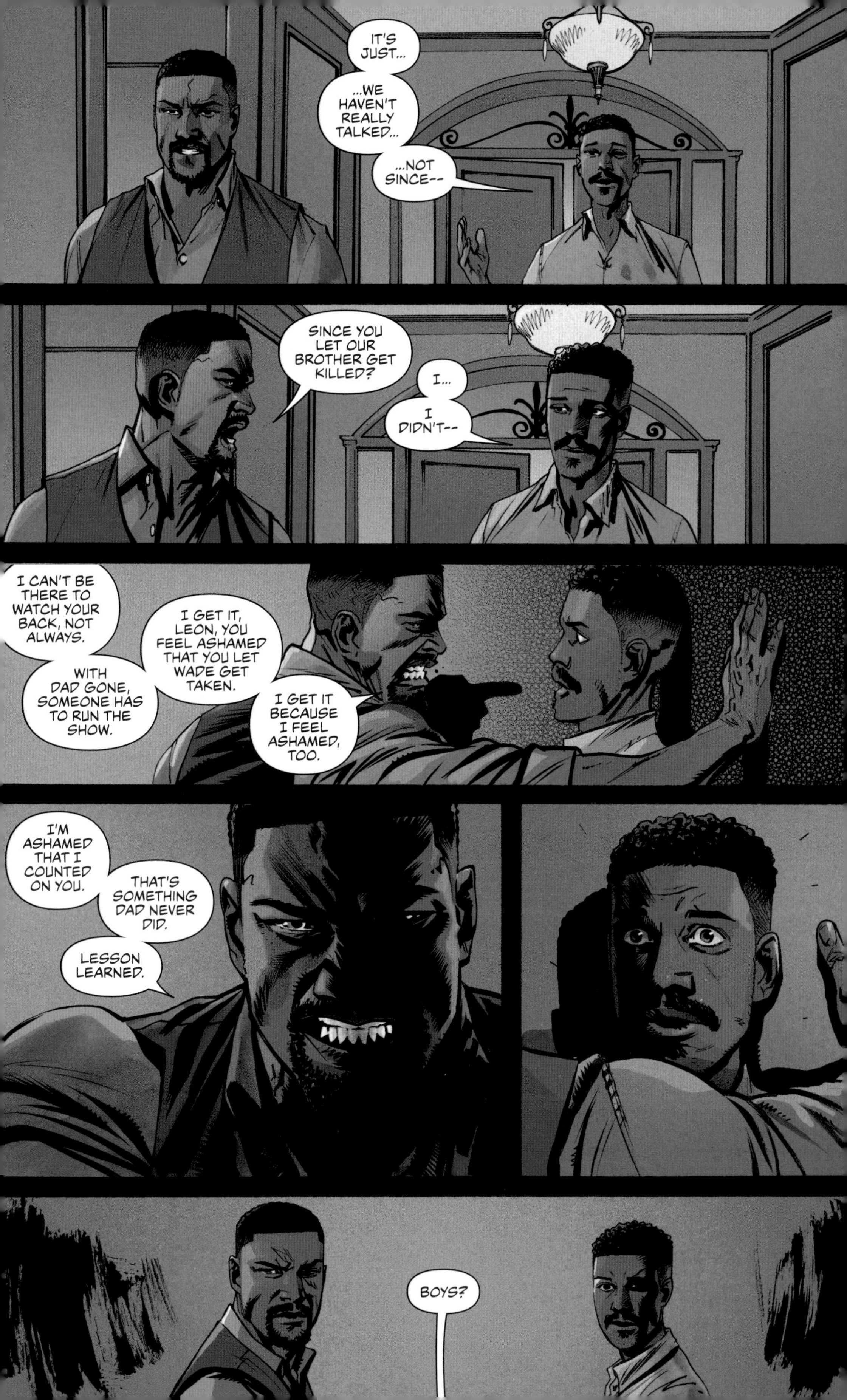
IT'S JUST...
...WE HAVEN'T REALLY TALKED...
...NOT SINCE--
SINCE YOU LET OUR BROTHER GET KILLED?
I...
I DIDN'T--
I CAN'T BE THERE TO WATCH YOUR BACK, NOT ALWAYS.
WITH DAD GONE, SOMEONE HAS TO RUN THE SHOW.
I GET IT, LEON, YOU FEEL ASHAMED THAT YOU LET WADE GET TAKEN.
I GET IT BECAUSE I FEEL ASHAMED, TOO.
I'M ASHAMED THAT I COUNTED ON YOU.
THAT'S SOMETHING DAD NEVER DID.
LESSON LEARNED.
BOYS?

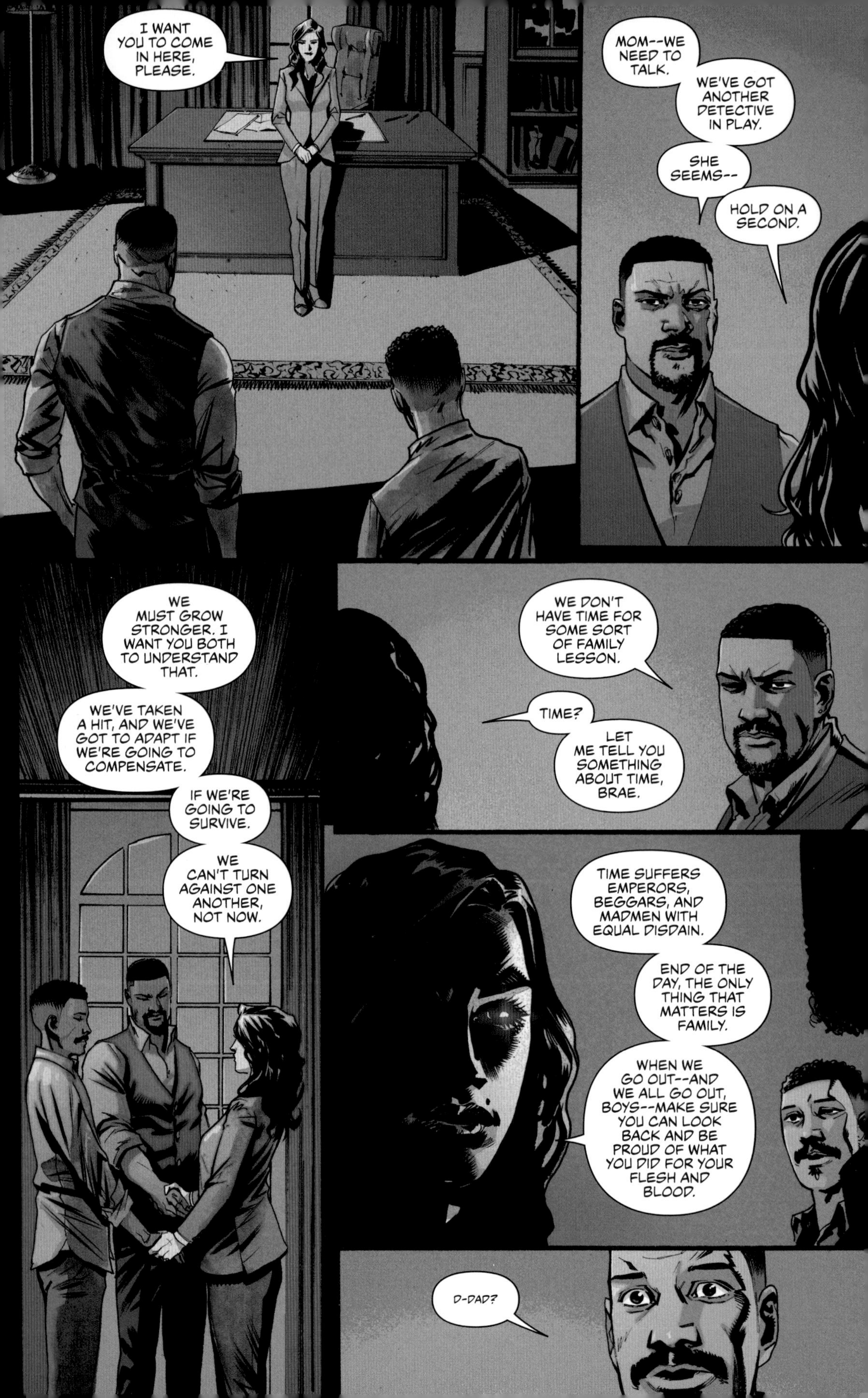
I WANT YOU TO COME IN HERE, PLEASE.
MOM--WE NEED TO TALK.
WE'VE GOT ANOTHER DETECTIVE IN PLAY.
SHE SEEMS--
HOLD ON A SECOND.
WE MUST GROW STRONGER. I WANT YOU BOTH TO UNDERSTAND THAT.
WE'VE TAKEN A HIT, AND WE'VE GOT TO ADAPT IF WE'RE GOING TO COMPENSATE.
IF WE'RE GOING TO SURVIVE.
WE CAN'T TURN AGAINST ONE ANOTHER, NOT NOW.
WE DON'T HAVE TIME FOR SOME SORT OF FAMILY LESSON.
TIME?
LET ME TELL YOU SOMETHING ABOUT TIME, BRAE.
TIME SUFFERS EMPERORS, BEGGARS, AND MADMEN WITH EQUAL DISDAIN.
END OF THE DAY, THE ONLY THING THAT MATTERS IS FAMILY.
WHEN WE GO OUT--AND WE ALL GO OUT, BOYS--MAKE SURE YOU CAN LOOK BACK AND BE PROUD OF WHAT YOU DID FOR YOUR FLESH AND BLOOD.
D-DAD?

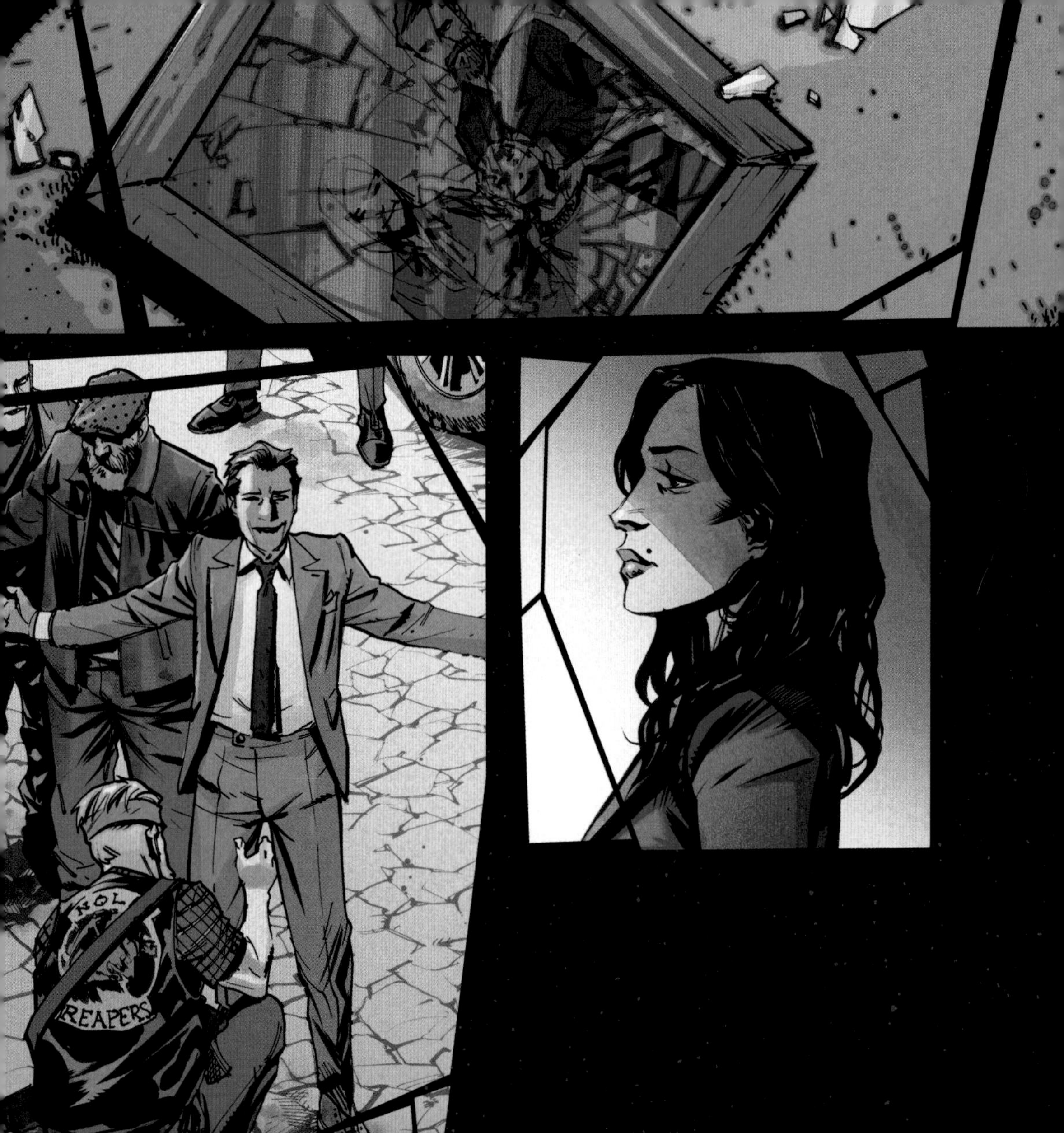
REAPERS

Chapter Seven

THE PAINS OF REBIRTH

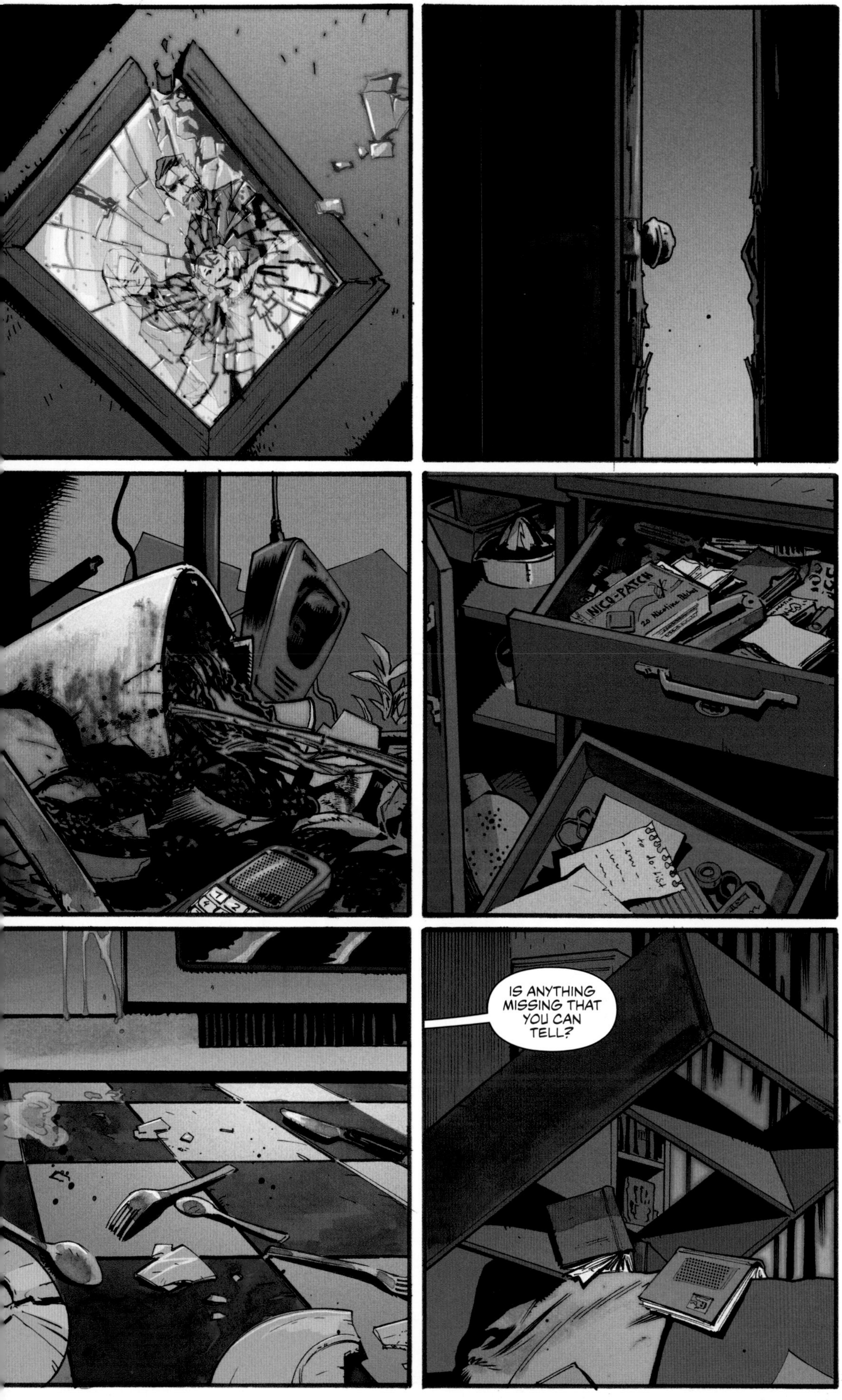
NICO-PATCH
20 Nicotine Patches
to do list
IS ANYTHING MISSING THAT YOU CAN TELL?

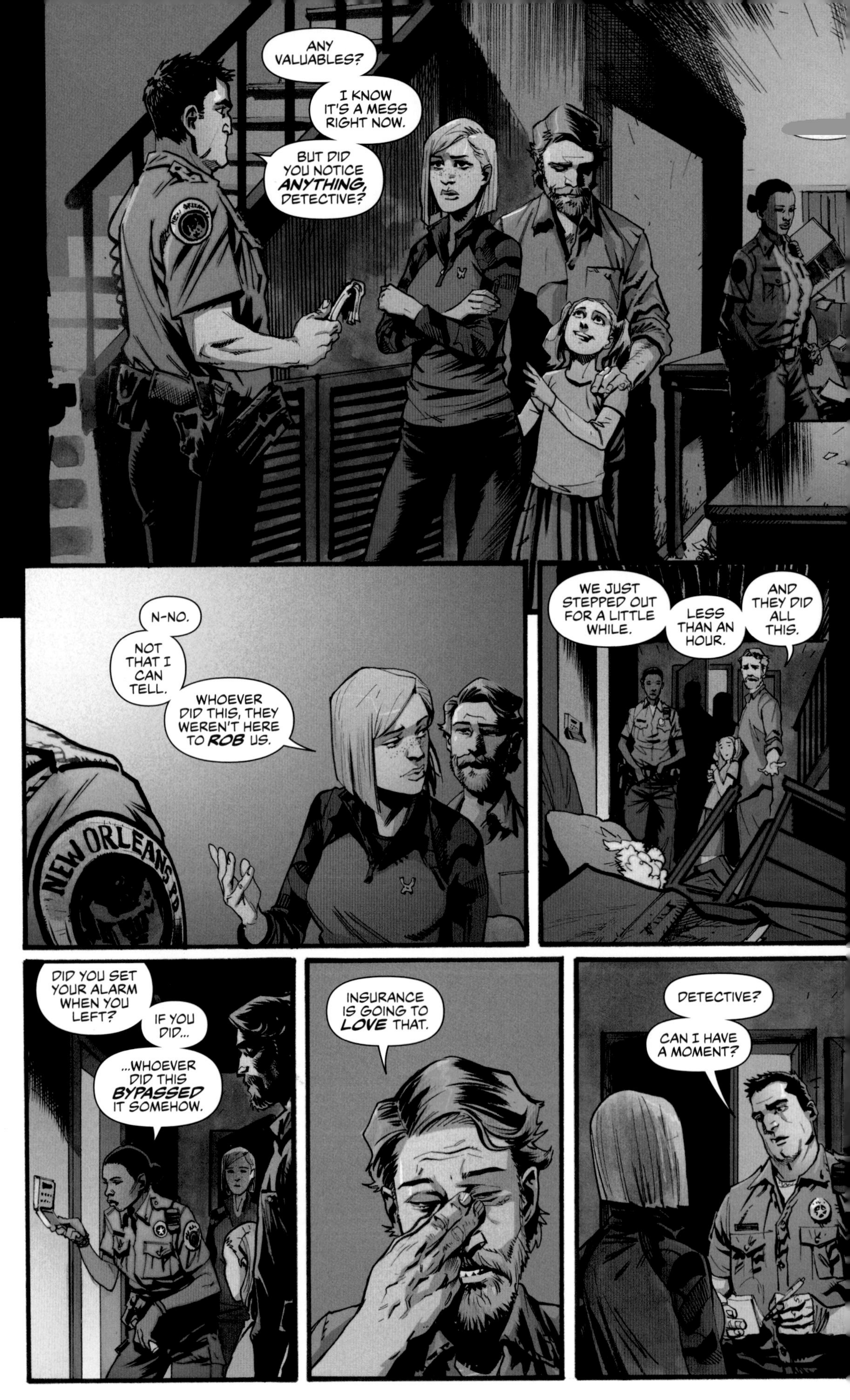
ANY VALUABLES?
I KNOW IT'S A MESS RIGHT NOW.
BUT DID YOU NOTICE ANYTHING, DETECTIVE?
N-NO.
NOT THAT I CAN TELL.
WHOEVER DID THIS, THEY WEREN'T HERE TO ROB US.
NEW ORLEANS PD
WE JUST STEPPED OUT FOR A LITTLE WHILE.
LESS THAN AN HOUR.
AND THEY DID ALL THIS.
DID YOU SET YOUR ALARM WHEN YOU LEFT?
IF YOU DID...
...WHOEVER DID THIS BYPASSED IT SOMEHOW.
INSURANCE IS GOING TO LOVE THAT.
DETECTIVE?
CAN I HAVE A MOMENT?

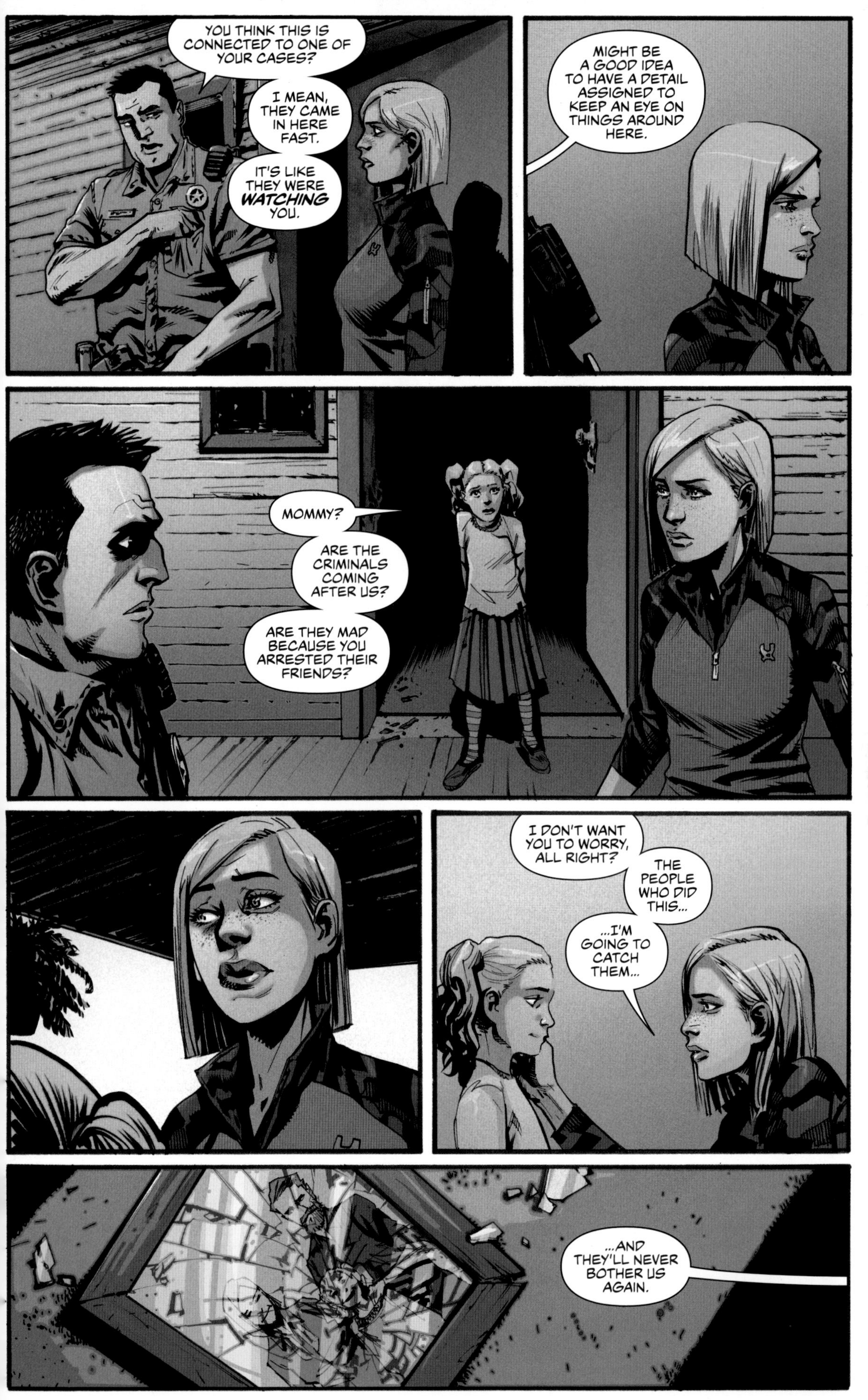
YOU THINK THIS IS CONNECTED TO ONE OF YOUR CASES?
I MEAN, THEY CAME IN HERE FAST.
IT'S LIKE THEY WERE WATCHING YOU.
MIGHT BE A GOOD IDEA TO HAVE A DETAIL ASSIGNED TO KEEP AN EYE ON THINGS AROUND HERE.
MOMMY?
ARE THE CRIMINALS COMING AFTER US?
ARE THEY MAD BECAUSE YOU ARRESTED THEIR FRIENDS?
I DON'T WANT YOU TO WORRY, ALL RIGHT?
THE PEOPLE WHO DID THIS...
...I'M GOING TO CATCH THEM...
...AND THEY'LL NEVER BOTHER US AGAIN.

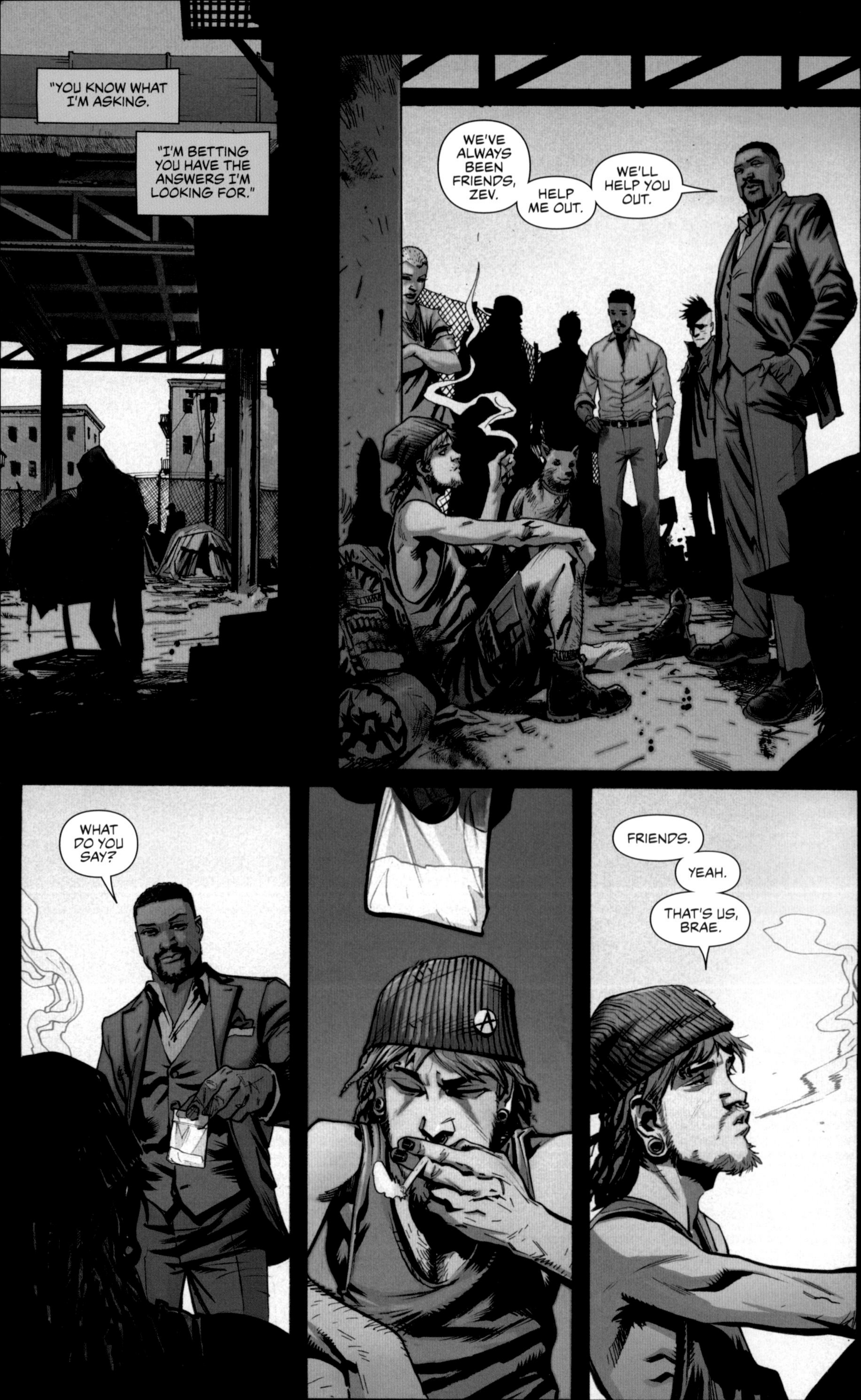
"YOU KNOW WHAT I'M ASKING.
"I'M BETTING YOU HAVE THE ANSWERS I'M LOOKING FOR."
WE'VE ALWAYS BEEN FRIENDS, ZEV.
HELP ME OUT.
WE'LL HELP YOU OUT.
WHAT DO YOU SAY?
FRIENDS.
YEAH.
THAT'S US, BRAE.

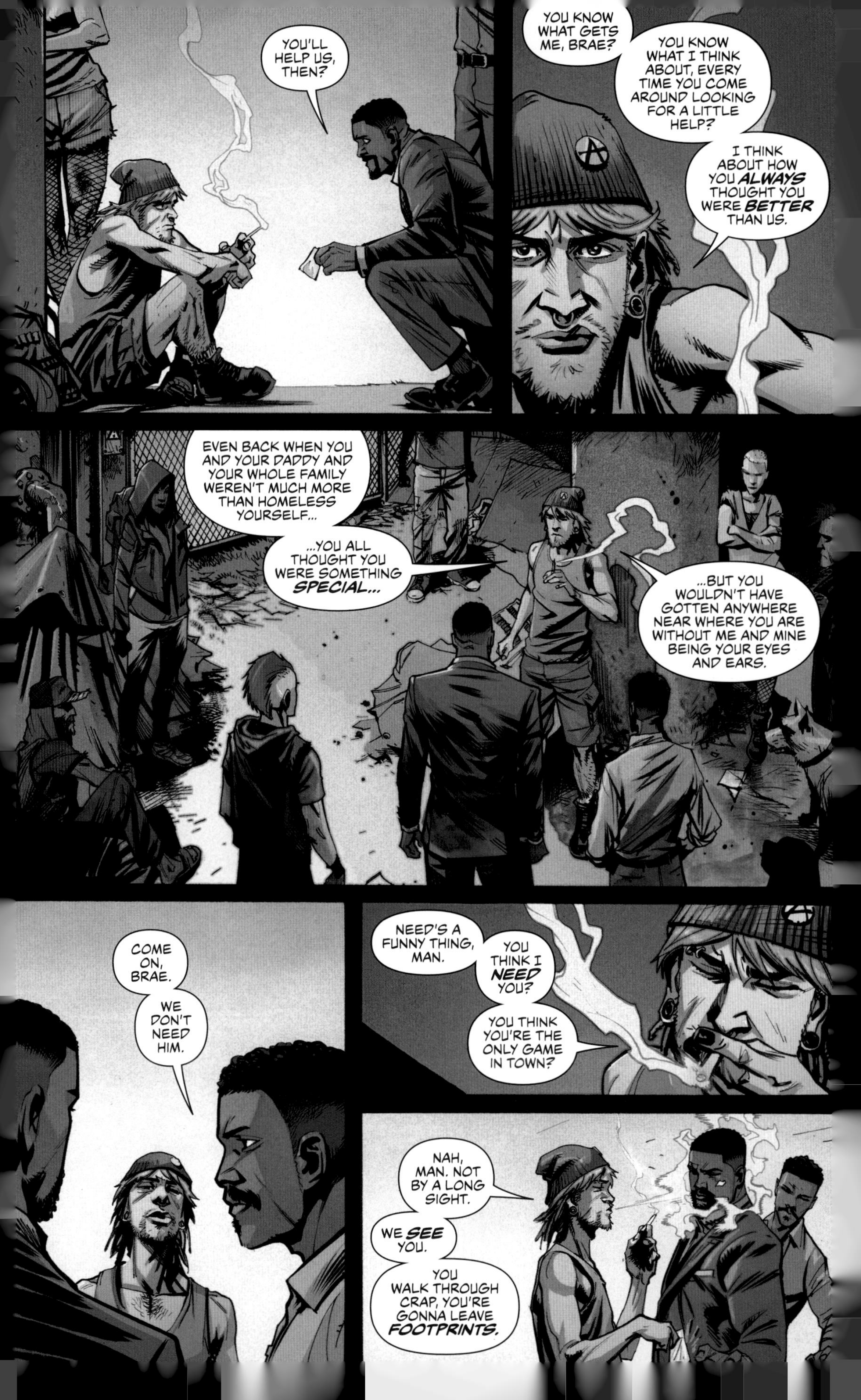
YOU'LL HELP US, THEN?
YOU KNOW WHAT GETS ME, BRAE?
YOU KNOW WHAT I THINK ABOUT, EVERY TIME YOU COME AROUND LOOKING FOR A LITTLE HELP?
I THINK ABOUT HOW YOU ALWAYS THOUGHT YOU WERE BETTER THAN US.
EVEN BACK WHEN YOU AND YOUR DADDY AND YOUR WHOLE FAMILY WEREN'T MUCH MORE THAN HOMELESS YOURSELF...
...YOU ALL THOUGHT YOU WERE SOMETHING SPECIAL...
...BUT YOU WOULDN'T HAVE GOTTEN ANYWHERE NEAR WHERE YOU ARE WITHOUT ME AND MINE BEING YOUR EYES AND EARS.
COME ON, BRAE.
WE DON'T NEED HIM.
NEED'S A FUNNY THING, MAN.
YOU THINK I NEED YOU?
YOU THINK YOU'RE THE ONLY GAME IN TOWN?
NAH, MAN. NOT BY A LONG SIGHT.
WE SEE YOU.
YOU WALK THROUGH CRAP, YOU'RE GONNA LEAVE FOOTPRINTS.

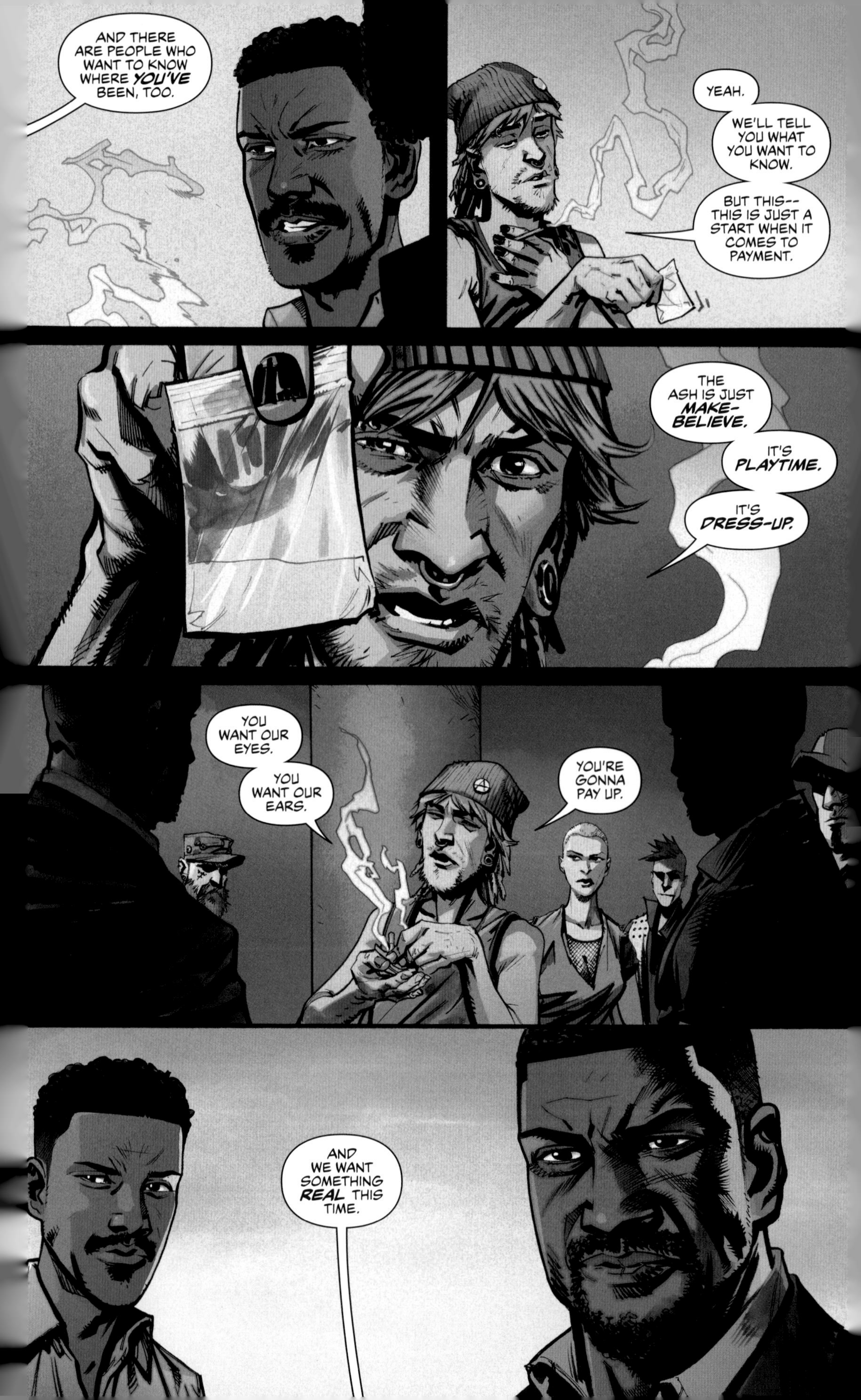
AND THERE ARE PEOPLE WHO WANT TO KNOW WHERE *YOU'VE* BEEN, TOO.
YEAH.
WE'LL TELL YOU WHAT YOU WANT TO KNOW.
BUT THIS-- THIS IS JUST A START WHEN IT COMES TO PAYMENT.
THE ASH IS JUST *MAKE-BELIEVE.*
IT'S *PLAYTIME.*
IT'S *DRESS-UP.*
YOU WANT OUR EYES.
YOU WANT OUR EARS.
YOU'RE GONNA PAY UP.
AND WE WANT SOMETHING *REAL* THIS TIME.

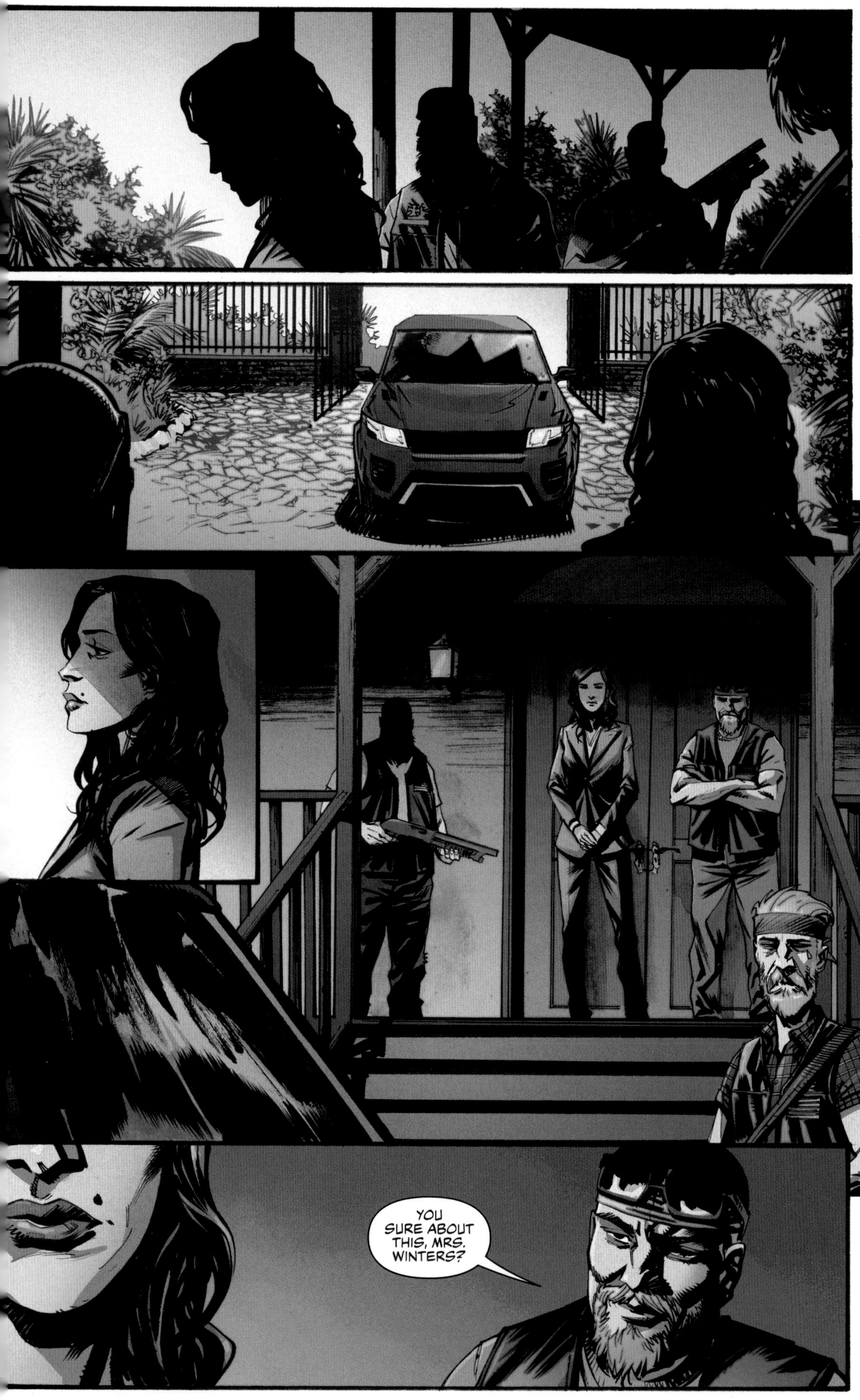
YOU SURE ABOUT THIS, MRS. WINTERS?

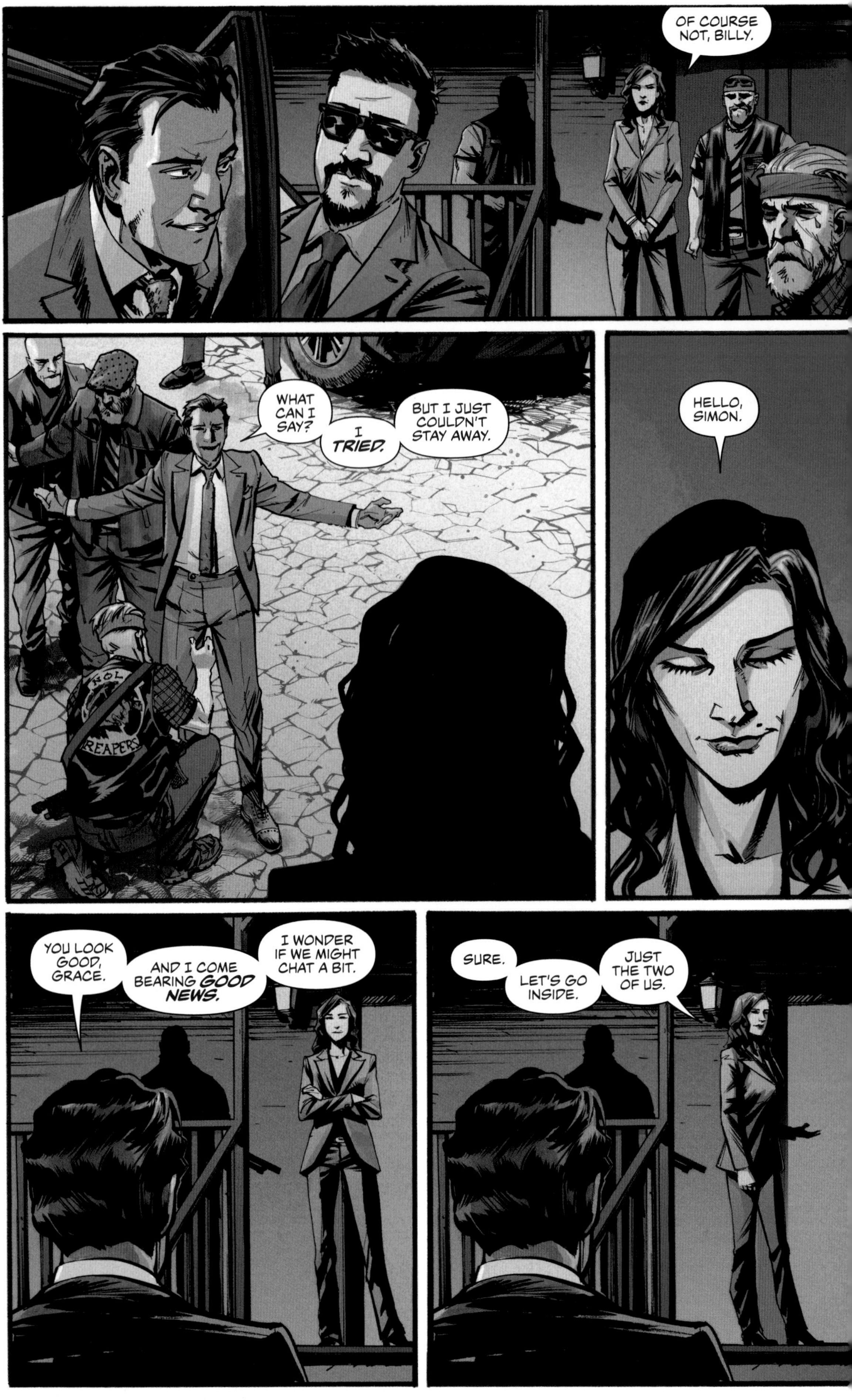
OF COURSE NOT, BILLY.
WHAT CAN I SAY?
I TRIED.
BUT I JUST COULDN'T STAY AWAY.
HELLO, SIMON.
YOU LOOK GOOD, GRACE.
AND I COME BEARING GOOD NEWS.
I WONDER IF WE MIGHT CHAT A BIT.
SURE.
LET'S GO INSIDE.
JUST THE TWO OF US.

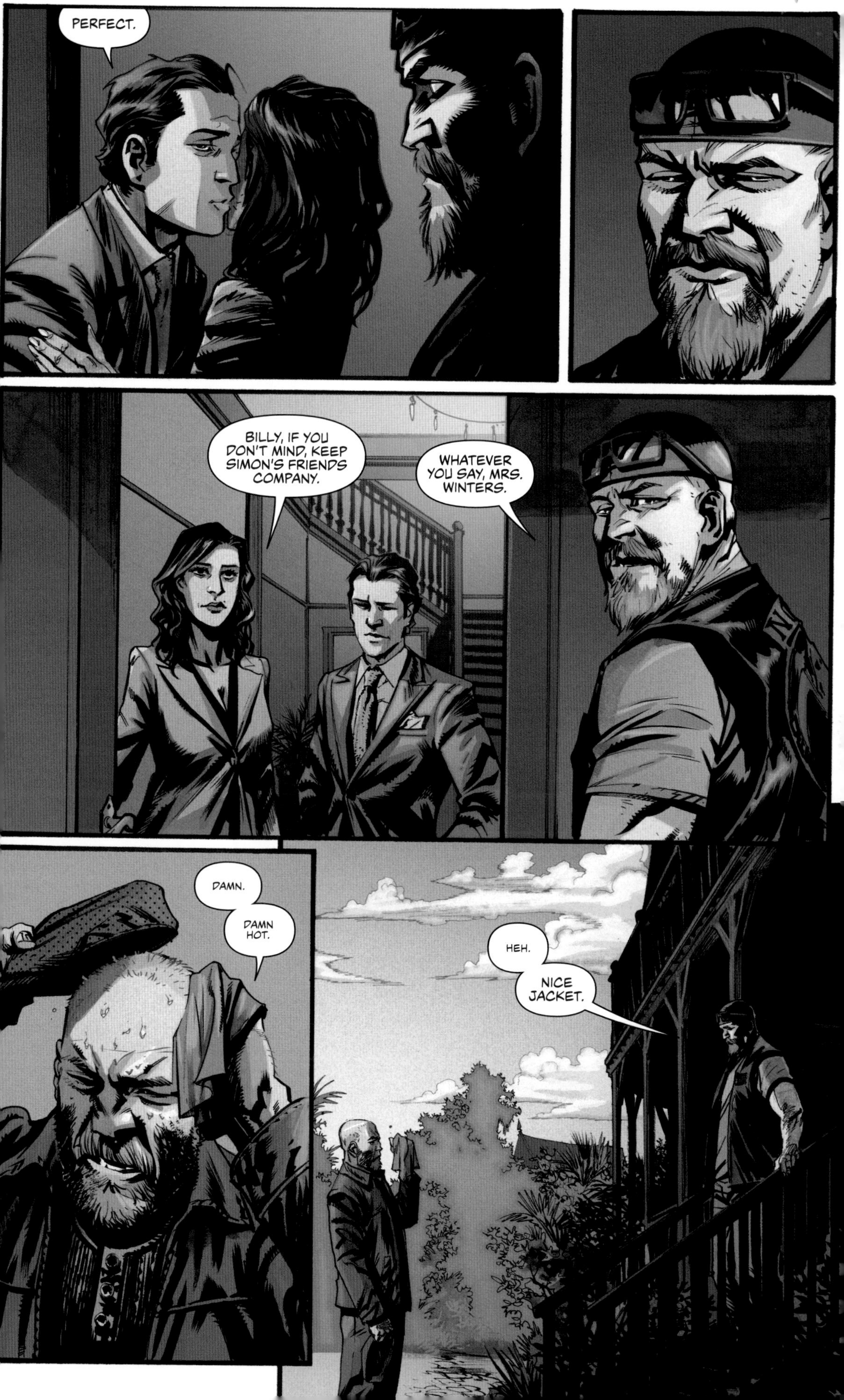
PERFECT.
BILLY, IF YOU DON'T MIND, KEEP SIMON'S FRIENDS COMPANY.
WHATEVER YOU SAY, MRS. WINTERS.
DAMN.
DAMN HOT.
HEH.
NICE JACKET.

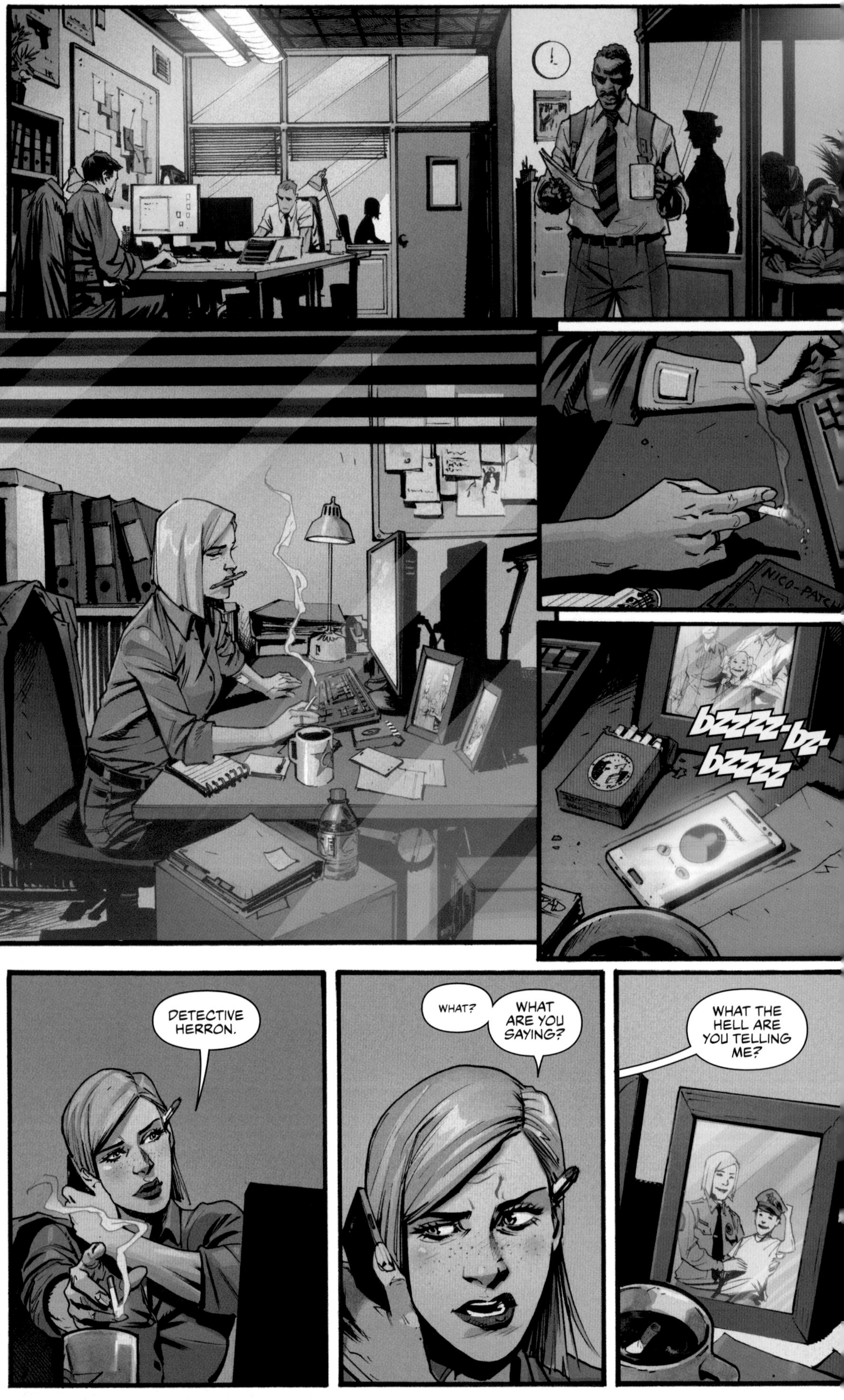
NICO-PATCH
bzzzz-bz-
bzzzz
DETECTIVE HERRON.
WHAT?
WHAT ARE YOU SAYING?
WHAT THE HELL ARE YOU TELLING ME?

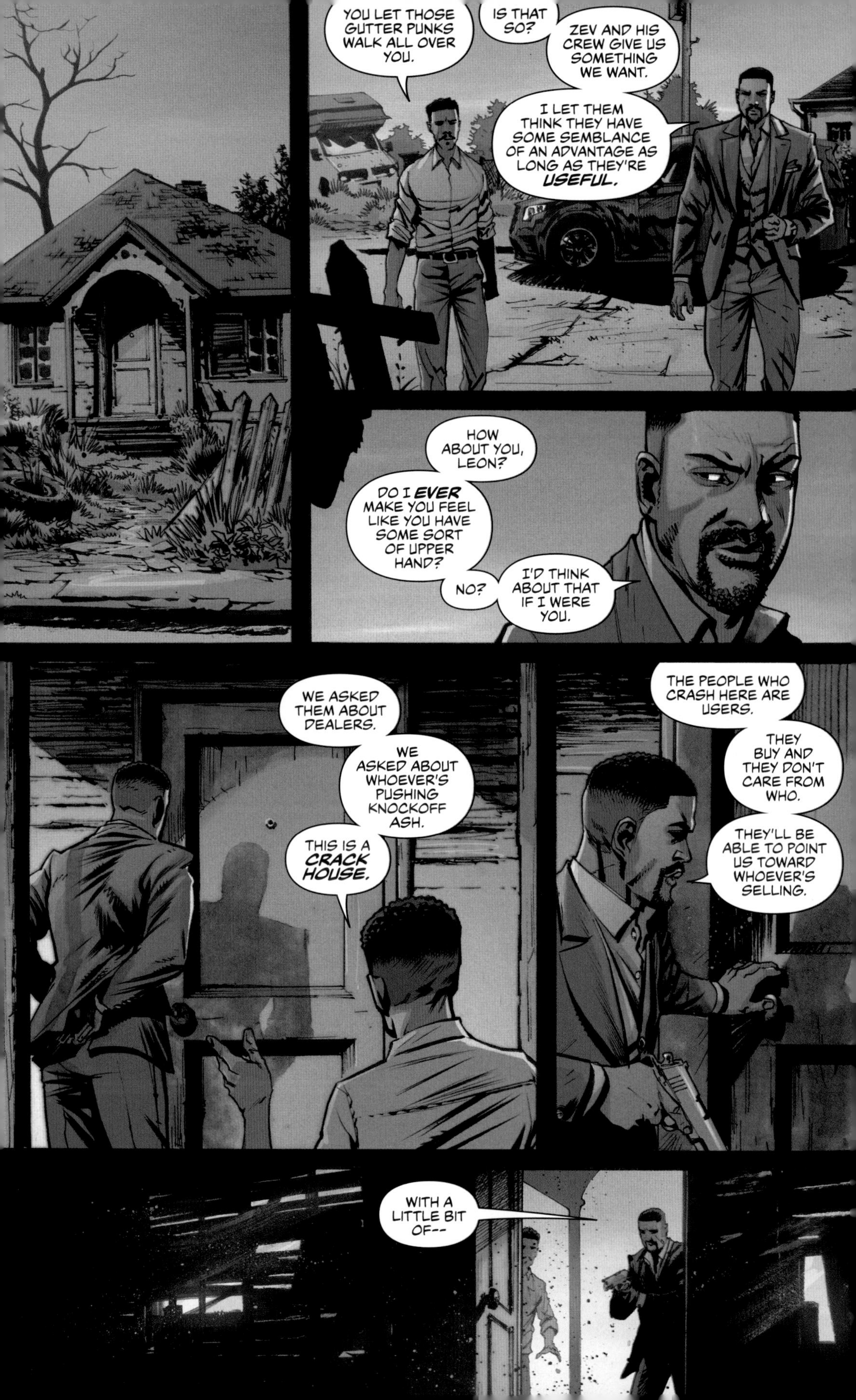
YOU LET THOSE GUTTER PUNKS WALK ALL OVER YOU.
IS THAT SO?
ZEV AND HIS CREW GIVE US SOMETHING WE WANT.
I LET THEM THINK THEY HAVE SOME SEMBLANCE OF AN ADVANTAGE AS LONG AS THEY'RE USEFUL.
HOW ABOUT YOU, LEON?
DO I EVER MAKE YOU FEEL LIKE YOU HAVE SOME SORT OF UPPER HAND?
NO?
I'D THINK ABOUT THAT IF I WERE YOU.
WE ASKED THEM ABOUT DEALERS.
WE ASKED ABOUT WHOEVER'S PUSHING KNOCKOFF ASH.
THIS IS A CRACK HOUSE.
THE PEOPLE WHO CRASH HERE ARE USERS.
THEY BUY AND THEY DON'T CARE FROM WHO.
THEY'LL BE ABLE TO POINT US TOWARD WHOEVER'S SELLING.
WITH A LITTLE BIT OF--

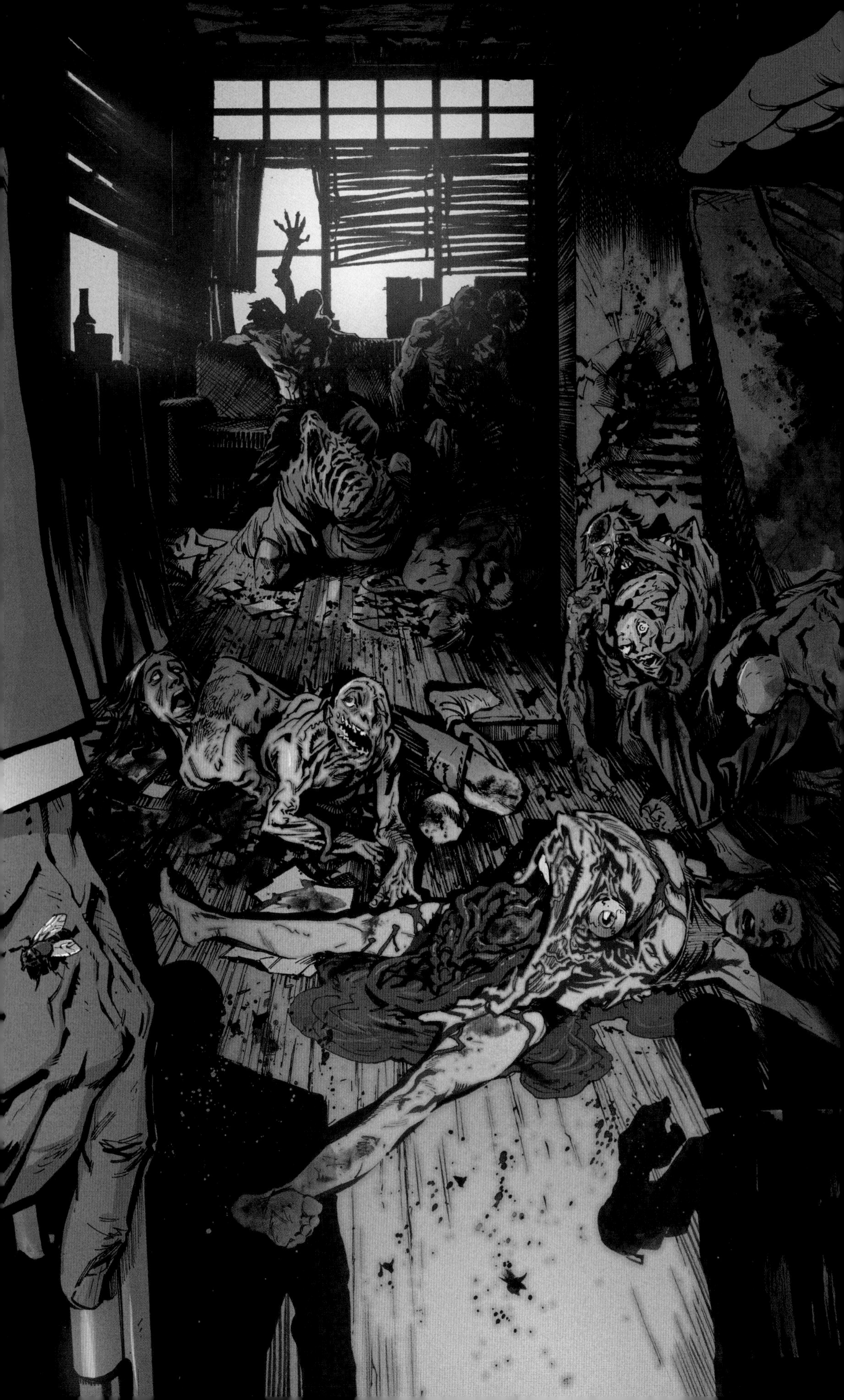

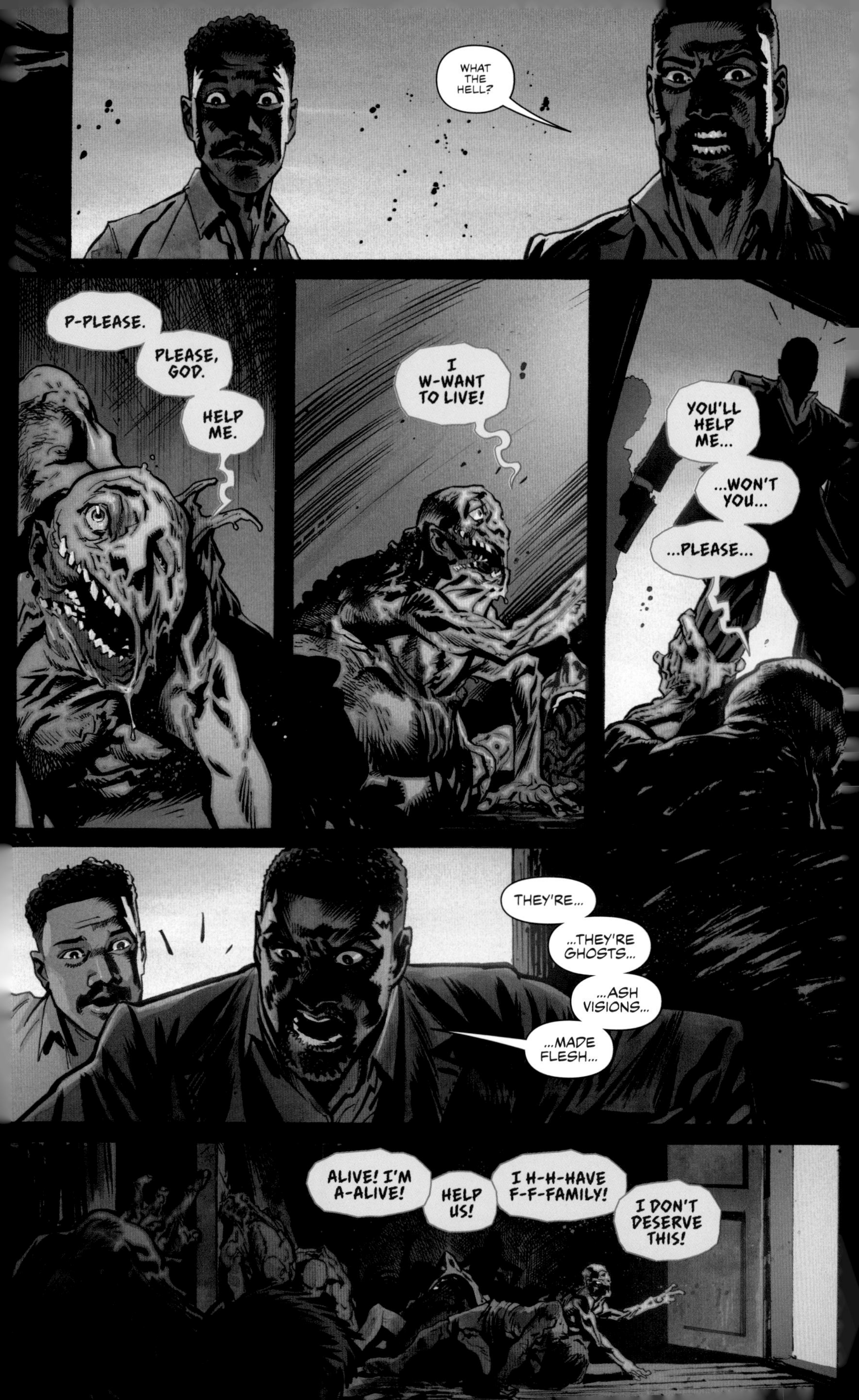
WHAT THE HELL?
P-PLEASE.
PLEASE, GOD.
HELP ME.
I W-WANT TO LIVE!
YOU'LL HELP ME...
...WON'T YOU...
...PLEASE...
THEY'RE...
...THEY'RE GHOSTS...
...ASH VISIONS...
...MADE FLESH...
ALIVE! I'M A-ALIVE!
HELP US!
I H-H-HAVE F-F-FAMILY!
I DON'T DESERVE THIS!

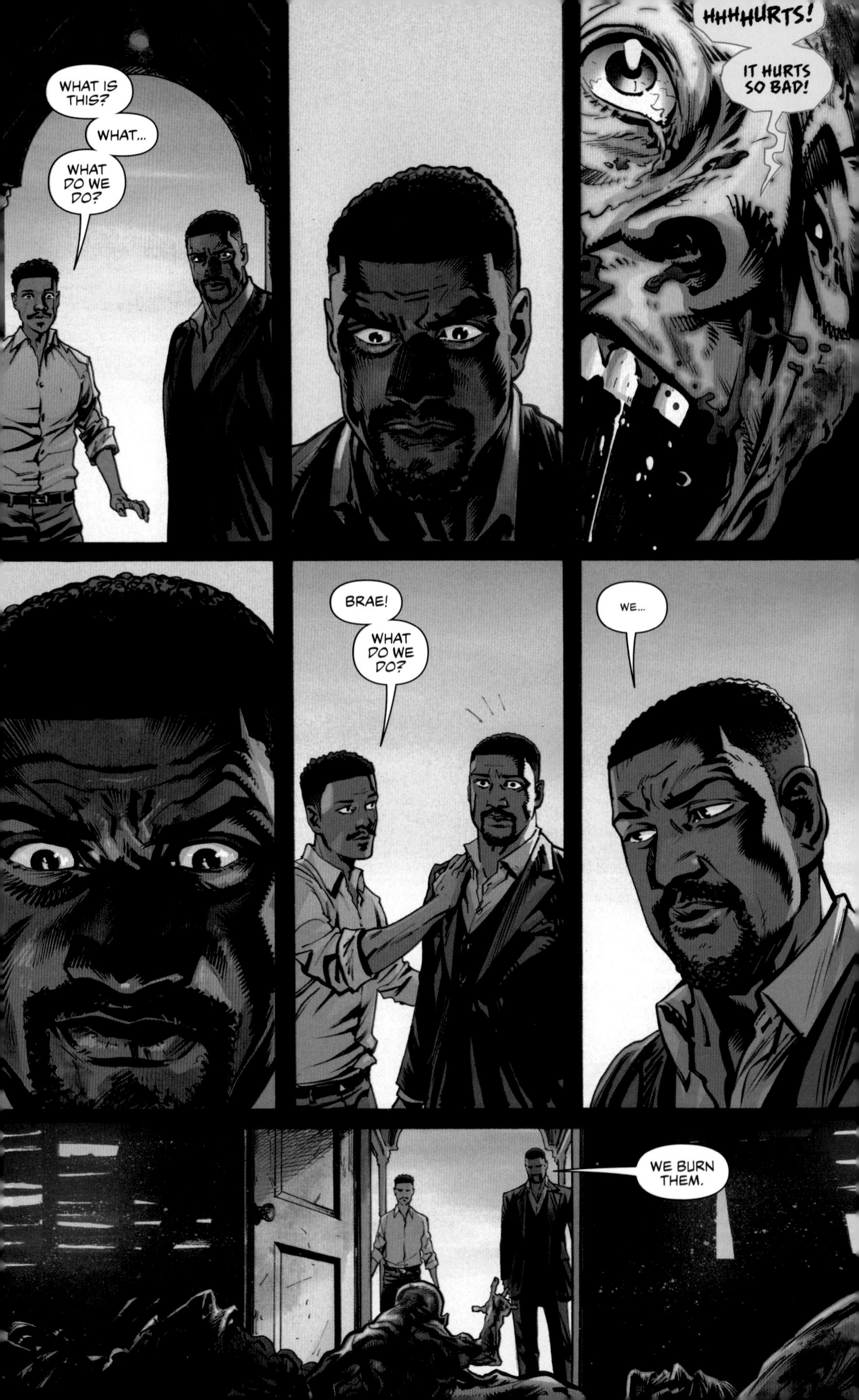
WHAT IS THIS?
WHAT...
WHAT DO WE DO?
HHHHURTS!
IT HURTS SO BAD!
BRAE!
WHAT DO WE DO?
WE...
WE BURN THEM.

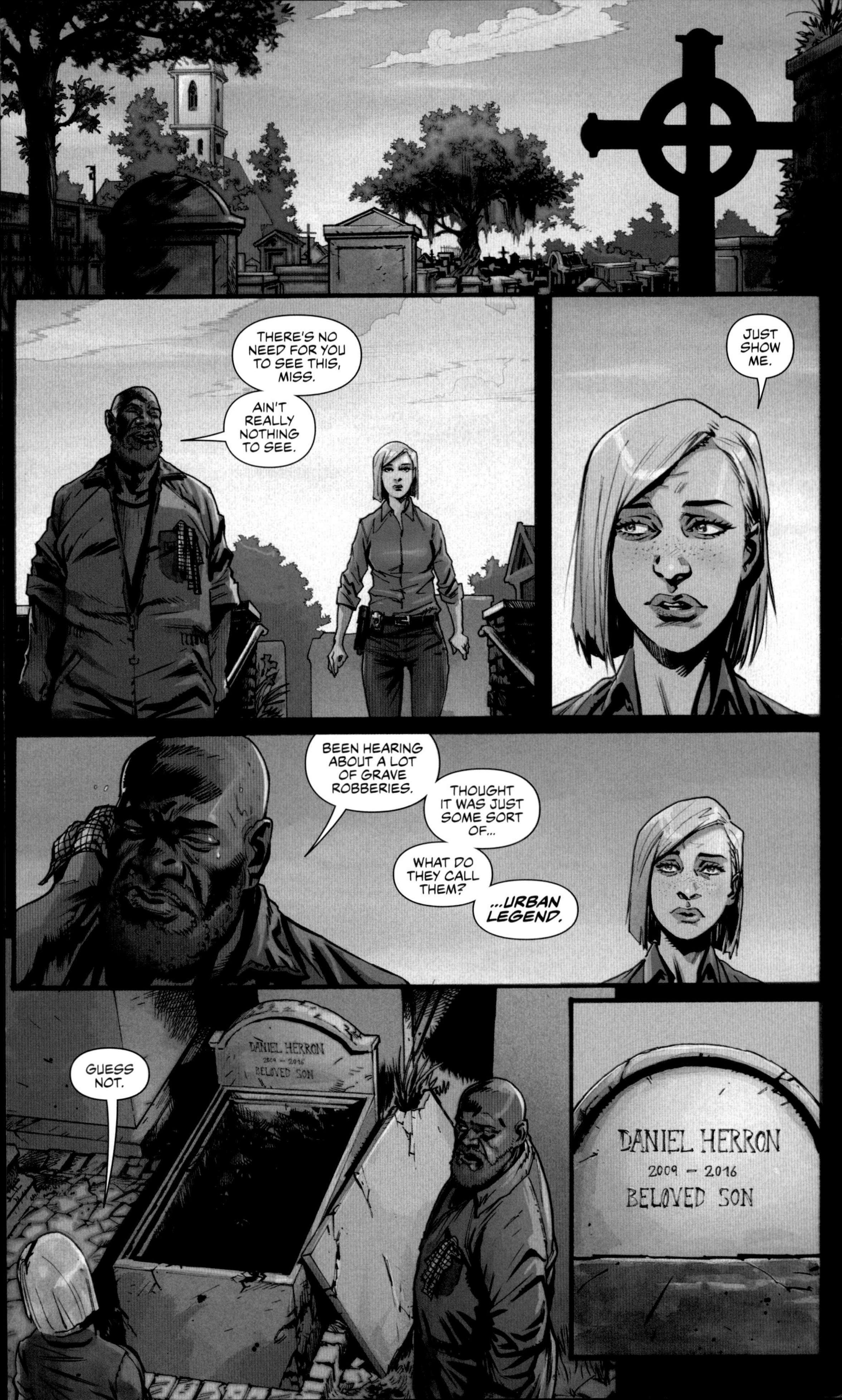
THERE'S NO NEED FOR YOU TO SEE THIS, MISS.
AIN'T REALLY NOTHING TO SEE.
JUST SHOW ME.
BEEN HEARING ABOUT A LOT OF GRAVE ROBBERIES.
THOUGHT IT WAS JUST SOME SORT OF...
WHAT DO THEY CALL THEM?
...URBAN LEGEND.
GUESS NOT.
DANIEL HERRON
2009 – 2016
BELOVED SON

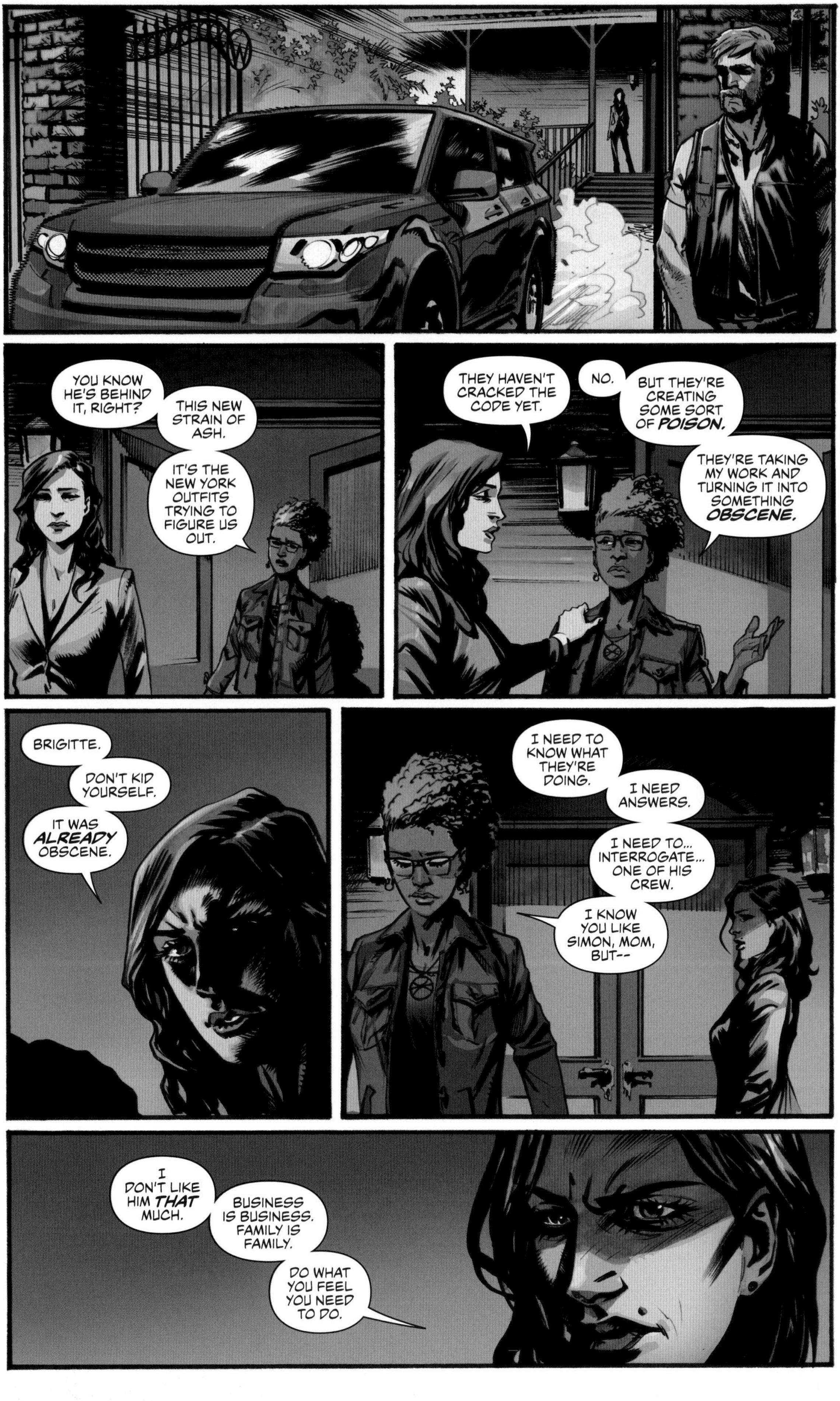

YOU KNOW HE'S BEHIND IT, RIGHT?
THIS NEW STRAIN OF ASH.
IT'S THE NEW YORK OUTFITS TRYING TO FIGURE US OUT.
THEY HAVEN'T CRACKED THE CODE YET.
NO.
BUT THEY'RE CREATING SOME SORT OF POISON.
THEY'RE TAKING MY WORK AND TURNING IT INTO SOMETHING OBSCENE.
BRIGITTE.
DON'T KID YOURSELF.
IT WAS ALREADY OBSCENE.
I NEED TO KNOW WHAT THEY'RE DOING.
I NEED ANSWERS.
I NEED TO... INTERROGATE... ONE OF HIS CREW.
I KNOW YOU LIKE SIMON, MOM, BUT--
I DON'T LIKE HIM THAT MUCH.
BUSINESS IS BUSINESS. FAMILY IS FAMILY.
DO WHAT YOU FEEL YOU NEED TO DO.

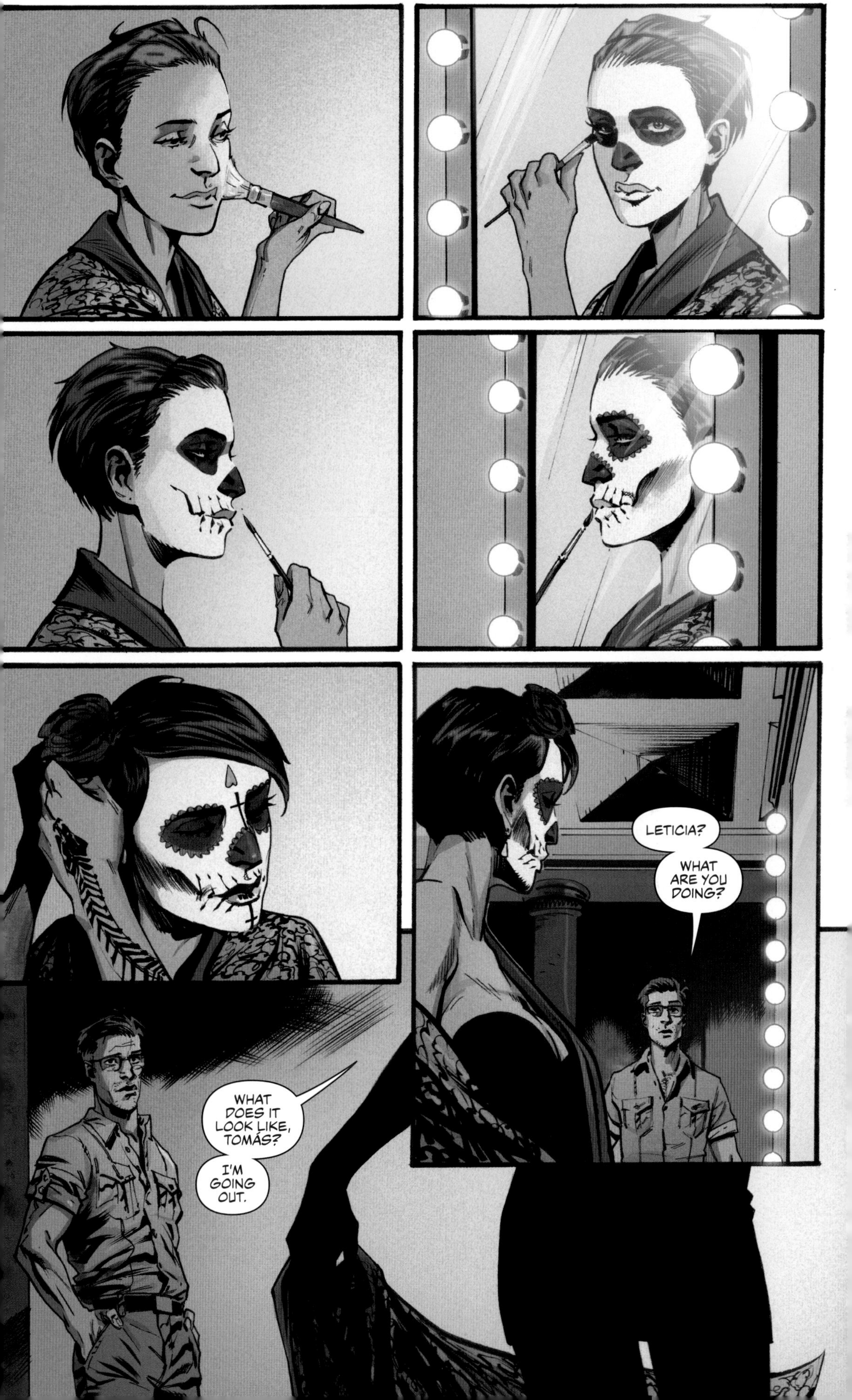
LETICIA?
WHAT ARE YOU DOING?
WHAT DOES IT LOOK LIKE, TOMÁS?
I'M GOING OUT.

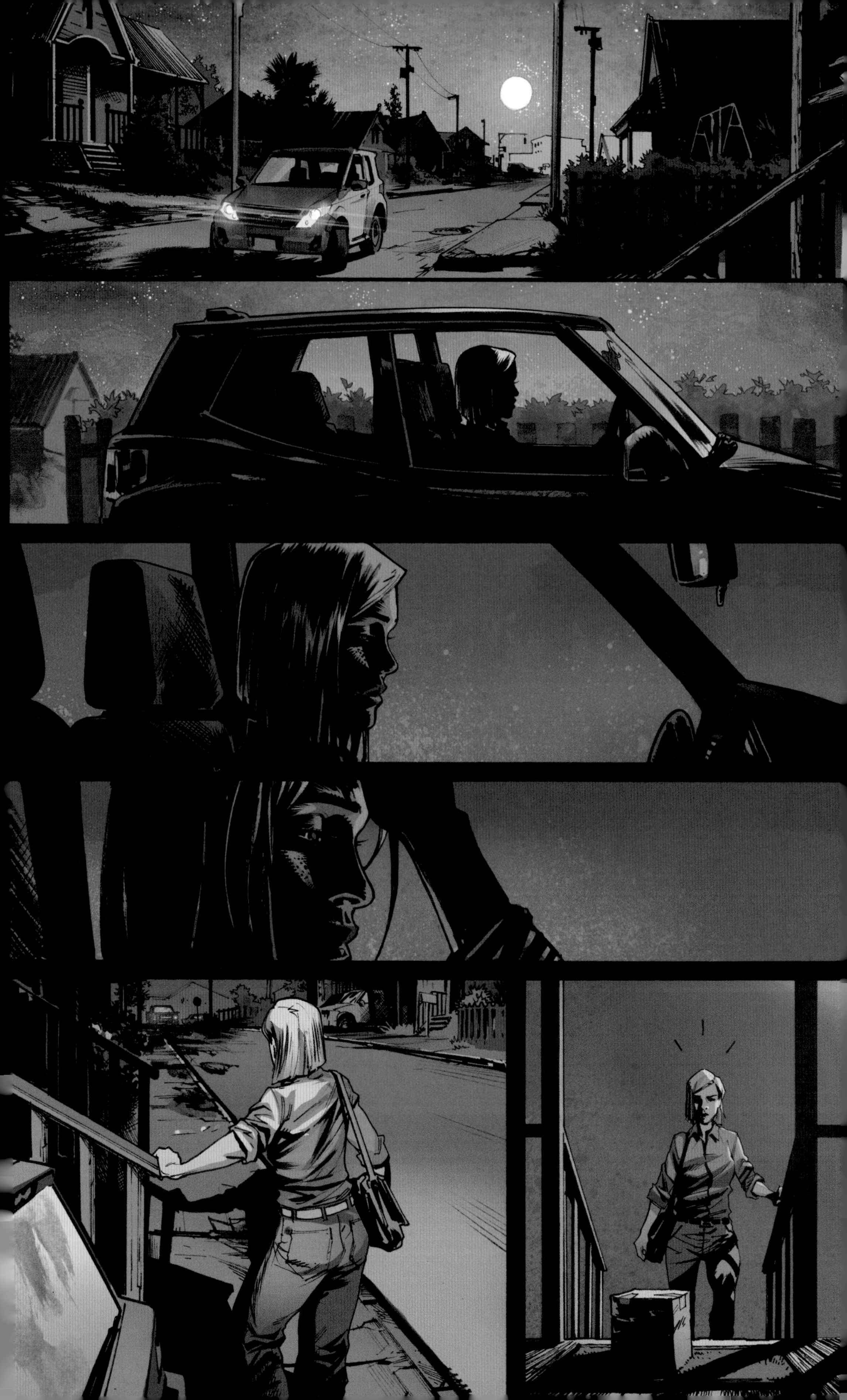

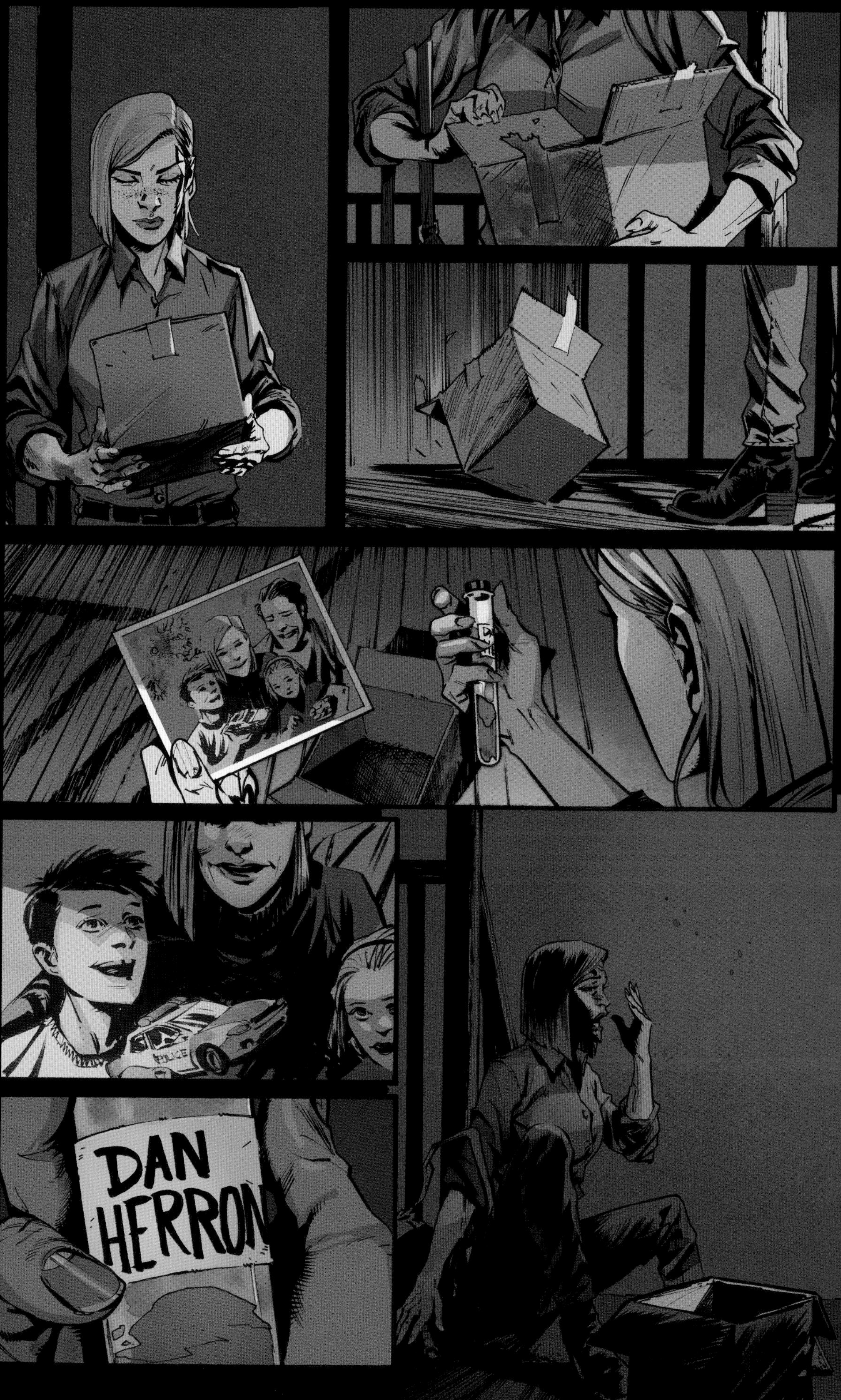
POLICE
DAN
HERRON

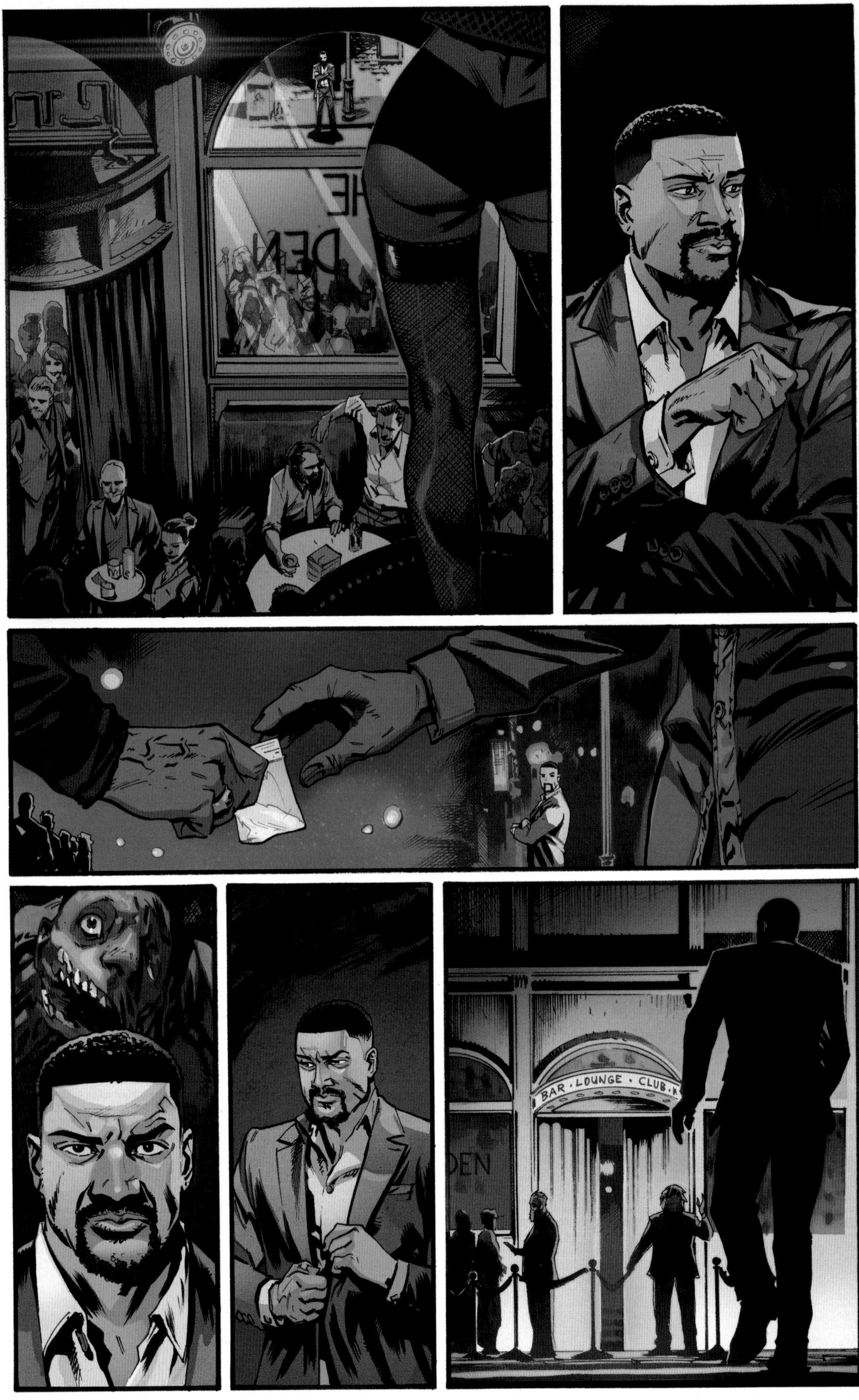
BAR · LOUNGE · CLUB
DEN

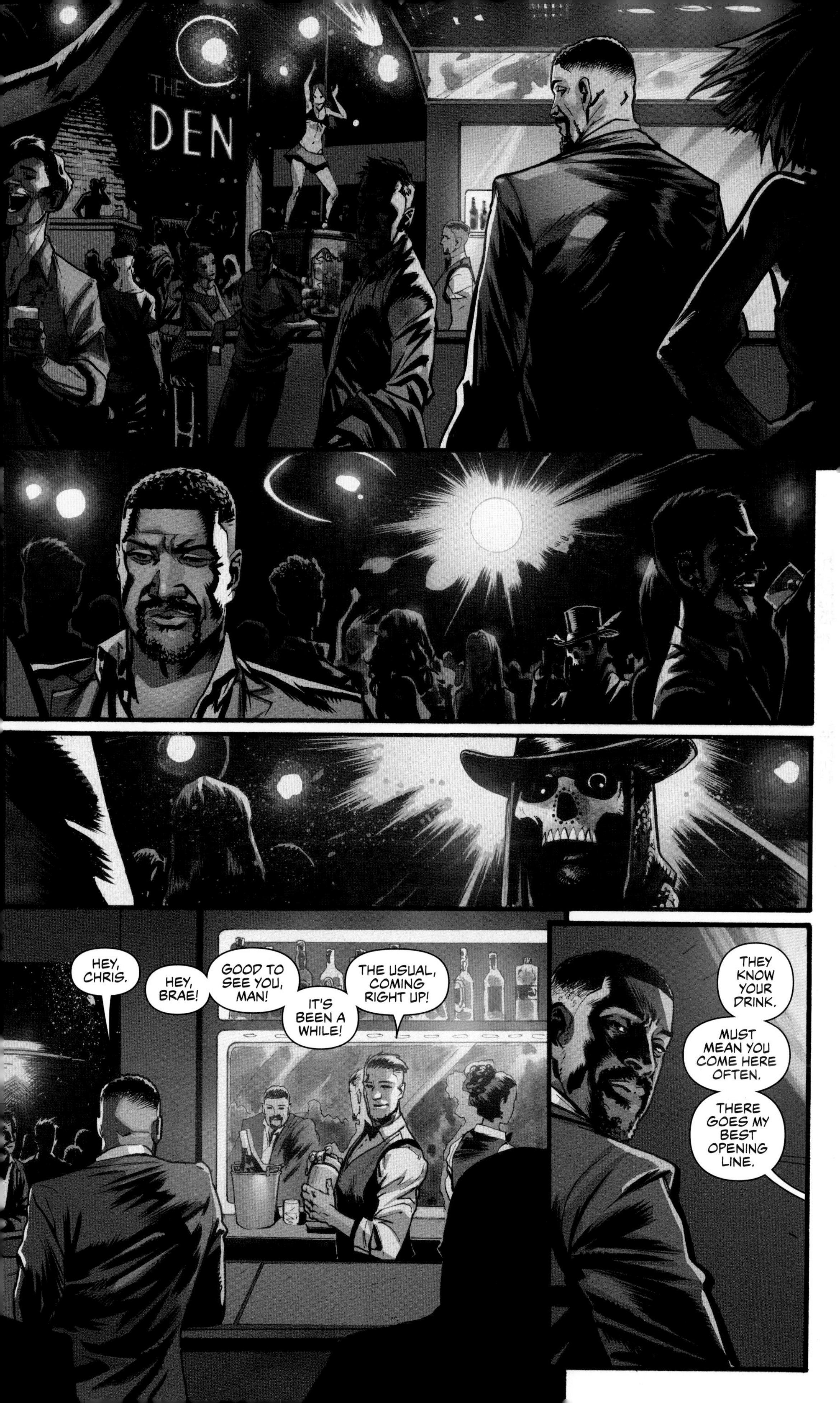
THE DEN
HEY, CHRIS.
HEY, BRAE!
GOOD TO SEE YOU, MAN!
IT'S BEEN A WHILE!
THE USUAL, COMING RIGHT UP!
THEY KNOW YOUR DRINK.
MUST MEAN YOU COME HERE OFTEN.
THERE GOES MY BEST OPENING LINE.

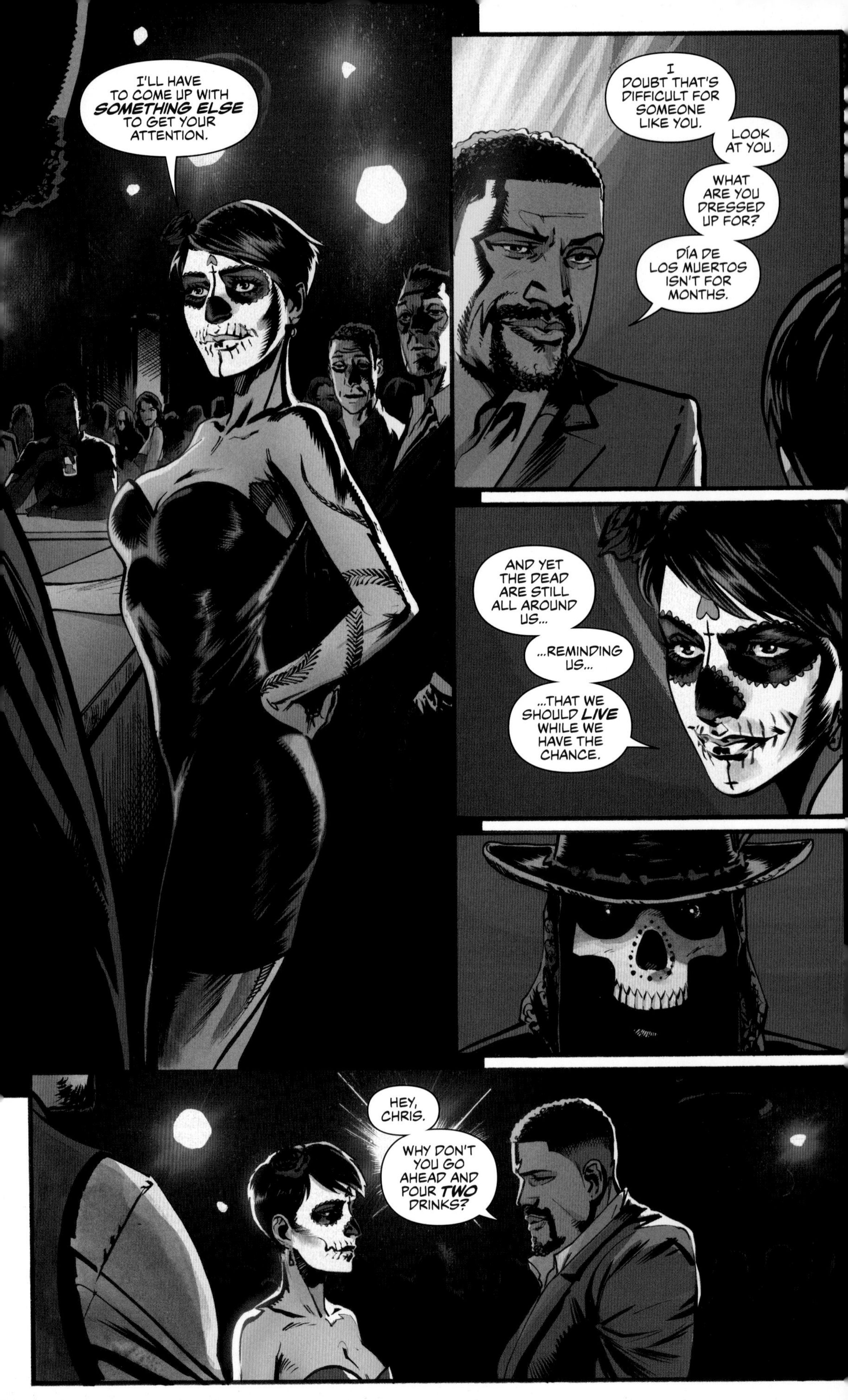
I'LL HAVE TO COME UP WITH SOMETHING ELSE TO GET YOUR ATTENTION.
I DOUBT THAT'S DIFFICULT FOR SOMEONE LIKE YOU.
LOOK AT YOU.
WHAT ARE YOU DRESSED UP FOR?
DÍA DE LOS MUERTOS ISN'T FOR MONTHS.
AND YET THE DEAD ARE STILL ALL AROUND US...
...REMINDING US...
...THAT WE SHOULD LIVE WHILE WE HAVE THE CHANCE.
HEY, CHRIS.
WHY DON'T YOU GO AHEAD AND POUR TWO DRINKS?

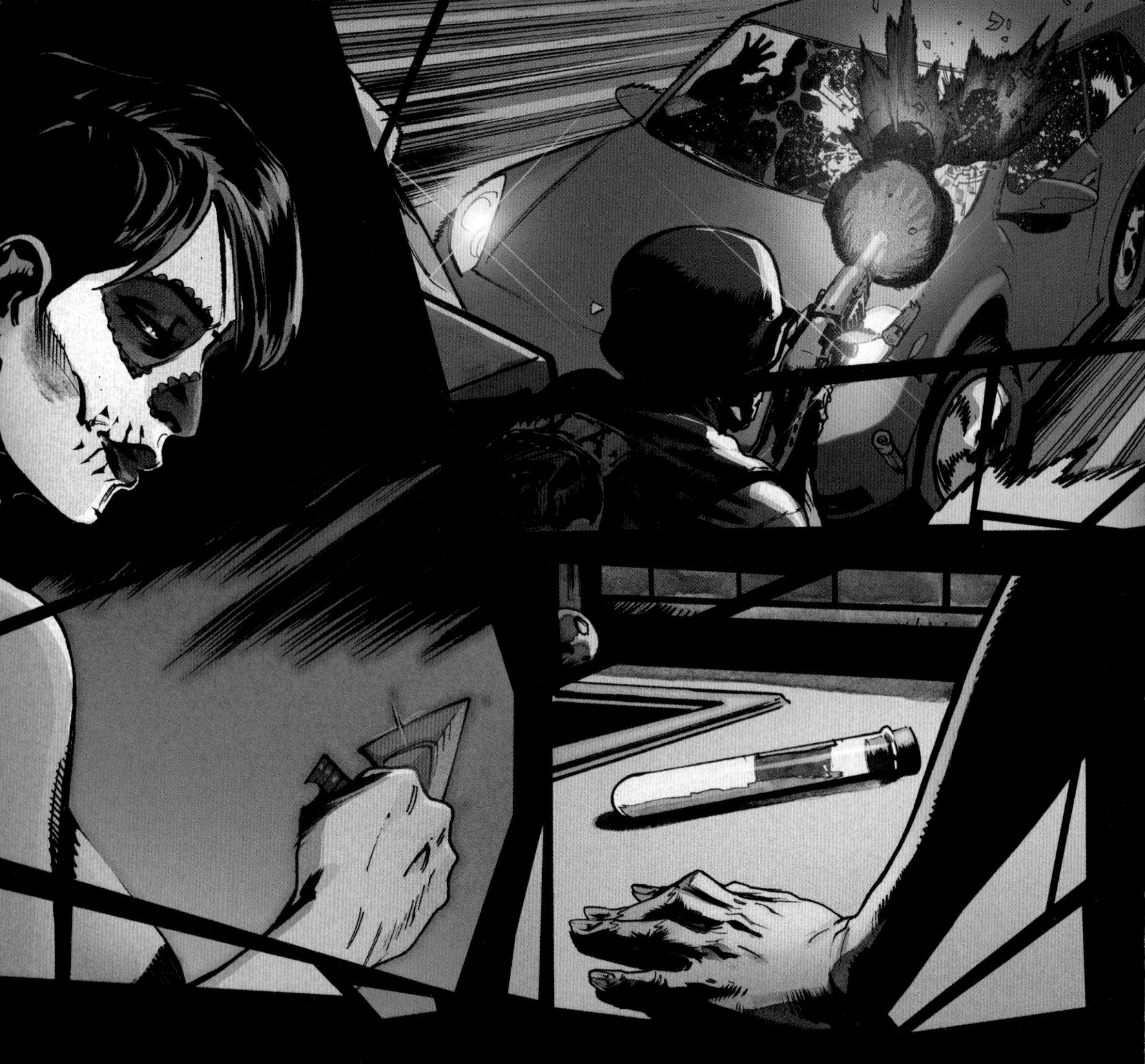

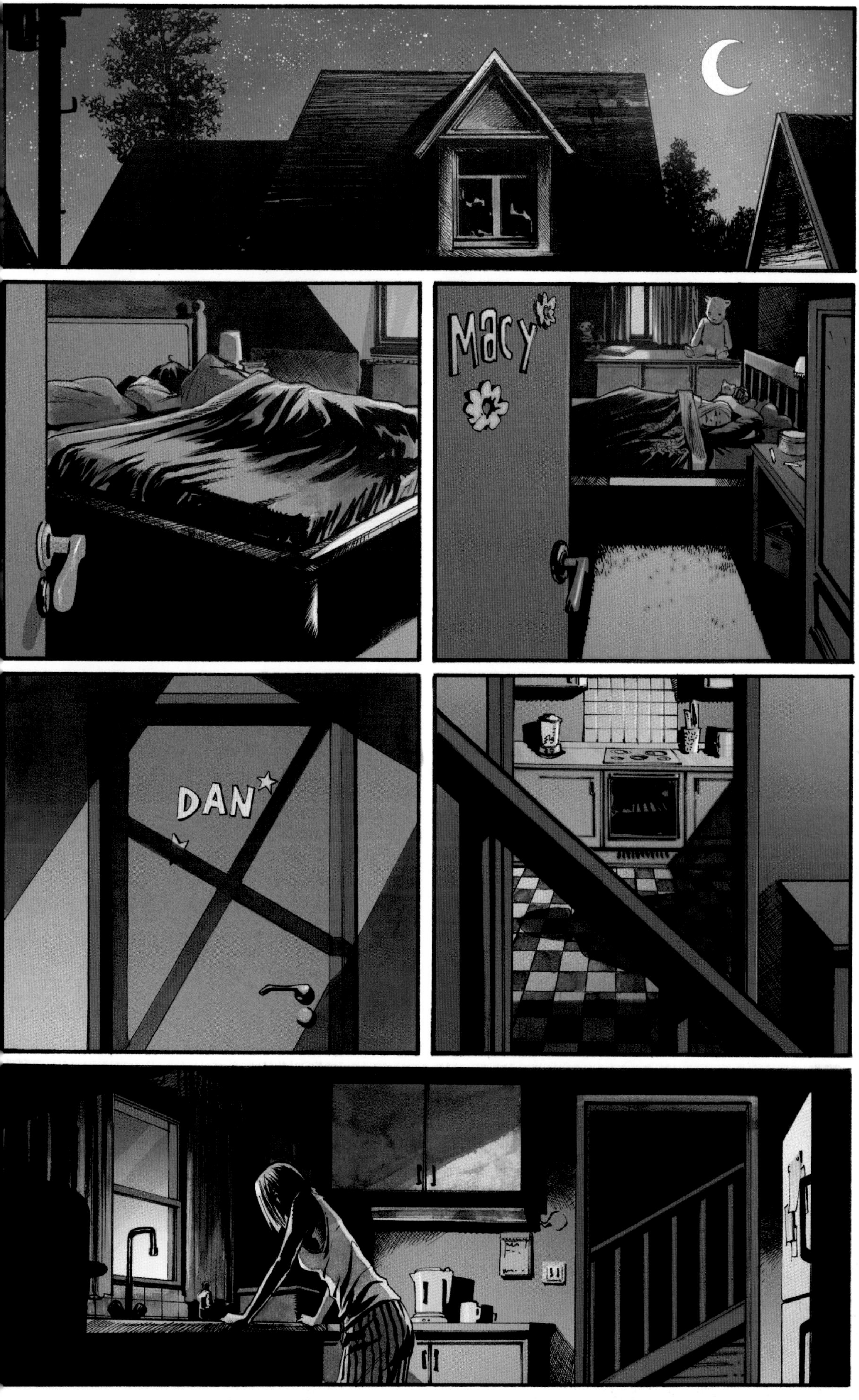
MACY
DAN

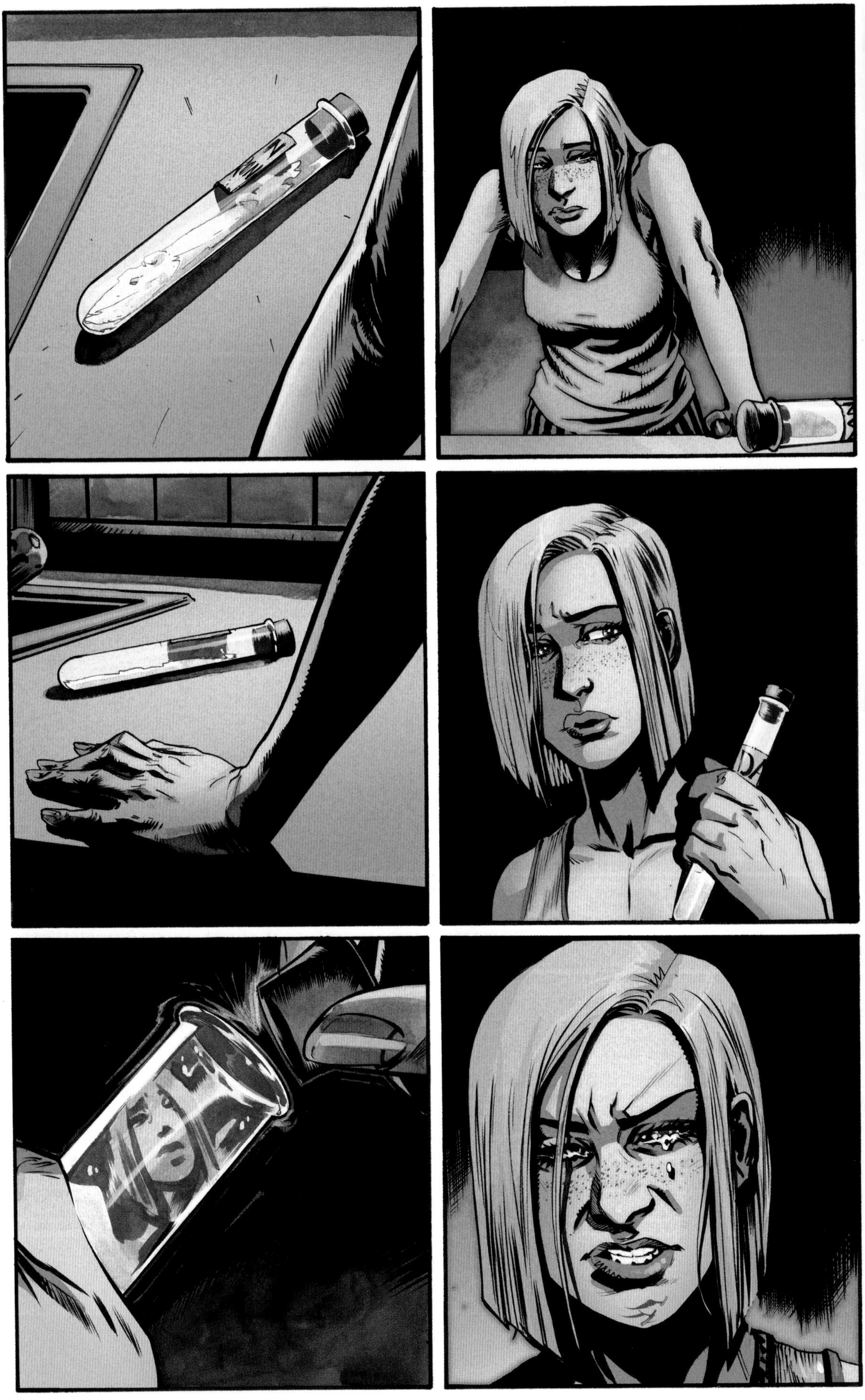

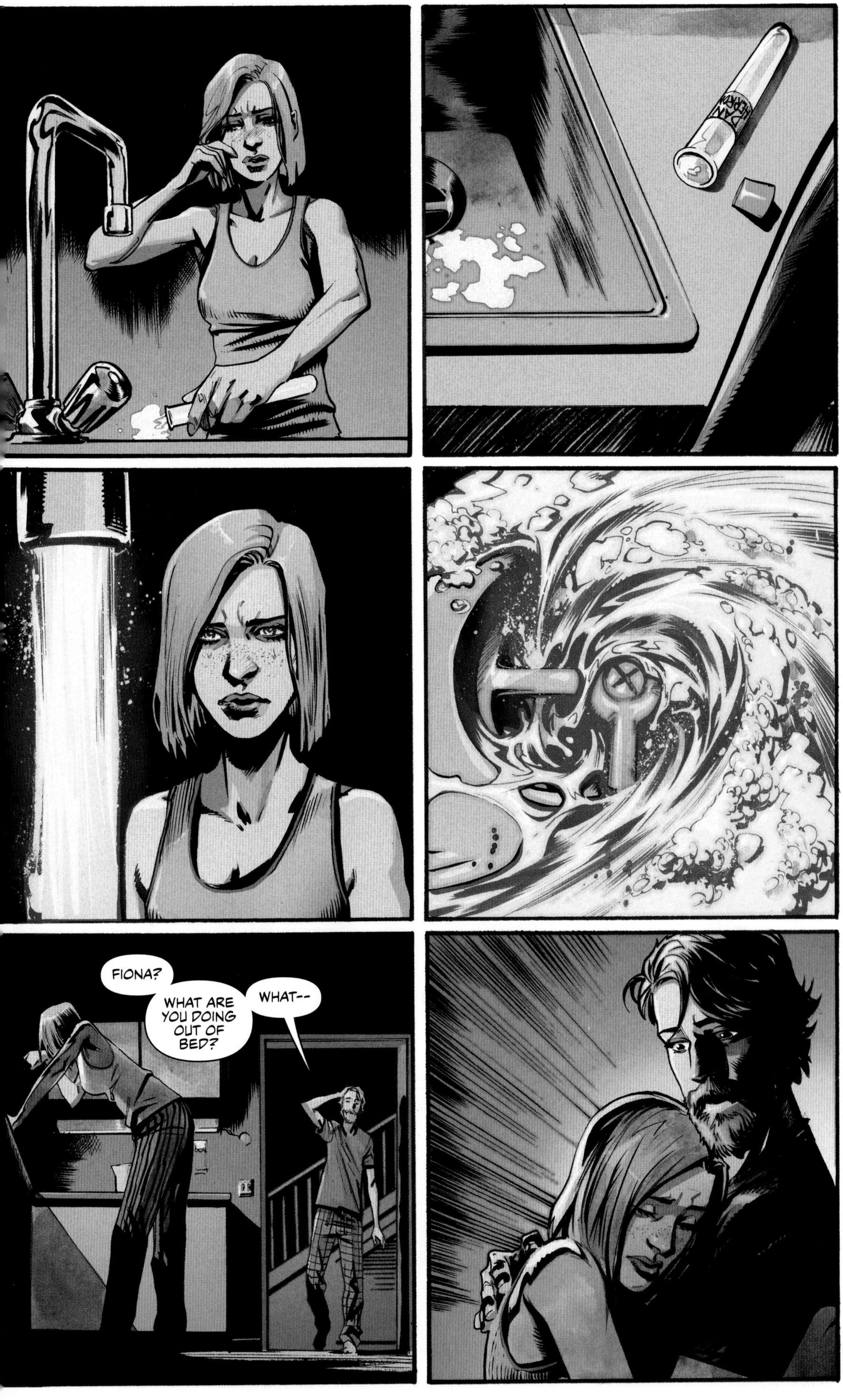
DAN
FIONA?
WHAT ARE YOU DOING OUT OF BED?
WHAT--

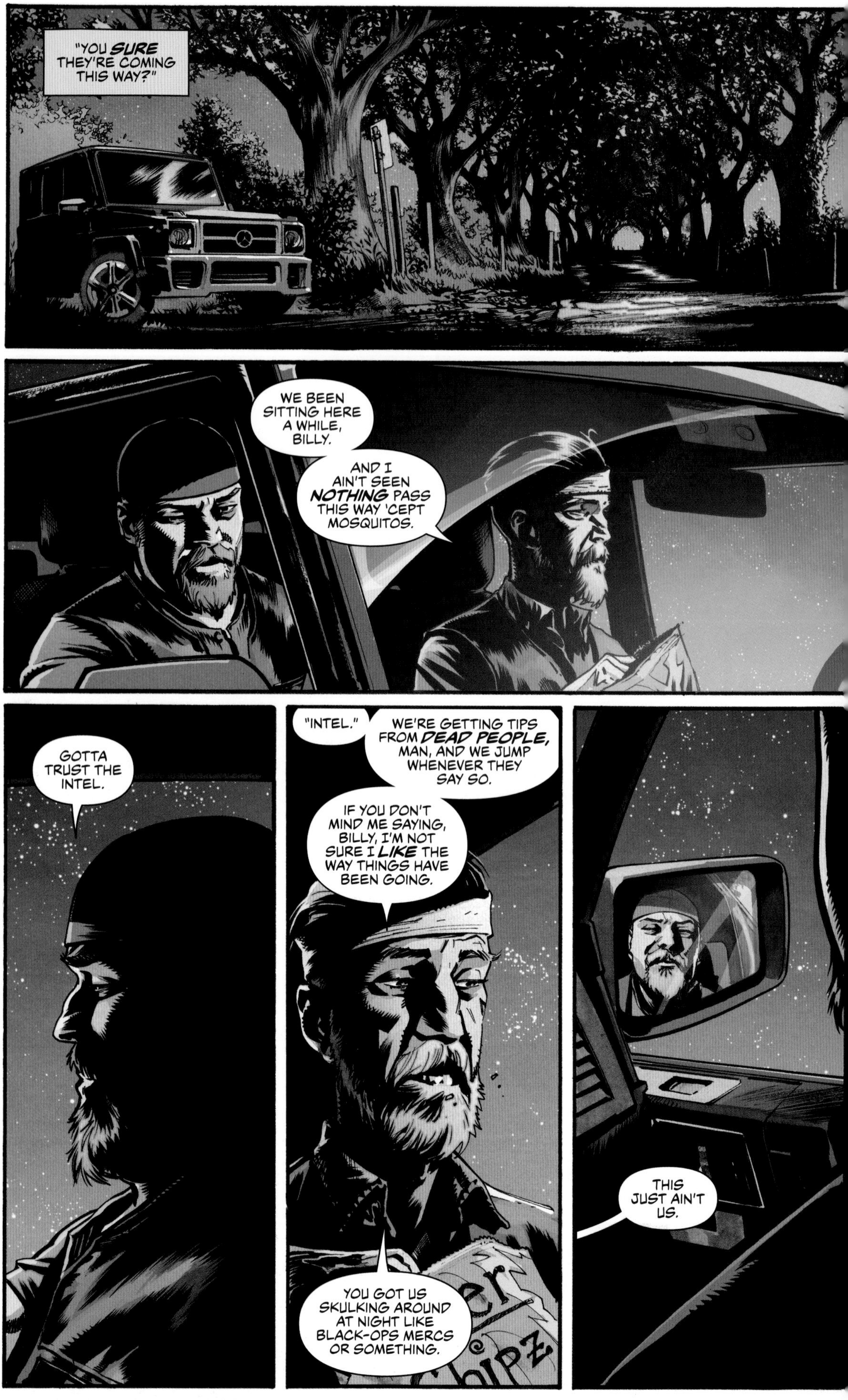
"YOU SURE THEY'RE COMING THIS WAY?"
WE BEEN SITTING HERE A WHILE, BILLY.
AND I AIN'T SEEN NOTHING PASS THIS WAY 'CEPT MOSQUITOS.
GOTTA TRUST THE INTEL.
"INTEL."
WE'RE GETTING TIPS FROM DEAD PEOPLE, MAN, AND WE JUMP WHENEVER THEY SAY SO.
IF YOU DON'T MIND ME SAYING, BILLY, I'M NOT SURE I LIKE THE WAY THINGS HAVE BEEN GOING.
YOU GOT US SKULKING AROUND AT NIGHT LIKE BLACK-OPS MERCS OR SOMETHING.
THIS JUST AIN'T US.

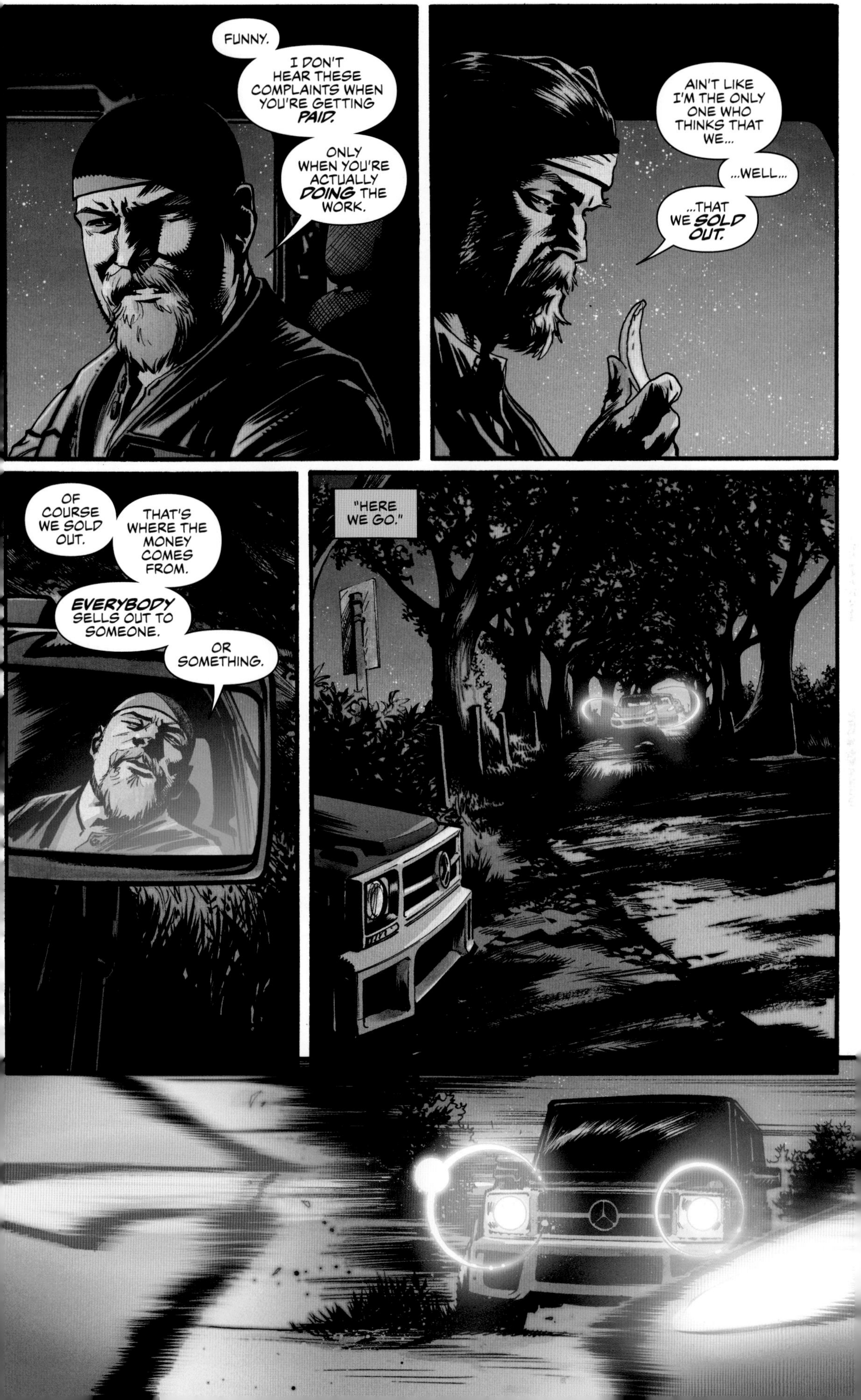
FUNNY.
I DON'T HEAR THESE COMPLAINTS WHEN YOU'RE GETTING PAID.
ONLY WHEN YOU'RE ACTUALLY DOING THE WORK.
AIN'T LIKE I'M THE ONLY ONE WHO THINKS THAT WE...
...WELL...
...THAT WE SOLD OUT.
OF COURSE WE SOLD OUT.
THAT'S WHERE THE MONEY COMES FROM.
EVERYBODY SELLS OUT TO SOMEONE.
OR SOMETHING.
"HERE WE GO."

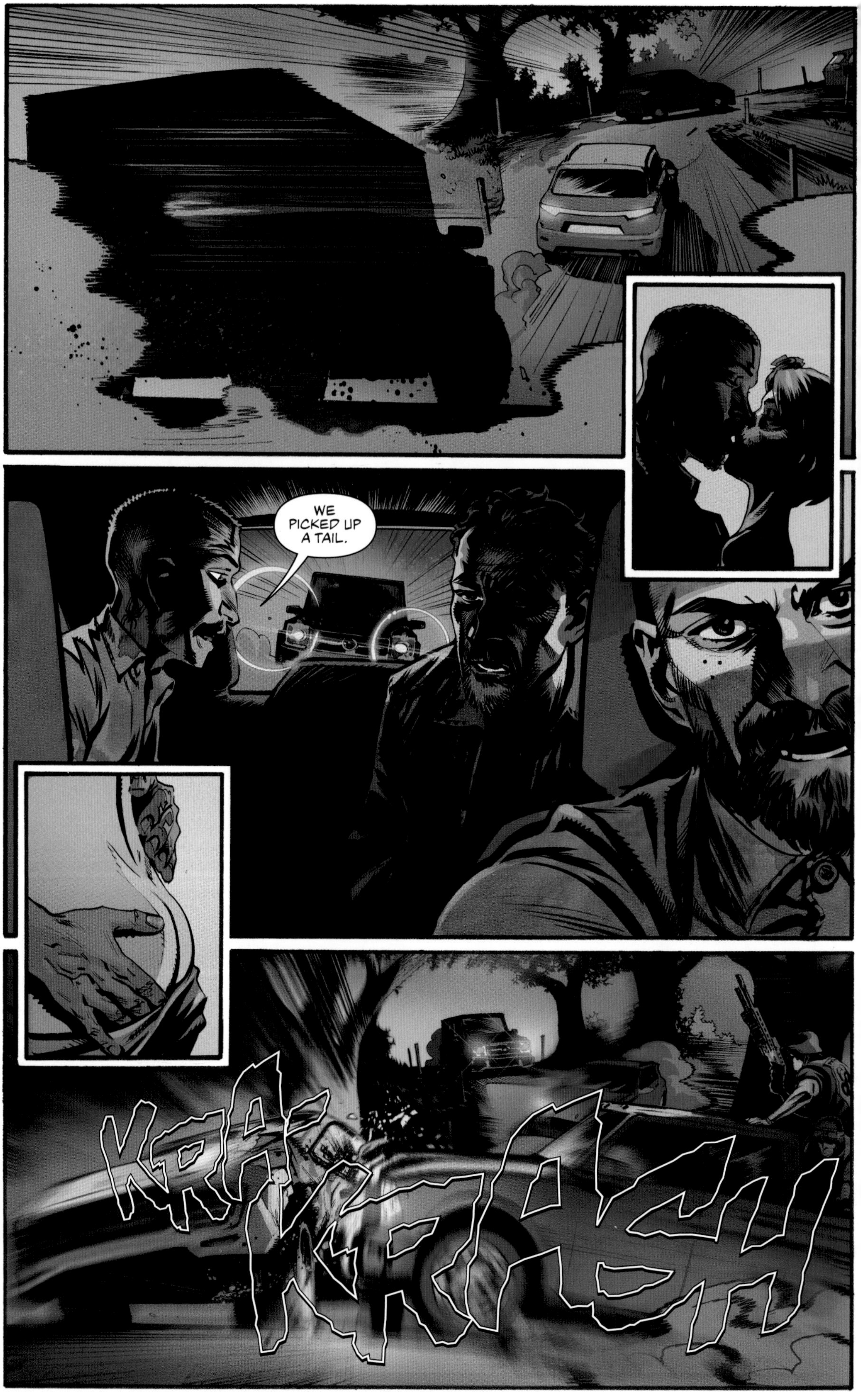
WE PICKED UP A TAIL.
KRA- KRASH

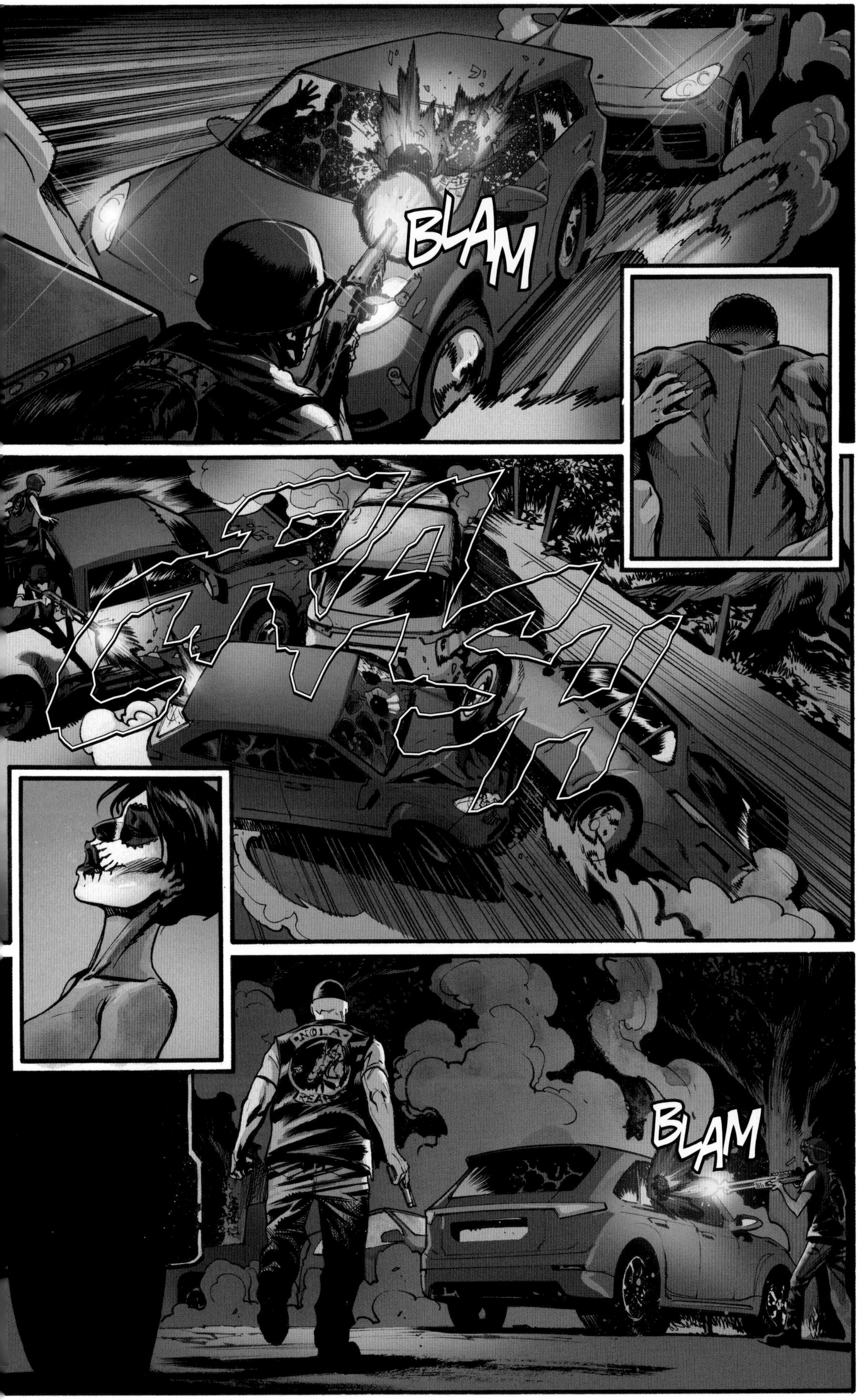
BLAM
CRASH
BLAM

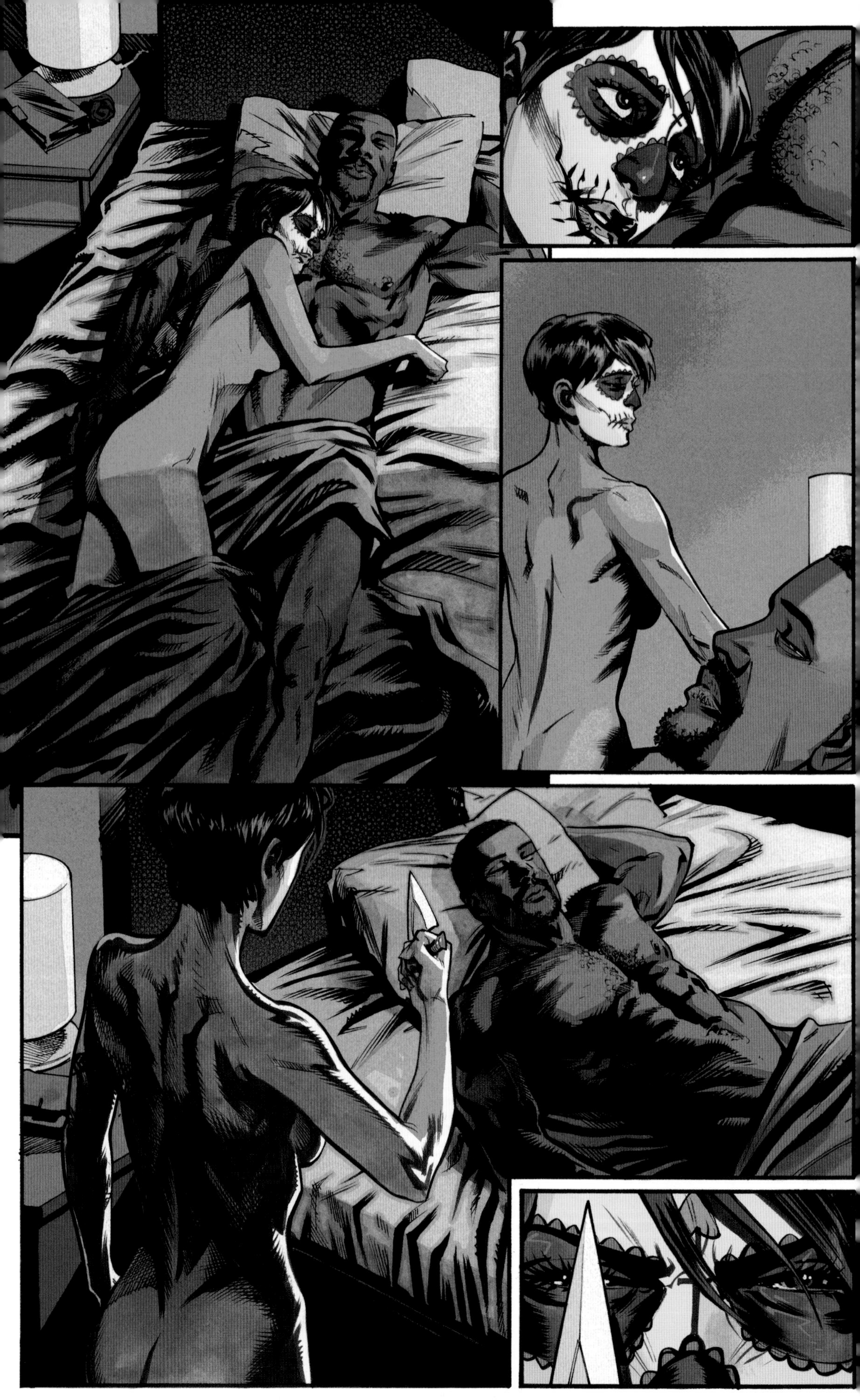

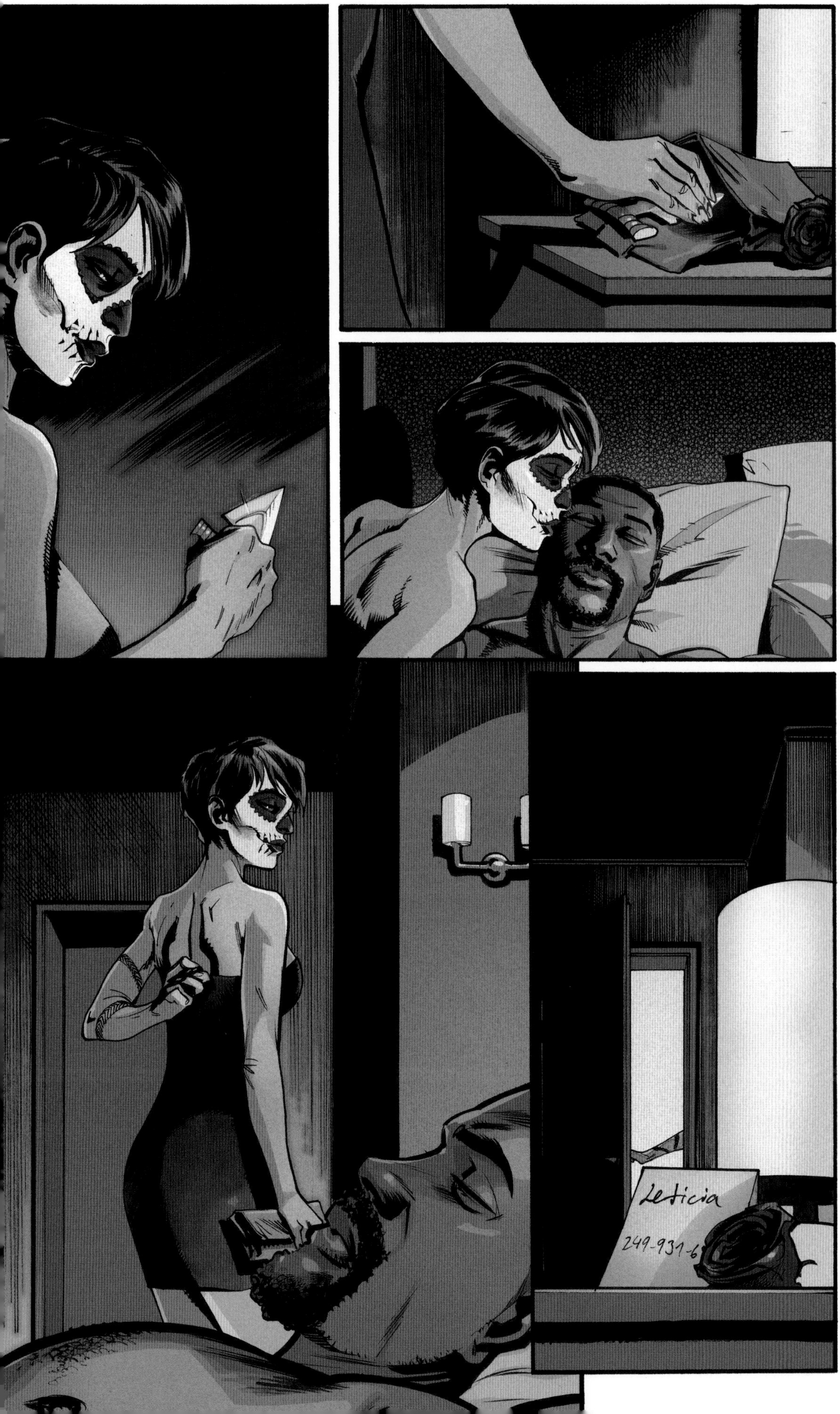
Leticia
249-931-6

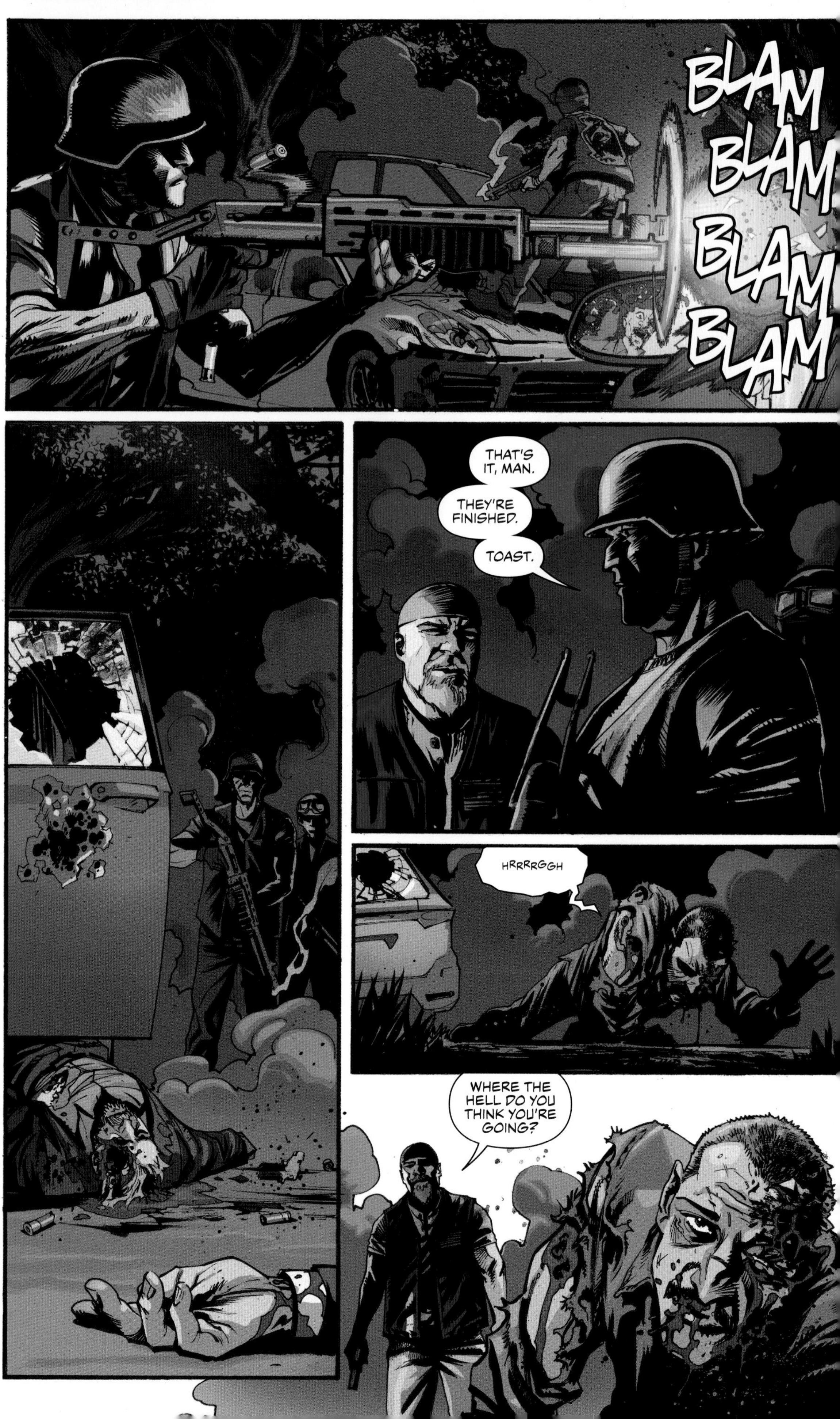
BLAM
BLAM
BLAM
BLAM
THAT'S IT, MAN.
THEY'RE FINISHED.
TOAST.
HRRRRGGH
WHERE THE HELL DO YOU THINK YOU'RE GOING?

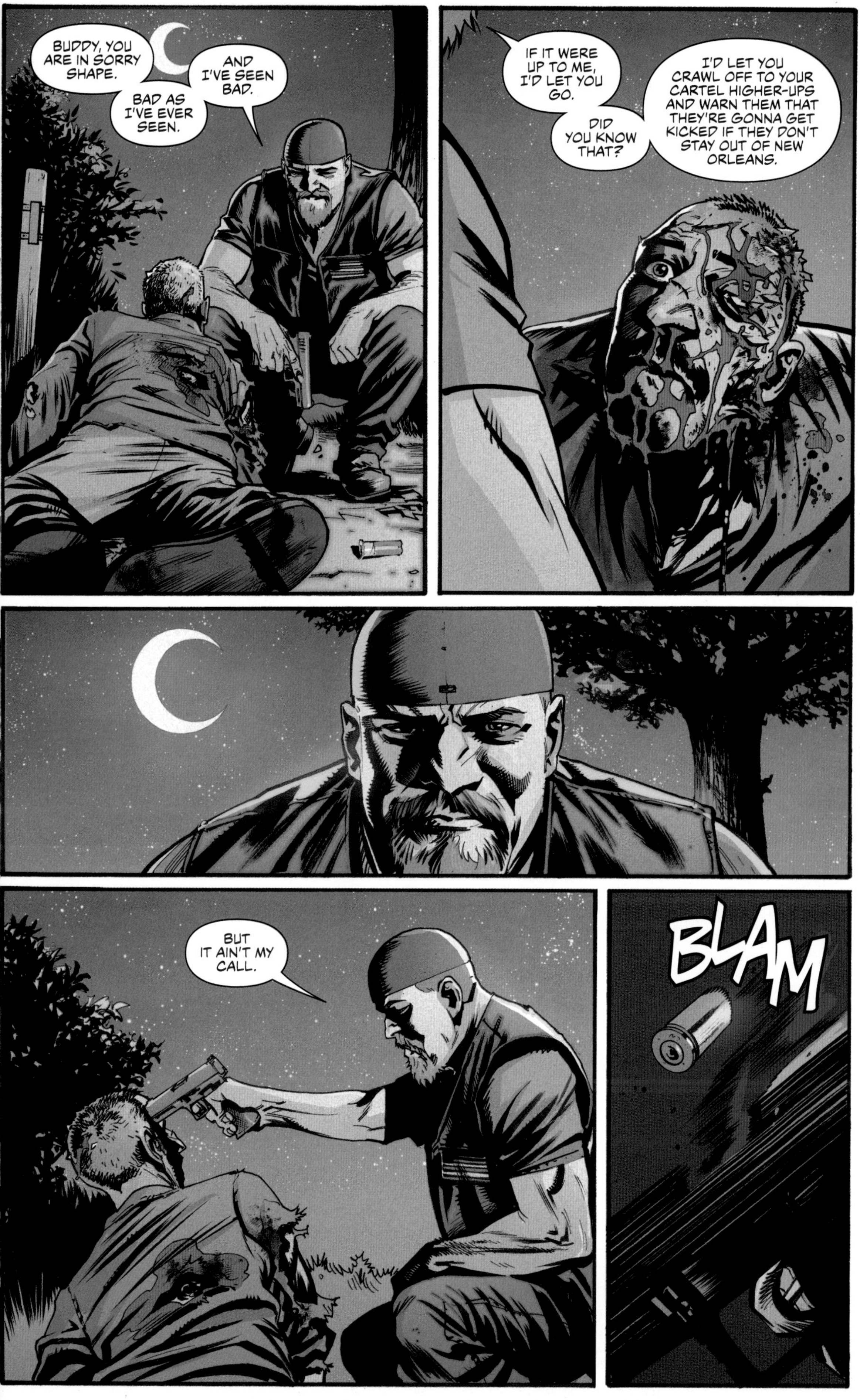
BUDDY, YOU ARE IN SORRY SHAPE.
BAD AS I'VE EVER SEEN.
AND I'VE SEEN BAD.
IF IT WERE UP TO ME, I'D LET YOU GO.
DID YOU KNOW THAT?
I'D LET YOU CRAWL OFF TO YOUR CARTEL HIGHER-UPS AND WARN THEM THAT THEY'RE GONNA GET KICKED IF THEY DON'T STAY OUT OF NEW ORLEANS.
BUT IT AIN'T MY CALL.
BLAM

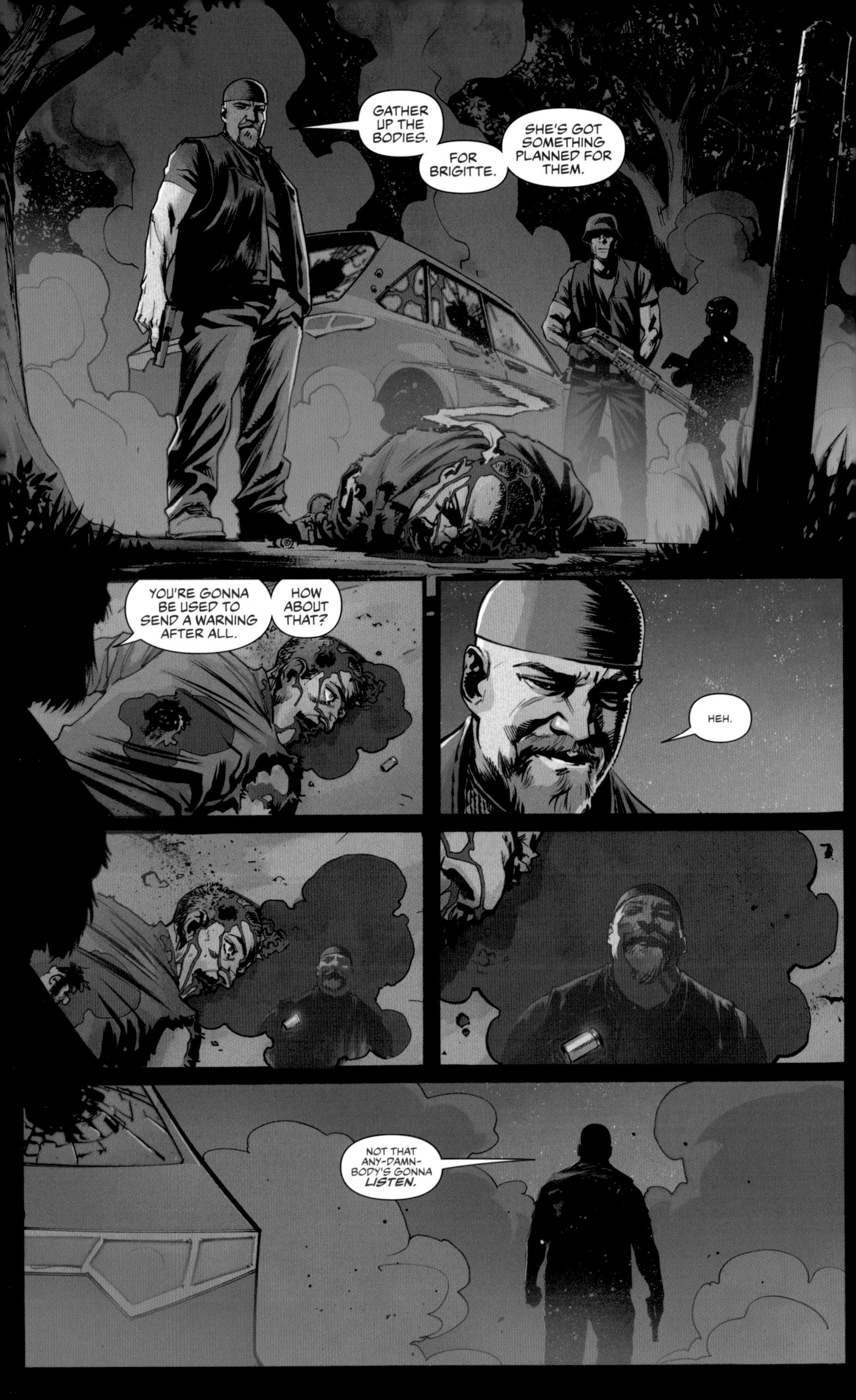
GATHER UP THE BODIES.
FOR BRIGITTE.
SHE'S GOT SOMETHING PLANNED FOR THEM.
YOU'RE GONNA BE USED TO SEND A WARNING AFTER ALL.
HOW ABOUT THAT?
HEH.
NOT THAT ANY-DAMN-BODY'S GONNA LISTEN.

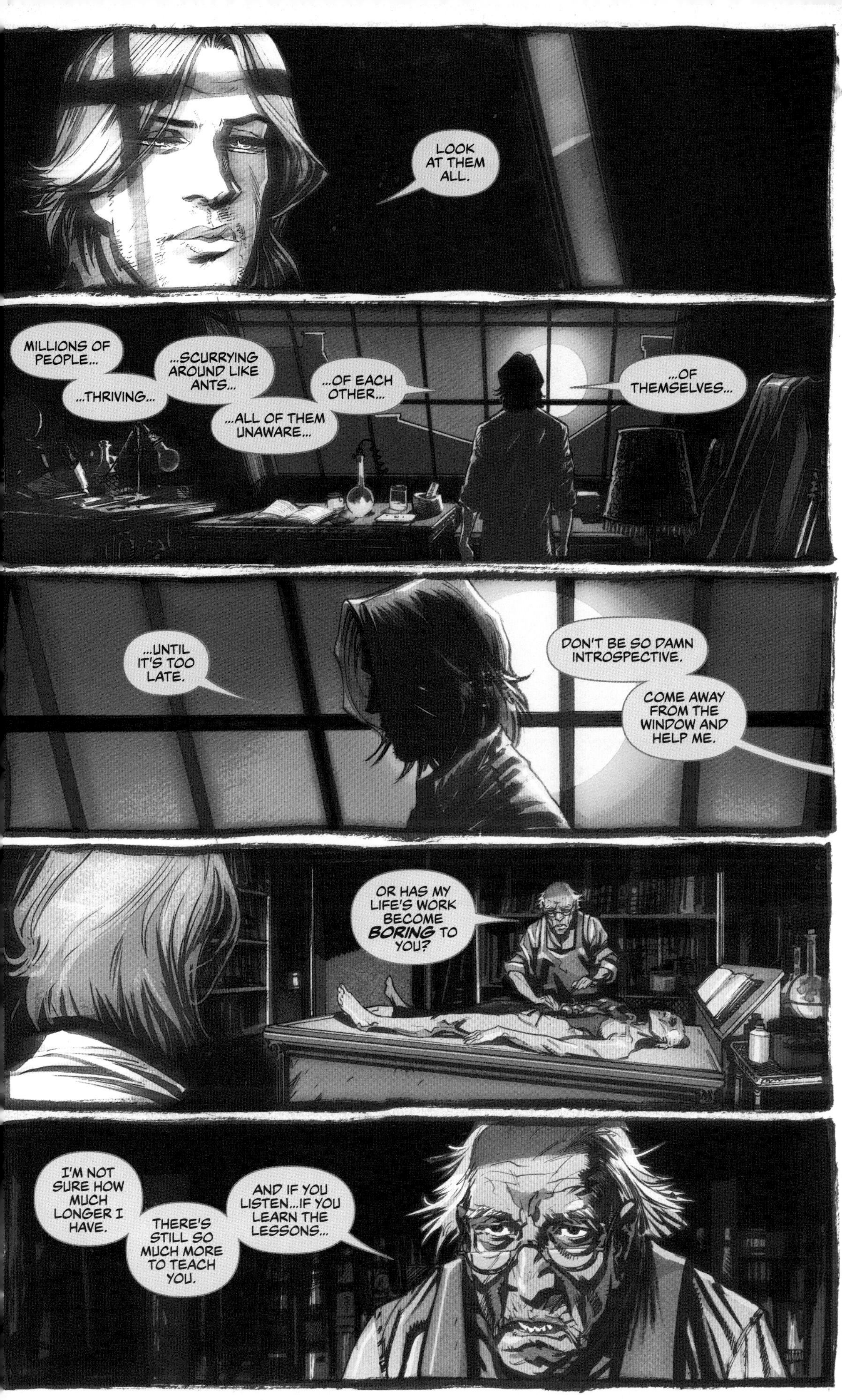
LOOK AT THEM ALL.
MILLIONS OF PEOPLE...
...THRIVING...
...SCURRYING AROUND LIKE ANTS...
...ALL OF THEM UNAWARE...
...OF EACH OTHER...
...OF THEMSELVES...
...UNTIL IT'S TOO LATE.
DON'T BE SO DAMN INTROSPECTIVE.
COME AWAY FROM THE WINDOW AND HELP ME.
OR HAS MY LIFE'S WORK BECOME BORING TO YOU?
I'M NOT SURE HOW MUCH LONGER I HAVE.
THERE'S STILL SO MUCH MORE TO TEACH YOU.
AND IF YOU LISTEN...IF YOU LEARN THE LESSONS...

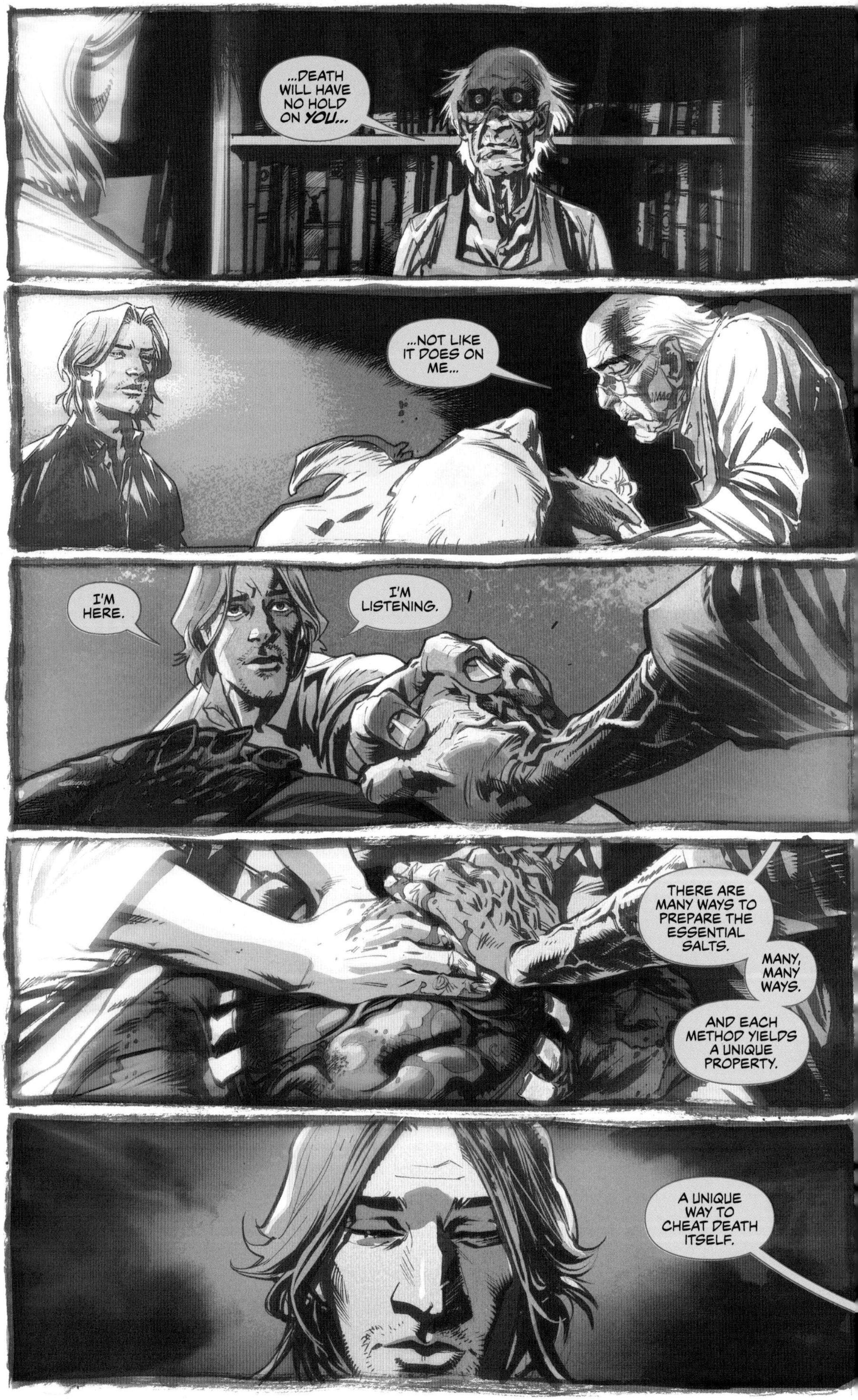
...DEATH WILL HAVE NO HOLD ON *YOU*...
...NOT LIKE IT DOES ON ME...
I'M HERE.
I'M LISTENING.
THERE ARE MANY WAYS TO PREPARE THE ESSENTIAL SALTS.
MANY, MANY WAYS.
AND EACH METHOD YIELDS A UNIQUE PROPERTY.
A UNIQUE WAY TO CHEAT DEATH ITSELF.

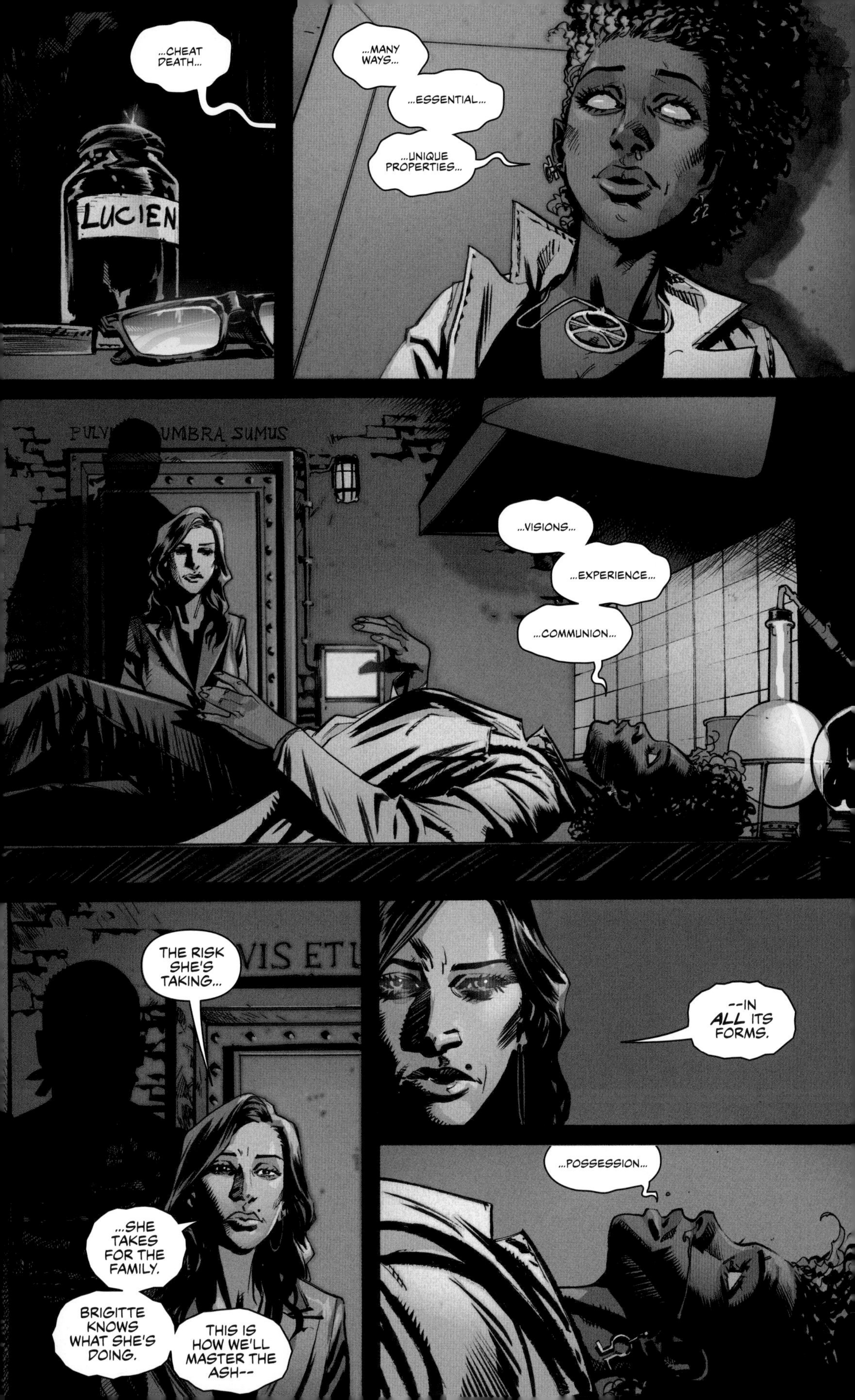
...CHEAT DEATH...
...MANY WAYS...
...ESSENTIAL...
...UNIQUE PROPERTIES...
LUCIEN
PULV UMBRA SUMUS
...VISIONS...
...EXPERIENCE...
...COMMUNION...
VIS ET U
THE RISK SHE'S TAKING...
...SHE TAKES FOR THE FAMILY.
BRIGITTE KNOWS WHAT SHE'S DOING.
THIS IS HOW WE'LL MASTER THE ASH--
--IN ALL ITS FORMS.
...POSSESSION...

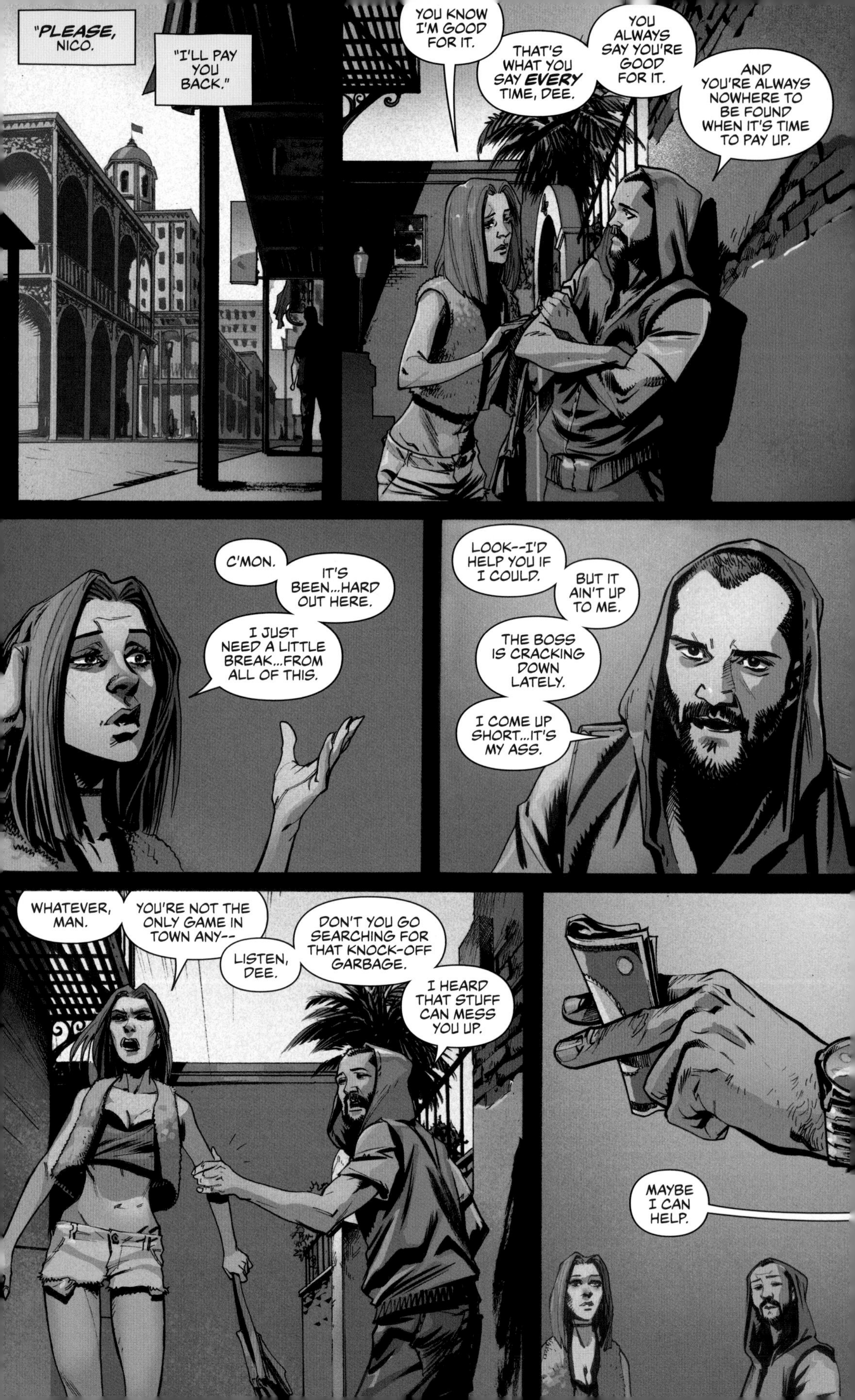
"PLEASE, NICO.
"I'LL PAY YOU BACK."
YOU KNOW I'M GOOD FOR IT.
THAT'S WHAT YOU SAY EVERY TIME, DEE.
YOU ALWAYS SAY YOU'RE GOOD FOR IT.
AND YOU'RE ALWAYS NOWHERE TO BE FOUND WHEN IT'S TIME TO PAY UP.
C'MON.
IT'S BEEN...HARD OUT HERE.
I JUST NEED A LITTLE BREAK...FROM ALL OF THIS.
LOOK--I'D HELP YOU IF I COULD.
BUT IT AIN'T UP TO ME.
THE BOSS IS CRACKING DOWN LATELY.
I COME UP SHORT...IT'S MY ASS.
WHATEVER, MAN.
YOU'RE NOT THE ONLY GAME IN TOWN ANY--
LISTEN, DEE.
DON'T YOU GO SEARCHING FOR THAT KNOCK-OFF GARBAGE.
I HEARD THAT STUFF CAN MESS YOU UP.
MAYBE I CAN HELP.

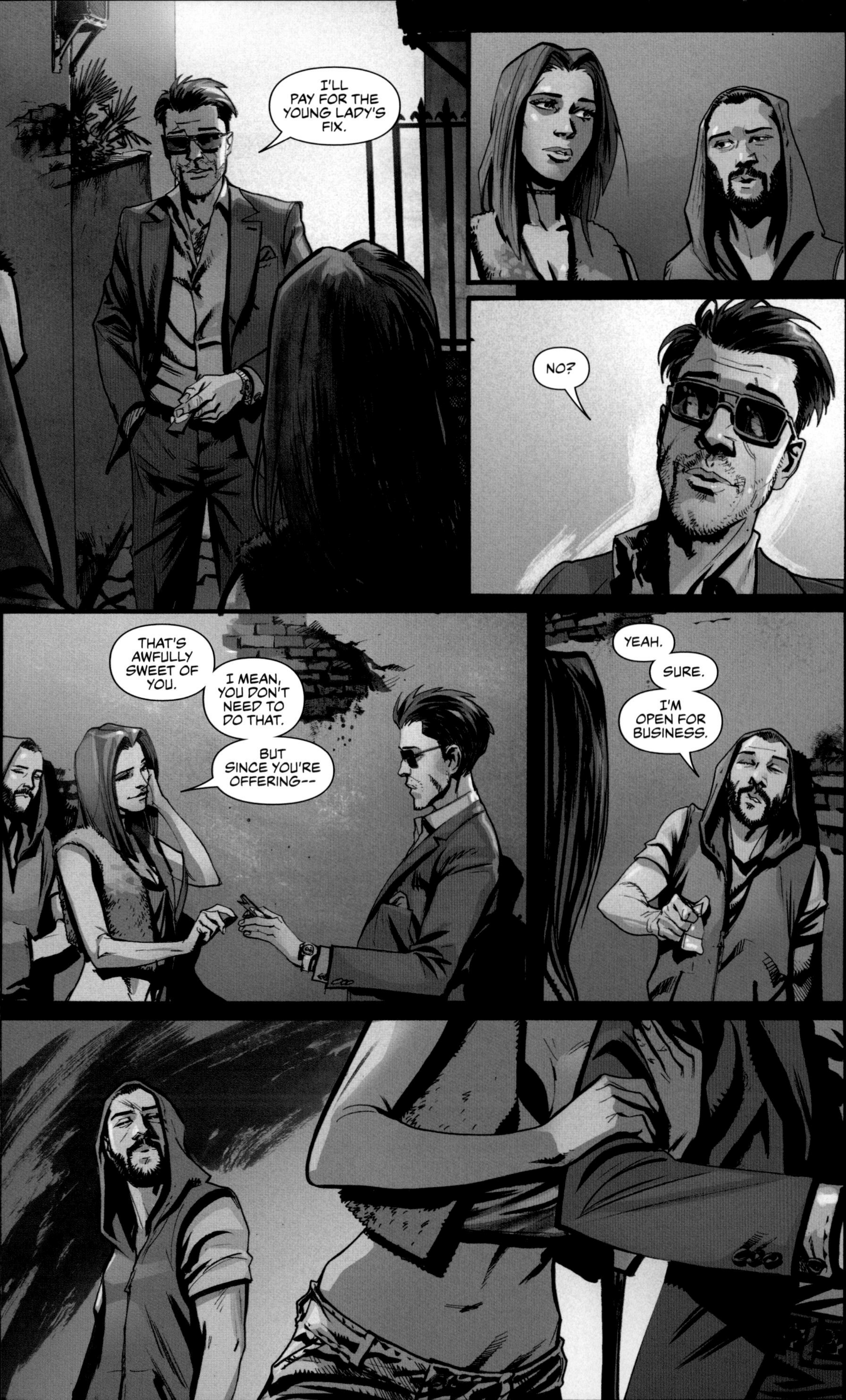
I'LL PAY FOR THE YOUNG LADY'S FIX.
NO?
THAT'S AWFULLY SWEET OF YOU.
I MEAN, YOU DON'T NEED TO DO THAT.
BUT SINCE YOU'RE OFFERING--
YEAH.
SURE.
I'M OPEN FOR BUSINESS.

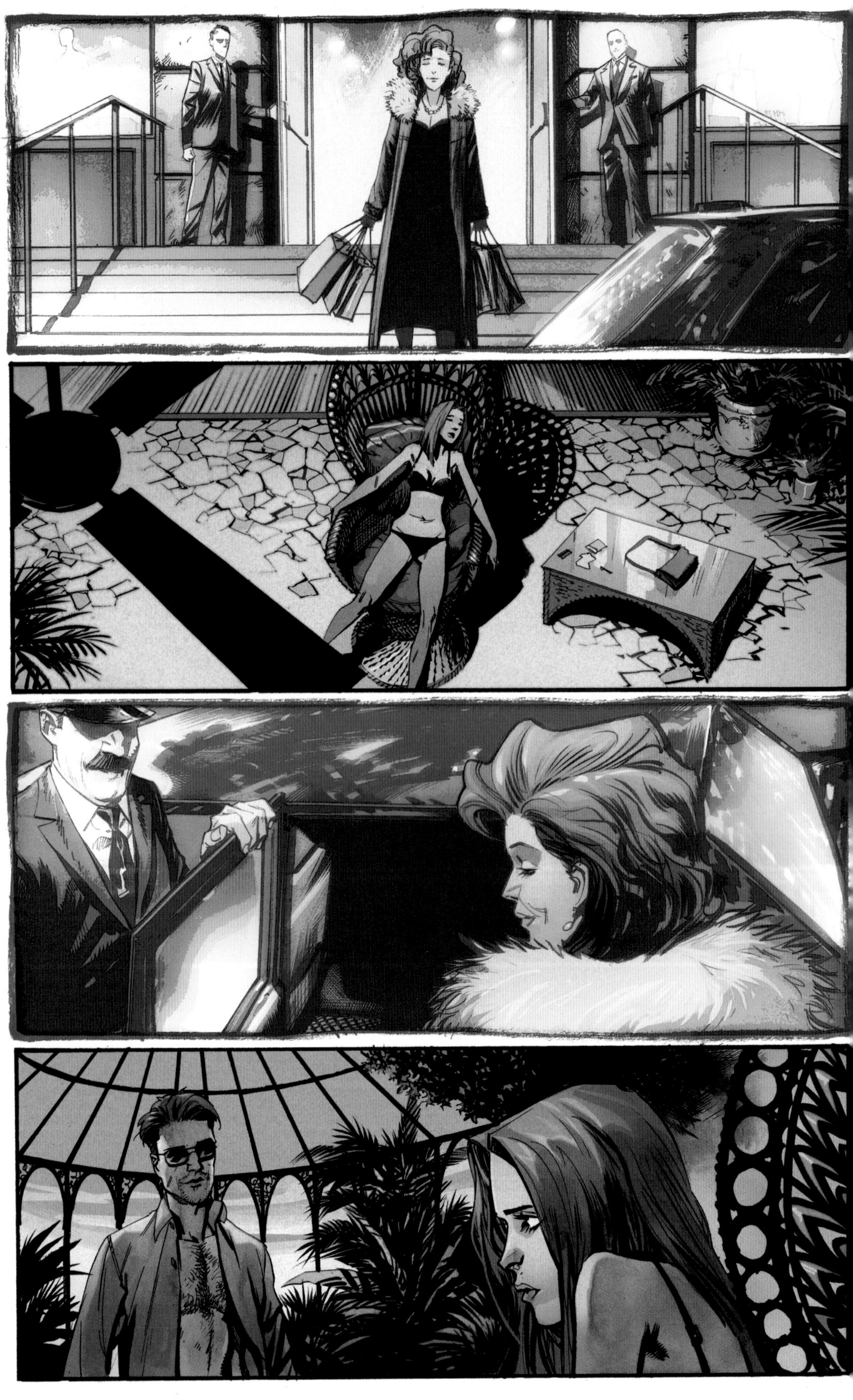

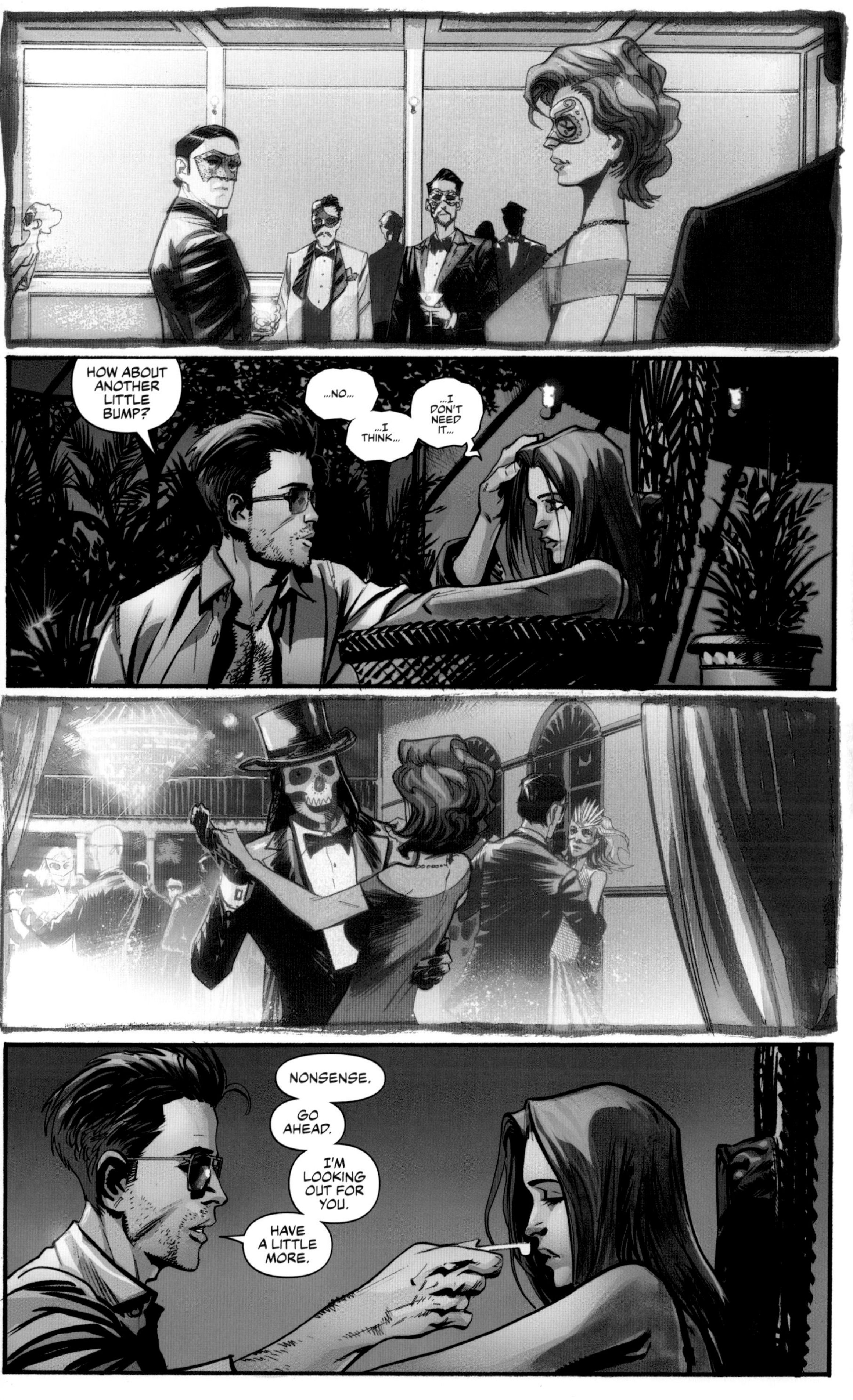
HOW ABOUT ANOTHER LITTLE BUMP?
...NO...
...I THINK...
...I DON'T NEED IT...
NONSENSE.
GO AHEAD.
I'M LOOKING OUT FOR YOU.
HAVE A LITTLE MORE.

NICO.

HEY, LEON.

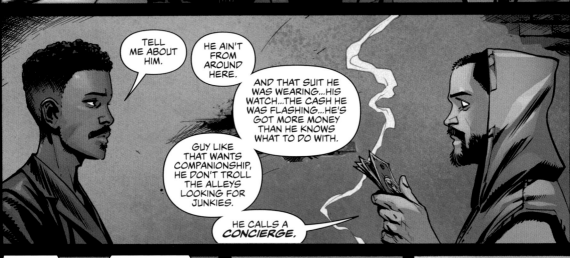

TELL ME ABOUT HIM.

HE AIN'T FROM AROUND HERE.

AND THAT SUIT HE WAS WEARING...HIS WATCH...THE CASH HE WAS FLASHING...HE'S GOT MORE MONEY THAN HE KNOWS WHAT TO DO WITH.

GUY LIKE THAT WANTS COMPANIONSHIP, HE DON'T TROLL THE ALLEYS LOOKING FOR JUNKIES.

HE CALLS A *CONCIERGE*,

AND THE GIRL?

DEE? SHE'S ALL RIGHT.

I FEEL SORRY FOR HER, I GUESS.

I GOT A SOFT SPOT FOR HER BROKE ASS.

YOU DID GOOD.

JUST LIKE YOU TOLD ME, RIGHT?

NEXT TIME YOU SEE THE GIRL...

...CALL *ME*,

I WANT TO TALK TO HER.

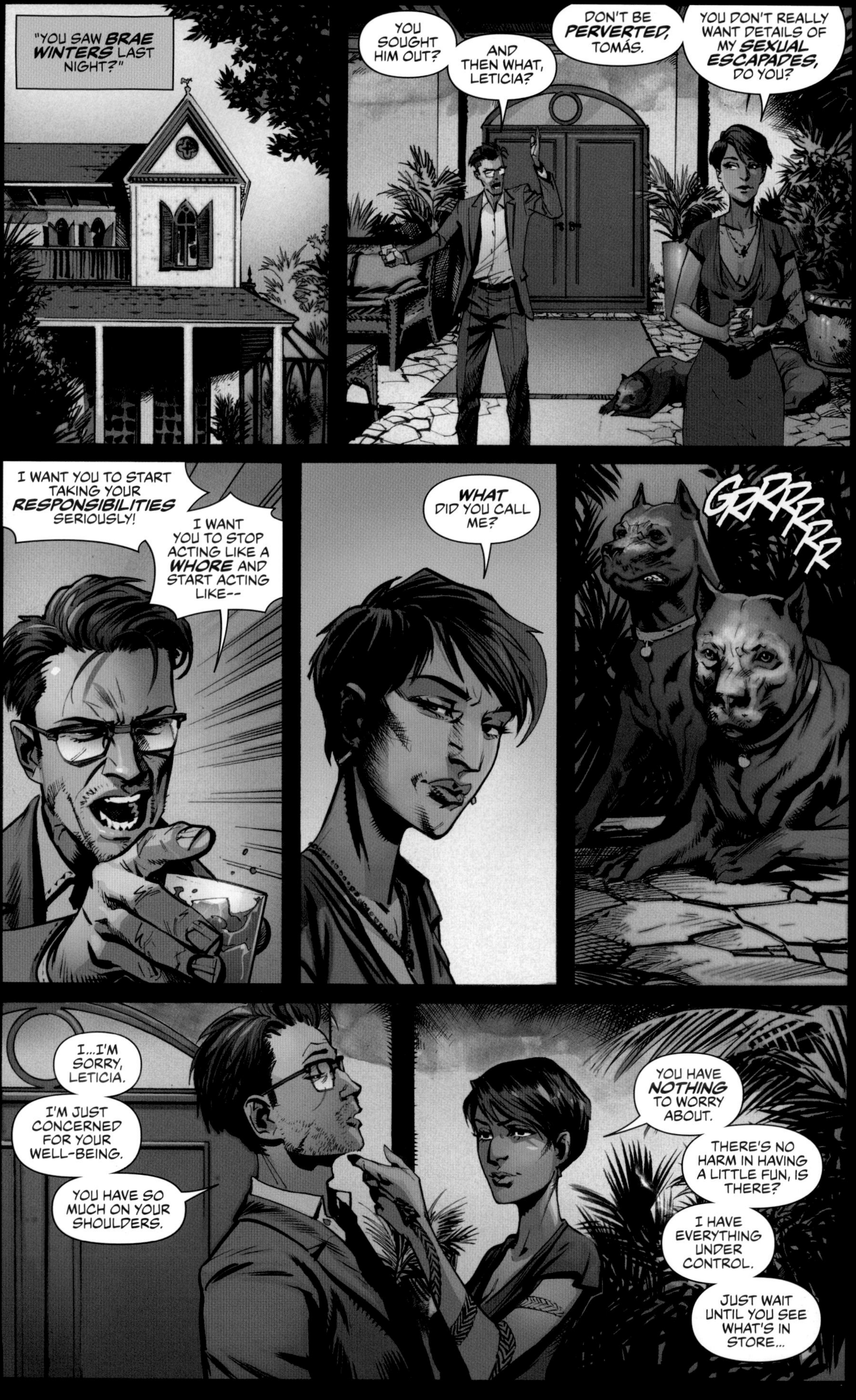
"YOU SAW BRAE WINTERS LAST NIGHT?"
YOU SOUGHT HIM OUT?
AND THEN WHAT, LETICIA?
DON'T BE PERVERTED, TOMÁS.
YOU DON'T REALLY WANT DETAILS OF MY SEXUAL ESCAPADES, DO YOU?
I WANT YOU TO START TAKING YOUR RESPONSIBILITIES SERIOUSLY!
I WANT YOU TO STOP ACTING LIKE A WHORE AND START ACTING LIKE--
WHAT DID YOU CALL ME?
GRRRRRR
I...I'M SORRY, LETICIA.
I'M JUST CONCERNED FOR YOUR WELL-BEING.
YOU HAVE SO MUCH ON YOUR SHOULDERS.
YOU HAVE NOTHING TO WORRY ABOUT.
THERE'S NO HARM IN HAVING A LITTLE FUN, IS THERE?
I HAVE EVERYTHING UNDER CONTROL.
JUST WAIT UNTIL YOU SEE WHAT'S IN STORE...

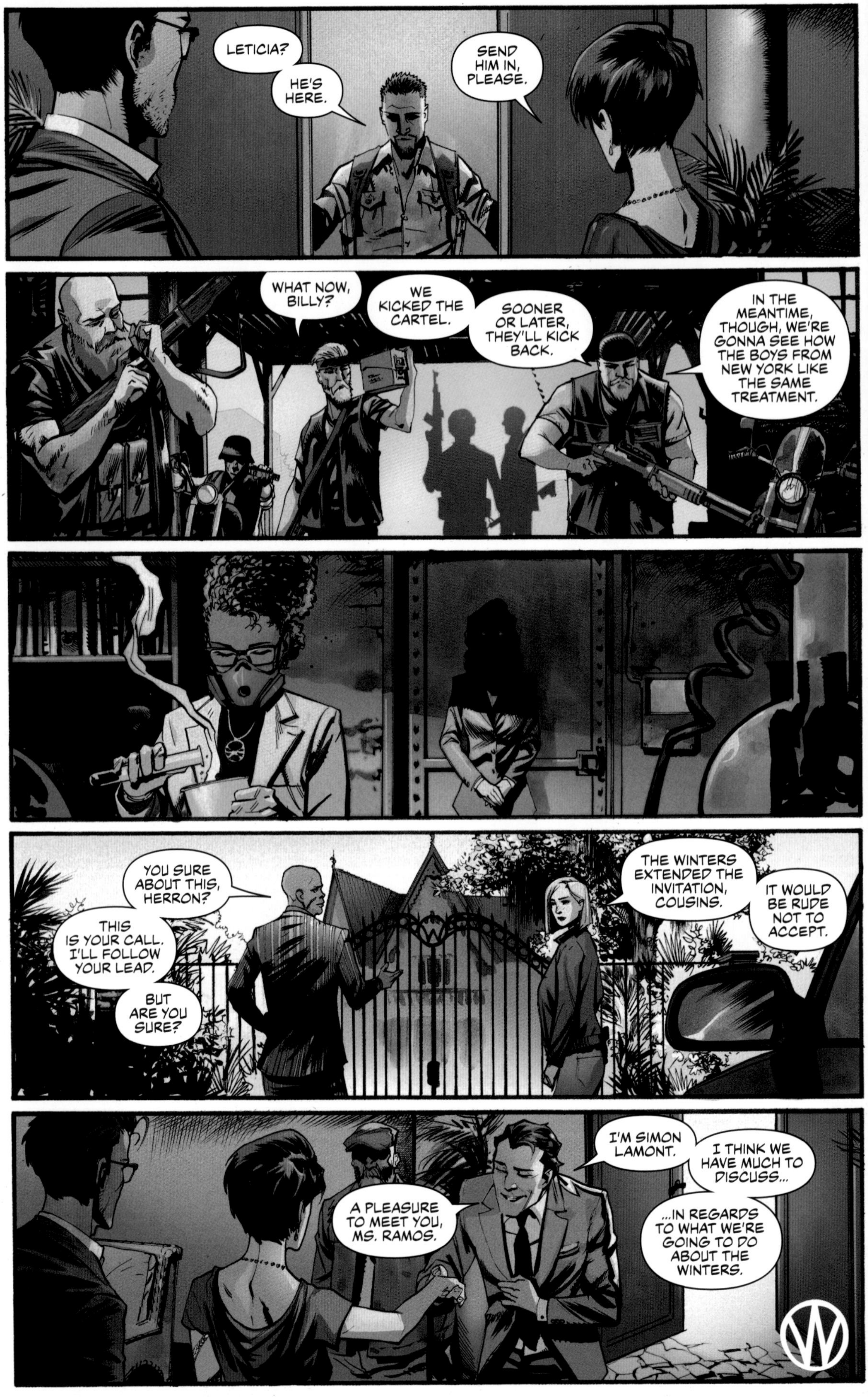
LETICIA?
HE'S HERE.
SEND HIM IN, PLEASE.
WHAT NOW, BILLY?
WE KICKED THE CARTEL.
SOONER OR LATER, THEY'LL KICK BACK.
IN THE MEANTIME, THOUGH, WE'RE GONNA SEE HOW THE BOYS FROM NEW YORK LIKE THE SAME TREATMENT.
YOU SURE ABOUT THIS, HERRON?
THIS IS YOUR CALL. I'LL FOLLOW YOUR LEAD.
BUT ARE YOU SURE?
THE WINTERS EXTENDED THE INVITATION, COUSINS.
IT WOULD BE RUDE NOT TO ACCEPT.
A PLEASURE TO MEET YOU, MS. RAMOS.
I'M SIMON LAMONT.
I THINK WE HAVE MUCH TO DISCUSS...
...IN REGARDS TO WHAT WE'RE GOING TO DO ABOUT THE WINTERS.

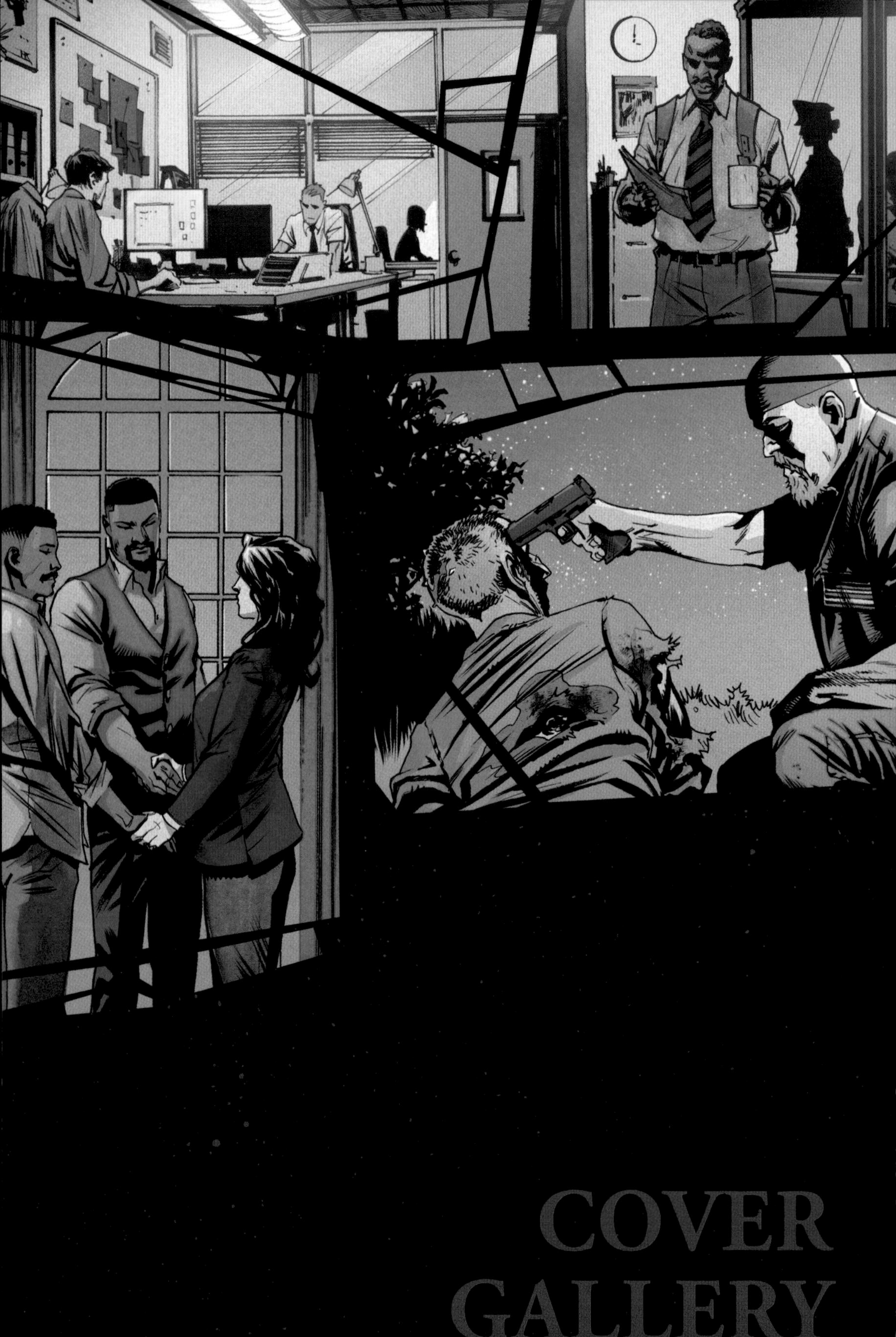

COVER GALLERY

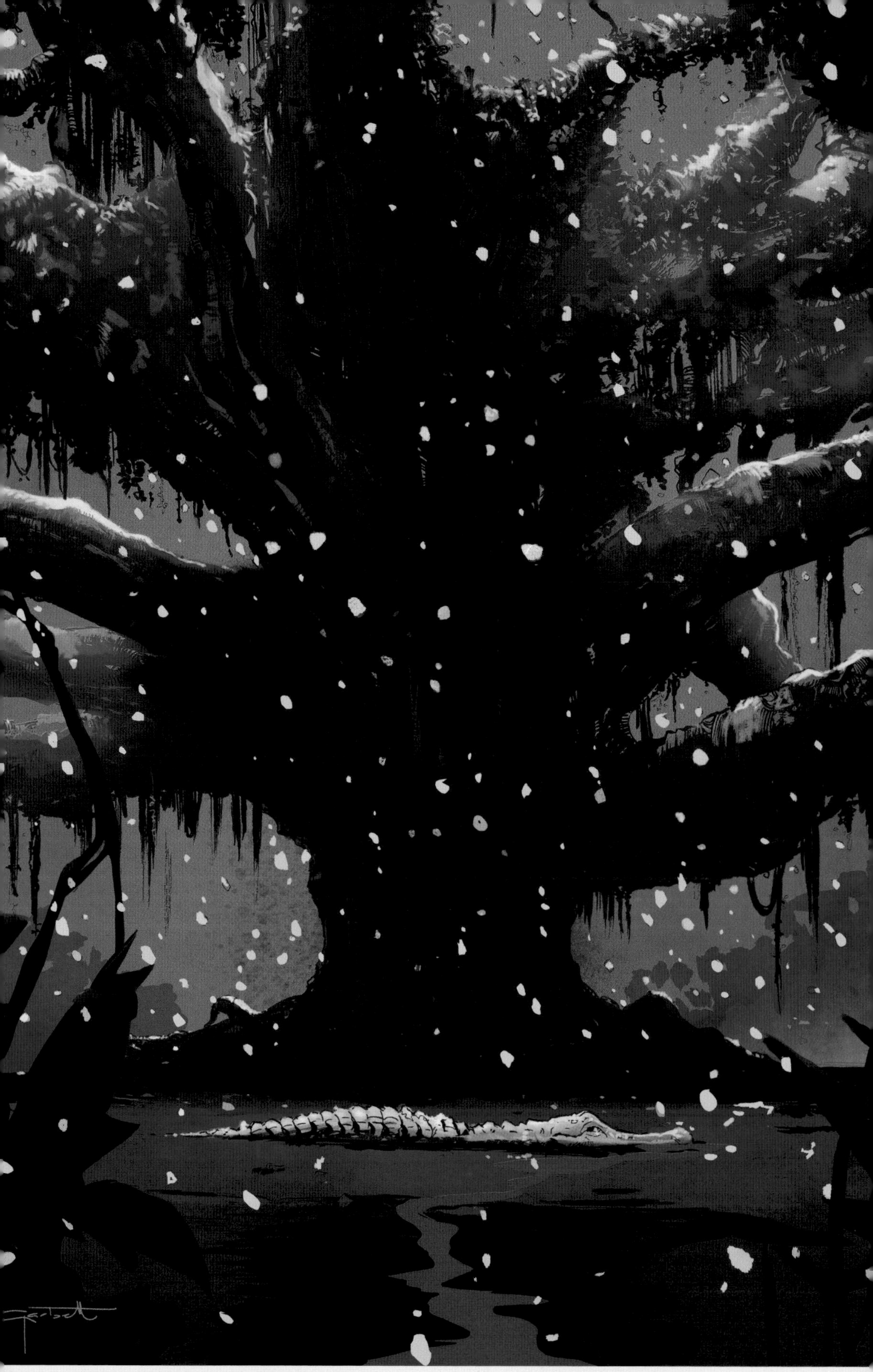

Issue Five Cover by **LEE GARBETT**

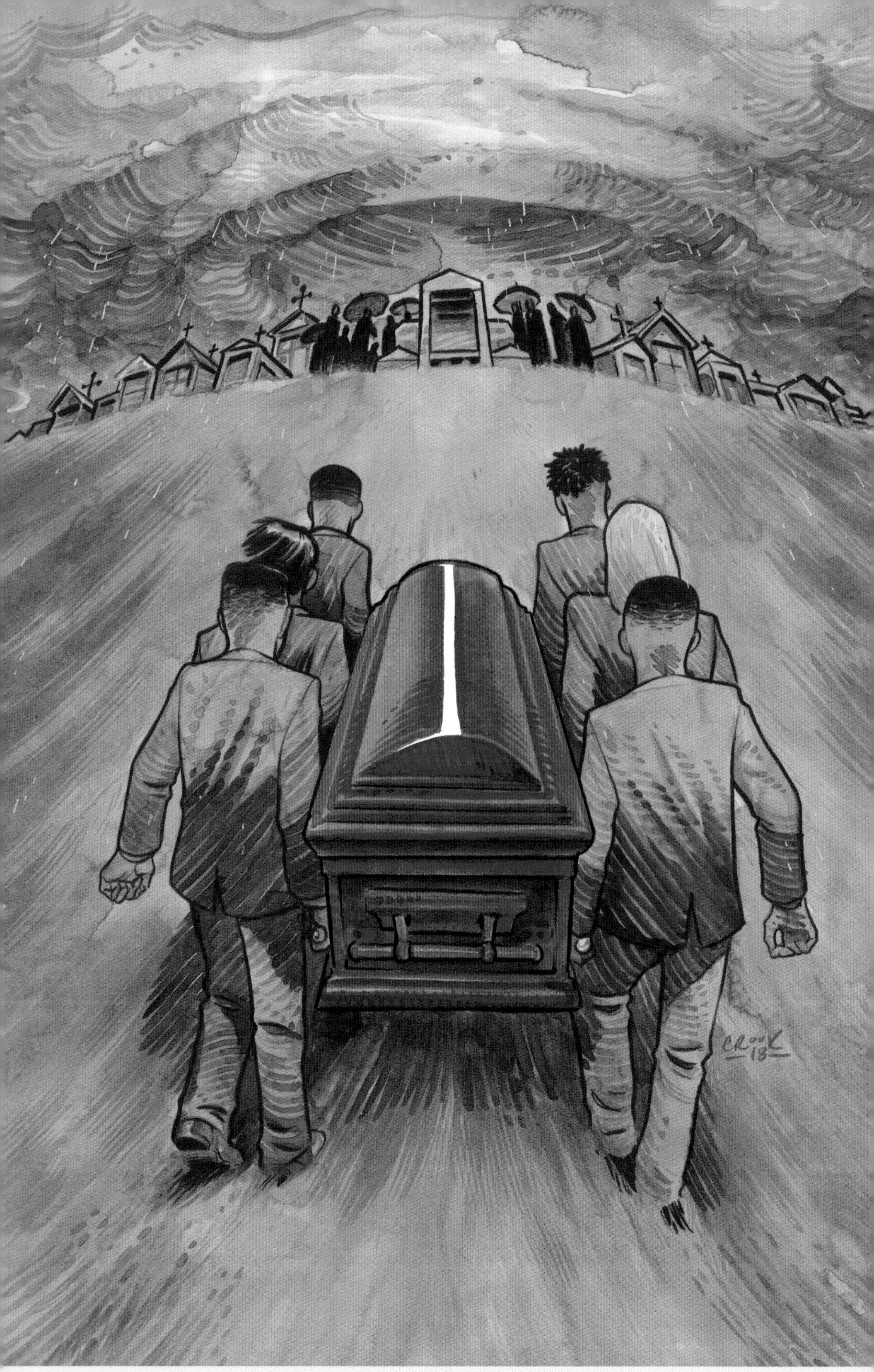
CROOK
18

Issue Five Cover by **TYLER CROOK**

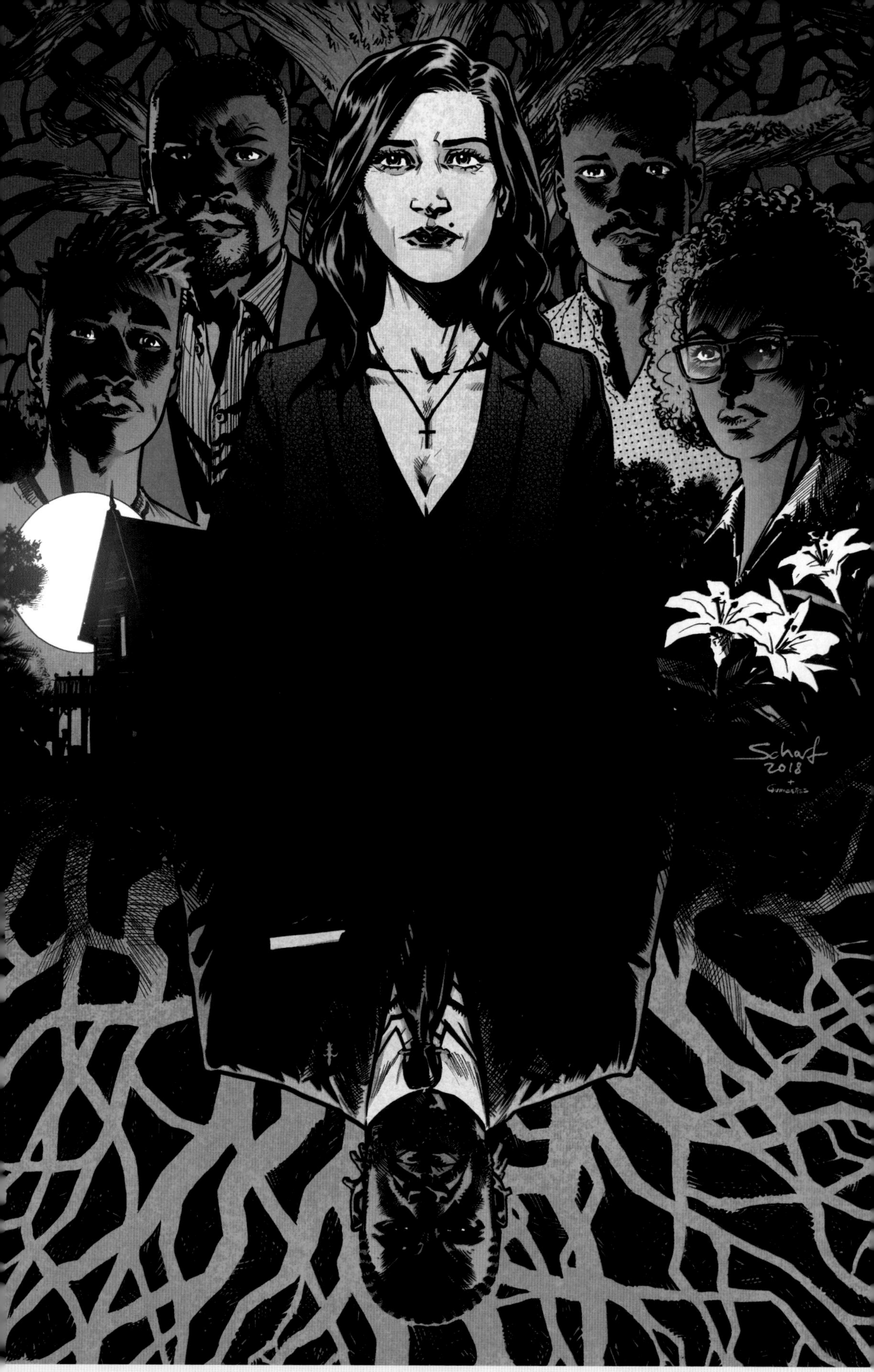
Scharf
2018

Issue Six Cover by **JONAS SCHARF** with colors by **ALEX GUIMARÃES**

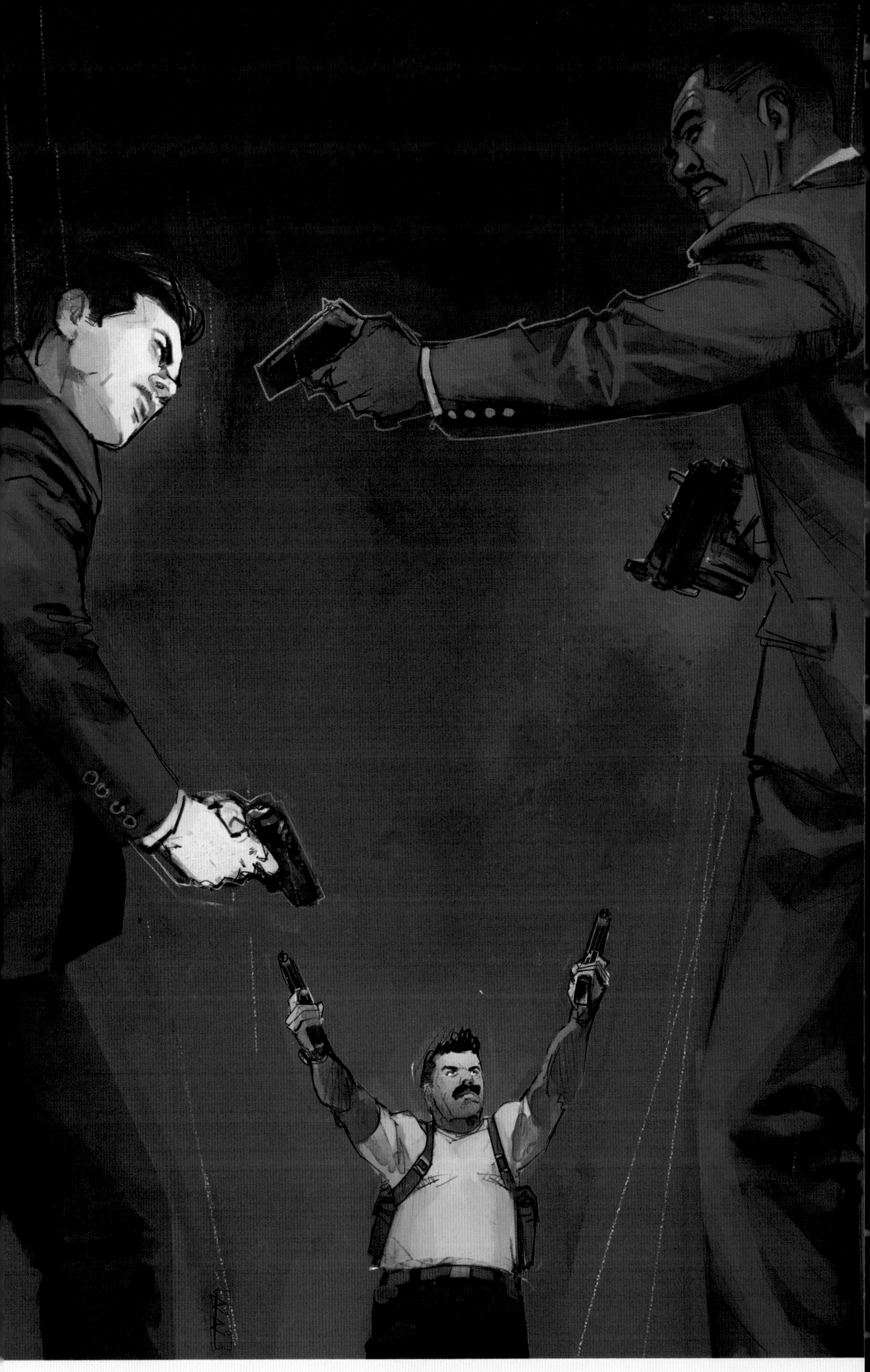

Issue Seven Cover by **ROD REIS**

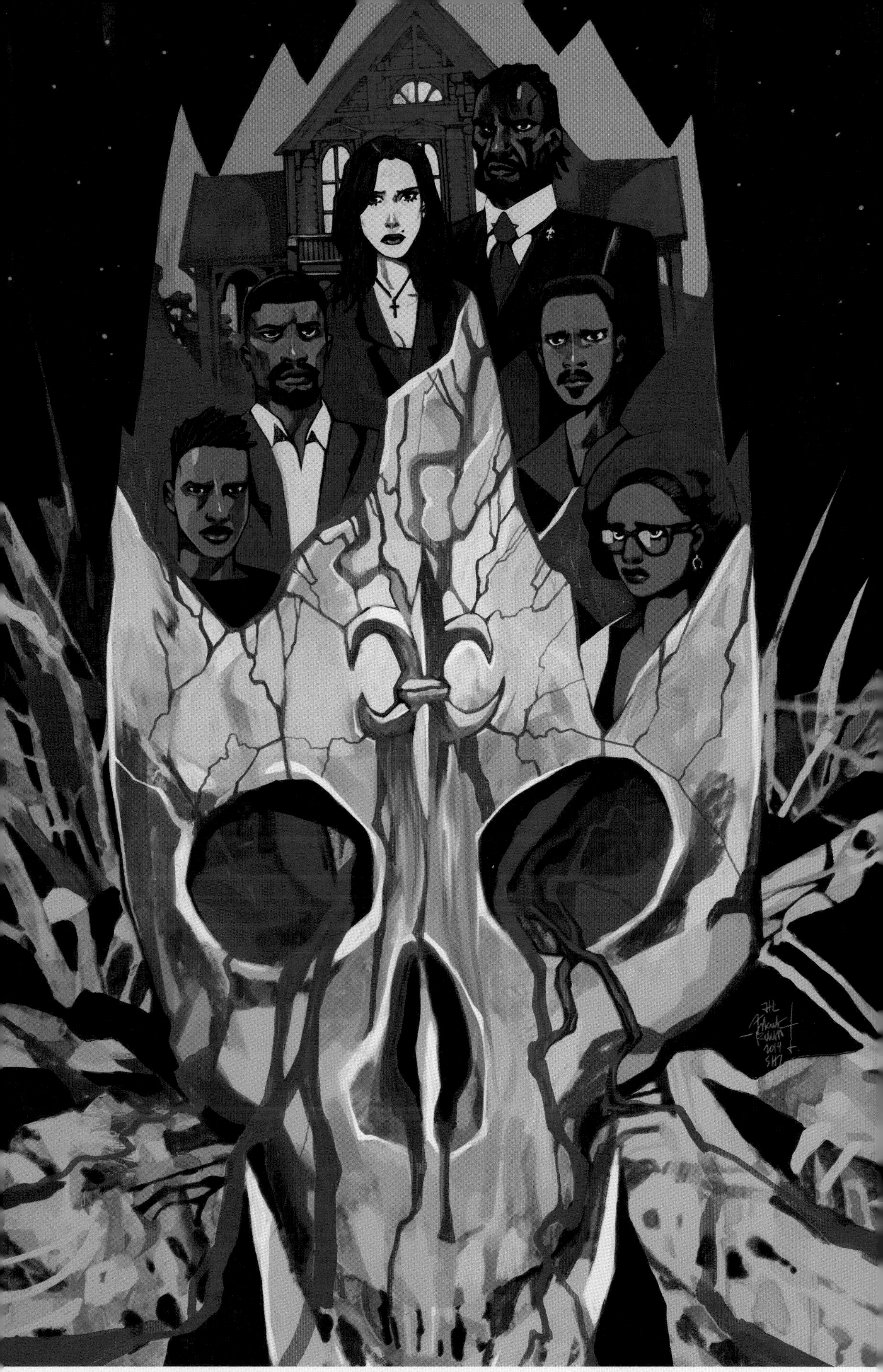

Issue Seven Cover by **JAKUB REBELKA**

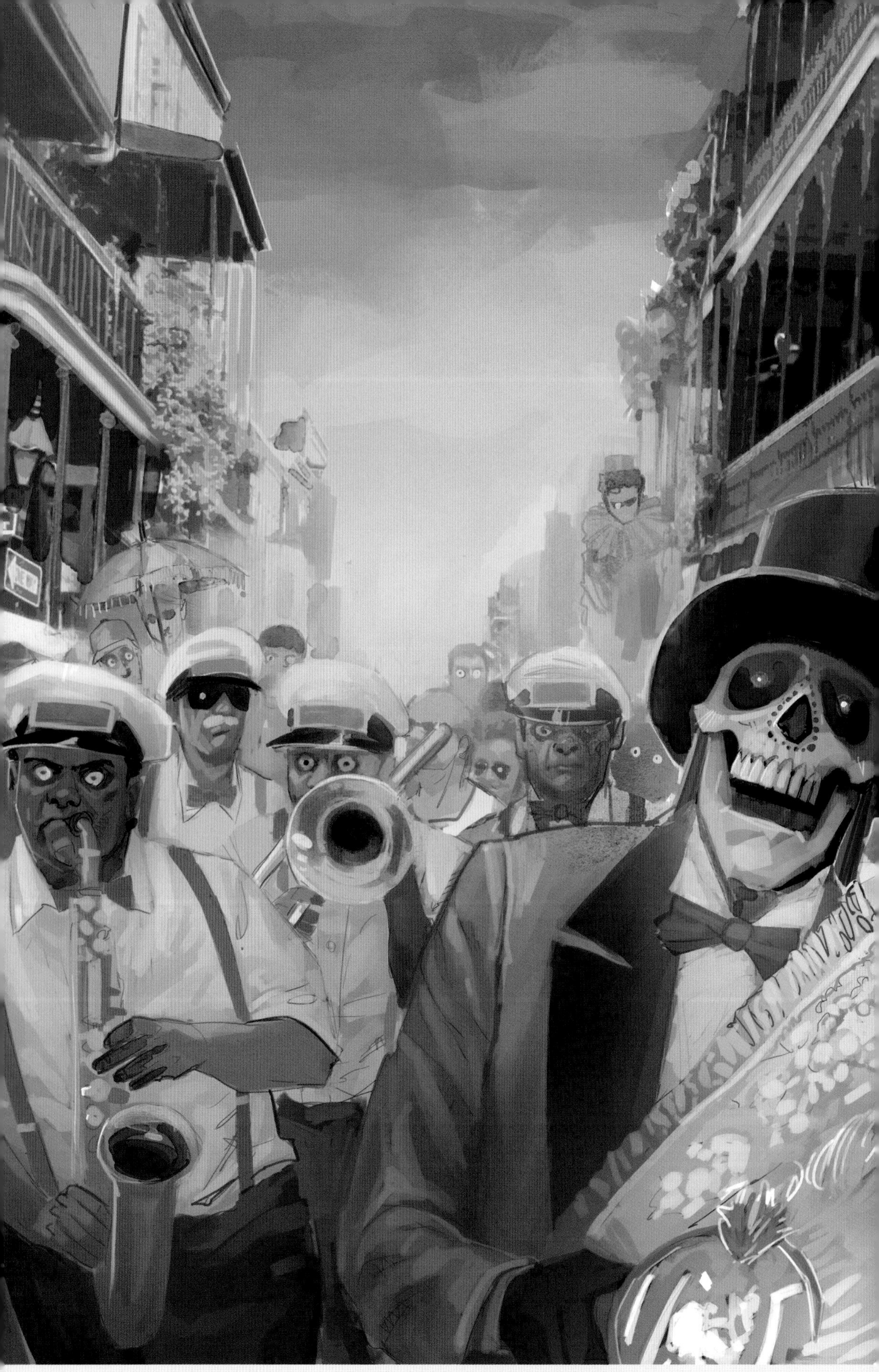

Issue Eight Cover by **ROD REIS**

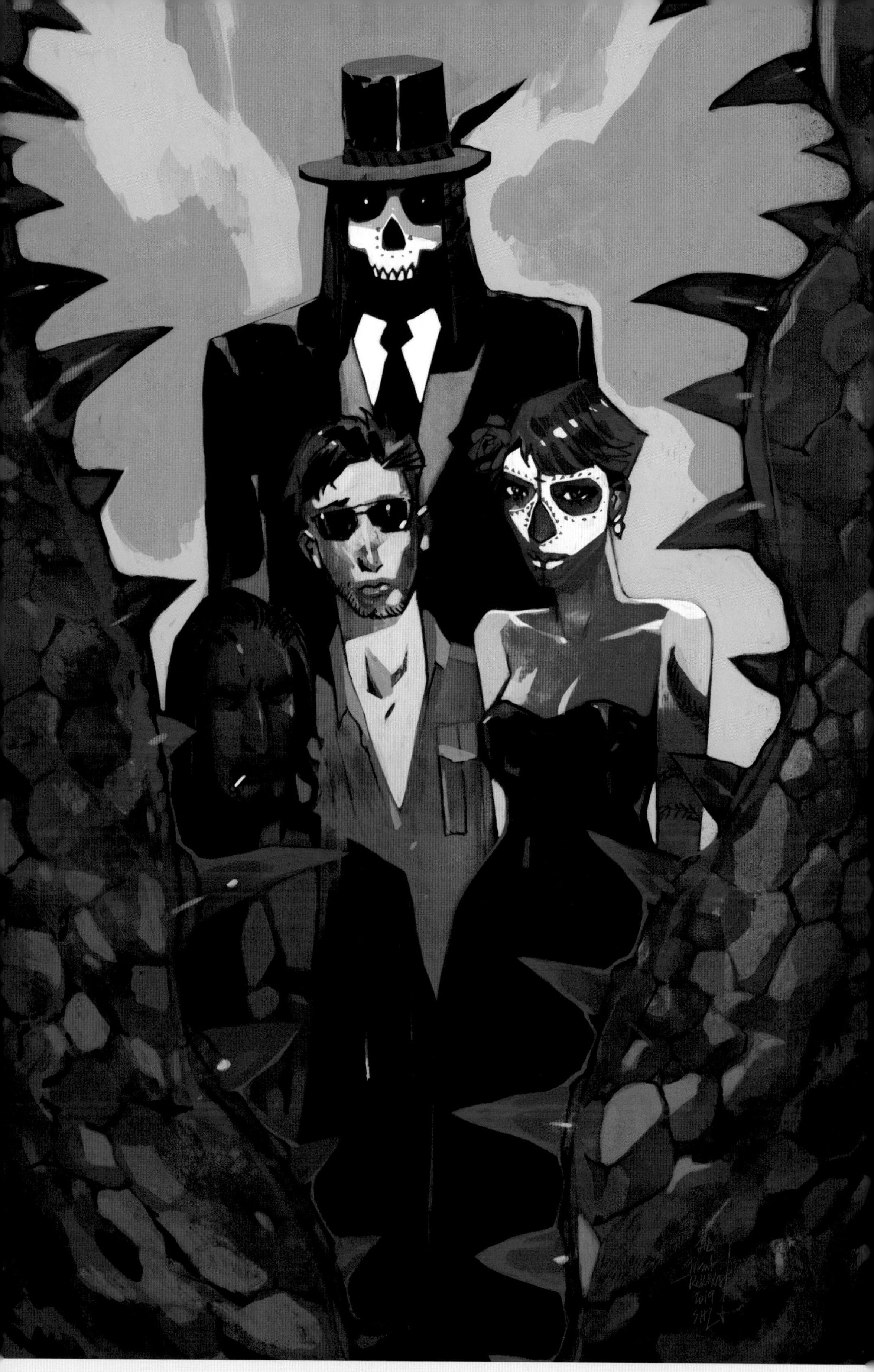

Issue Eight Cover by **JAKUB REBELKA**

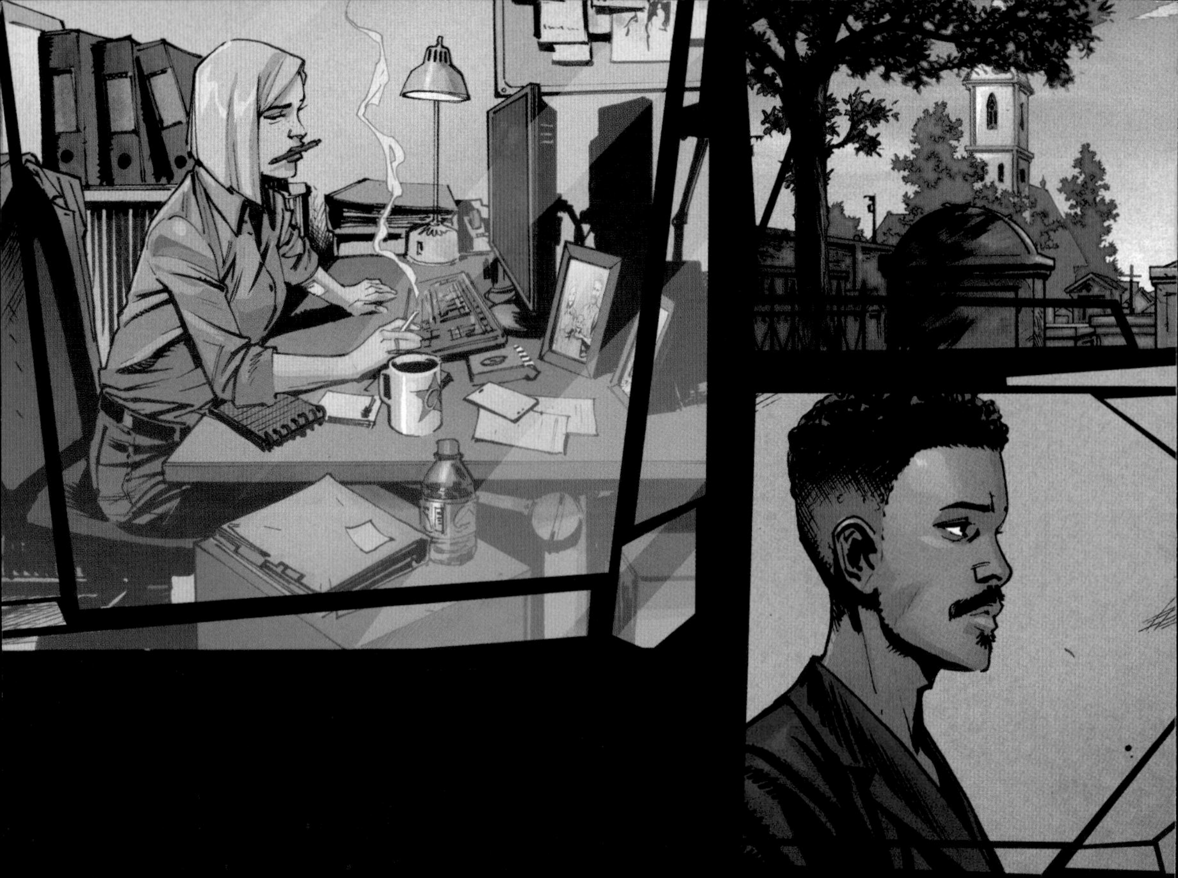

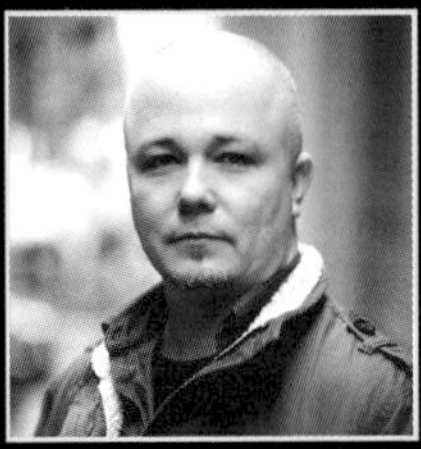

CULLEN BUNN

Cullen Bunn writes graphic novels, comic books, short fiction, and novels. He has written *The Sixth Gun, The Damned, Helheim,* and *The Tooth* for Oni Press; *Harrow County* for Dark Horse; *The Empty Man, The Unsound,* and *Bone Parish* for BOOM! Studios; *Dark Ark, Unholy Grail,* and *Brothers Dracul* for AfterShock Comics; and *Regression* and *Cold Spots* for Image Comics. He also writes titles such as *Asgardians of the Galaxy* and numerous *Deadpool* series for Marvel Comics.

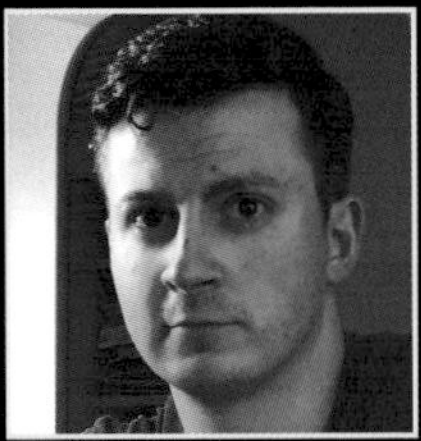

JONAS SCHARF

As a kid, young **Jonas Scharf** fell in love with comics and drawing and, being the daydreamer that he was, decided he would one day be a comic book artist. After doing the reasonable thing for a while, getting a solid education and a bachelor's degree, he decided it was time to do the unreasonable thing and pursued a career in comics. In 2016, shortly after his graduation, he was offered his first book and hasn't stopped drawing since. So far he is mostly known for his work on titles like *Warlords of Appalachia, War for the Planet of the Apes,* and *Mighty Morphin Power Rangers* for BOOM! Studios. Other works include illustrations for the crowdfunded horror series *Blood and Gourd* and *House of Waxwork* for

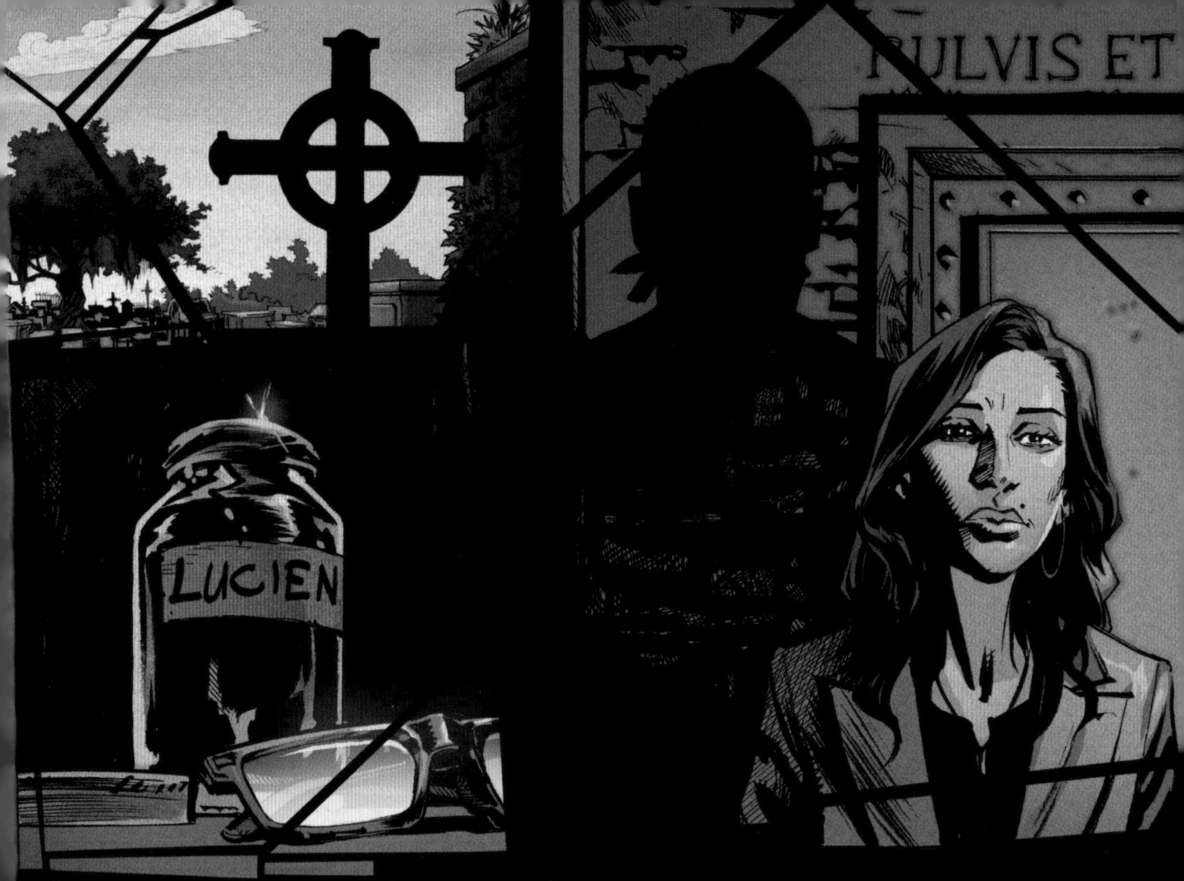
ULVIS ET
LUCIEN

ALEX GUIMARÃES

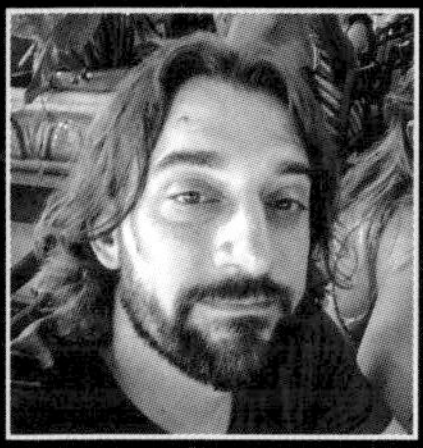

Alex Guimarães is a colorist from Brazil. He has been working in comics since 2000, with publishers like Dynamite, DC Comics, 2000 AD, and many others. He started working with BOOM! Studios two years ago, and has had a lot of fun with the variety of projects and characters, from *Planet of the Apes* to *Bill & Ted*. He considers *Bone Parish* a career highlight and his best work so far. In addition to *Bone Parish*, he is also currently working on *Invaders* for Marvel Comics.

ED DUKESHIRE

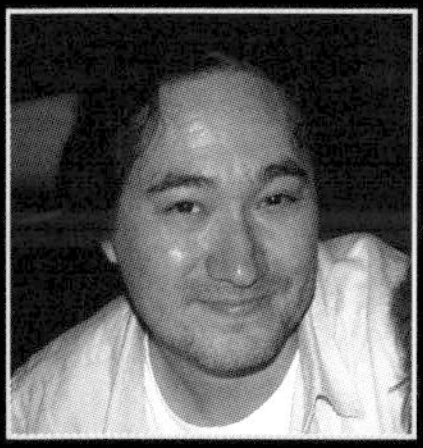

Born in Seoul, Korea, **Ed Dukeshire** is a graphic artist and Harvey-nominated comic book letterer who has worked in the biz since 2001. He has lettered titles from mainstream to creator-owned favorites. He also owns and operates the Digital Webbing website, a gathering place for comic creators. And you may even catch him playing video games once in a while.

DISCOVER
THRILLING NEW TALES

CULLEN BUNN
BONE PARISH
JONAS SCHARF ALEX GUIMARÃES
VOLUME ONE

CULLEN BUNN
VANESA R. DEL REY
MICHAEL GARLAND
THE EMPTY MAN

CULLEN BUNN
JESÚS HERVÁS
NIKO GUARDIA
THE EMPTY MAN
RECURRENCE

THE UNSOUND
CULLEN BUNN • JACK T. COLE

DAVID F. WALKER · JONAS SCHARF · JASON WORDIE
WAR FOR THE PLANET OF THE APES

PHILLIP KENNEDY JOHNSON
JONAS SCHARF
DOUG GARBARK
WARLORDS OF APPALACHIA
—JAMES TYNION IV
(DETECTIVE COMICS)

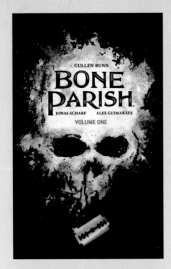

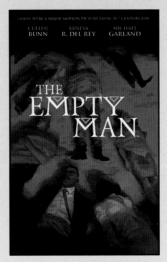

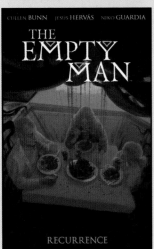

Bone Parish
Cullen Bunn, Jonas Scharf
Volume 1
978-1-68415-354-1 | $14.99
Volume 2
978-1-68415-425-8 | $14.99

The Empty Man
Cullen Bunn, Vanesa R. Del Rey
978-1-60886-720-2 | $19.99

The Empty Man: Recurrence
Cullen Bunn, Jesús Hervás
978-1-68415-356-5 | $14.99

The Unsound
Cullen Bunn, Jack T. Cole
978-1-68415-178-3 | $19.99

War for the Planet of the Apes
David F. Walker, Jonas Scharf
978-1-68415-213-1 | $14.99

Warlords of Appalachia
Phillip Kennedy Johnson, Jonas Scharf
978-1-68415-000-7 | $19.99

Abbott
Saladin Ahmed, Sami Kivelä
978-1-68415-245-2 | $17.99

Black Badge
Matt Kindt, Tyler Jenkins, Hilary Jenkins
Volume 1
978-1-68415-353-4 | $29.99

Victor LaValle's Destroyer
Victor LaValle, Dietrich Smith
978-168415-055-7 | $19.99

BOOM! STUDIOS

AVAILABLE AT YOUR LOCAL COMICS SHOP AND BOOKSTORE
To find a comics shop in your area, visit www.comicshoplocator.com
WWW.**BOOM-STUDIOS**.COM